WHO WILL ROCK THE CRADLE?

WHO WILL ROCK THE CRADLE?

THE BATTLE FOR CONTROL OF CHILD CARE IN AMERICA

EDITED BY PHYLLIS SCHLAFLY

WORD PUBLISHING
Dallas · London · Sydney · Singapore

Originally published by
Eagle Forum Education & Legal Defense Fund
316 Pennsylvania Avenue, S.E., Suite 203
Washington, D.C. 20003
(202) 544-0353

Two Conferences on Child Care were sponsored by the Eagle Forum Education & Legal Defense Fund: one in St. Louis on September 23-25, 1988, and the other in Washington, D.C. on January 9-10, 1989. The 18 addresses in this volume were given at one or the other, or both, of these Conferences. The addresses present different facets of this subject and represent varying points of view. Two additional addresses are included in the Appendix to add other perspectives and give a more complete presentation of the subject.

Library of Congress Catalog Card Number 89-83720

ISBN 0-8499-3198-3

Printed in the United States of America

012349 AGF 987654321

First printing of Word Publishing Edition — 1990

TABLE OF CONTENTS

INTRODUCTION

With all the media coverage currently given to the topics of child care and daycare, with one hundred bills introduced into the 100th Congress and the attention devoted to the subject by the 1988 Presidential candidates, this issue has become a preeminent concern of our time. Nearly all the television newscasts, documentaries and public affairs programs have editorialized in behalf of those who are demanding federally financed and federally regulated daycare. It is important that other voices and other points of view be heard.

We need to ask some definitional questions. Are we talking about child care, which means the care of children? Or, are we talking about support for daycare, which is the baby-sitting of preschool children — even infants — by persons other than their own parents? Or, are we talking only about federal financing and regulation of institutional daycare, something that is freely chosen by only about ten percent of parents?

It is important to look at mother care and "other care" from the child's point of view. The question is not "is woman's place in the home?" but "is the child's place in the home?" We must ask questions such as, do children want and benefit from daycare? What does modern research say about whether or not daycare is beneficial or harmful to a child? Can we, as a society, afford to start financing a large-scale program that may administer long-term harms to the next generation?

It is important to look at the child care issue in relation to broad social trends, tax policies, and the cultural environment of our modern American society. We should study the financial and social incentives and pressures that now influence parental decision-making about child care. We should examine the ideologies, the assumptions, and the objectives of the groups so actively promoting nonparental care of young children.

It is important to look at daycare from the point of view of who would get the benefits and who would pay the costs. We must ask questions such as, would a federally financed program unfairly discriminate against some families and in favor of others? Would federally financed daycare layer another national and costly injustice on the backs of families who are raising their own children without government assistance?

It is important to look at daycare from the point of view of the parents who have the primary responsibility and should have the freedom of choice to make their own child care decisions without government compulsion or financial incentives or disincentives. We must look at the choices parents are freely making today in the absence of federal intrusion in this field, and we must resist pressures to dictate parental choices.

We should do nothing to discourage mothers from caring for their own children in their own home. It is important, in the necessary absence of the mother, that we do nothing that discourages families from having young children cared for by other family members. It is important, in the necessary absence of the mother, that we do nothing that discourages families from having young children cared for by neighborhood daycare mothers who provide a home setting for the children. It is important that we do nothing to harm the curriculum, independence, or financial solvency of religious daycare, which is a principal form of daycare for the urban poor.

We must respect the family as the fundamental institution of health, education and welfare for the next generation. We must do nothing that tends to discourage families from taking care of their own, or assuming responsibility for their own children and other family members.

Perhaps the ultimate question is not who will raise our children, but who will control the raising of our children: the government or the family?

Phyllis Schlafly

Chapter 1

THE POWERFUL ECONOMICS OF MOTHERING
by Allan Carlson

An economist and historian explains federal tax policies in relation to the family and how changes in tax rates, credits, deductions, joint returns, and targeted benefits have been variously pro-family and anti-family. He recommends pro-family tax policies and predicts beneficial results.

Dr. Allan C. Carlson has been President of the Rockford Institute in Rockford, Illinois since 1986. He is a Reagan appointee to the National Commission on Children.

Dr. Carlson formerly served as executive vice president of the Rockford Institute and editor of the Institute's monthly publication, Persuasion At Work. *During the 1970s, he was assistant director of the Governmental Affairs Office of the Lutheran Council in the U.S.A., a Visiting Fellow at the American Enterprise Institute in Washington, D.C., and Assistant to the President and Lecturer in History at Gettysburg College in Pennsylvania.*

Allan Carlson received his B.A. degree from Augustana College (1971) and his Ph.D. in Modern European History from Ohio University (1978). Among other appointments, he has been a visiting scholar in Stockholm, Sweden and a manuscript reader for the Governmental Studies Program of the Brookings Institution. He received research grants from Ohio University, the American-Scandinavian Foundation, the National Endowment for the Humanities, and the Institute for Educational Affairs.

Dr. Carlson has written extensively on the subjects of modern social history, family policy, the relationship between foreign and domestic policies, the interaction of economics and culture, and modern religion. His book Family Questions: Reflections on the American Social Crisis *was published in 1988 by Transaction*

Press (Rutgers University). He has contributed to many anthologies, including The Future of American Culture, The Wealth of Families, The Family in the Modern World, *and* Directions for America in the 21st Century. *Dr. Carlson's essays have appeared in many magazines, including* The Public Interest, Policy Review, The American Spectator, The Human Life Review, *and* Modern Age. *He has contributed articles to* The Washington Post, The Wall Street Journal, San Francisco Chronicle, USA Today, Baltimore Sun, The International Herald-Tribune, The Detroit News, *and* The Atlanta Journal.

Dr. Carlson has lectured at many universities and testified before numerous Congressional committees on subjects such as tax fairness for families and family life in the emerging economy. He is married and has four children.

It's sometimes difficult to make economics — particularly micro-economics — interesting. Certainly back in the 19th century, this discipline fully earned its informal title "the dismal science," as the thoughts and theories of Thomas Robert Malthus spread widely, particularly his contention that "overpopulation" was our premier problem and the birth of a new child something to fret about or lament, rather than celebrate.

In our own time, too, the "economics" of any subject can seem a little dry. Perhaps that is why we have one contemporary definition of an economist — a fellow who wanted to be an accountant but didn't have the personality for it.

Then, too, there is the problem of economic lingo. Only a modern economist, for example, can look at the miracle of his newborn babe and see "marginal human capital"; only an economist can look at the wonders and mysteries of marriage and see "a utility function"; and only a modern economist can contemplate the power of human love, and relabel it "psychic income."

Despite the absence of poetry in economics, we all have a great deal to learn from this discipline, as we turn to the status of mothering in the latter 1980s. This is particularly true as the question turns to the economic pressures which determine the choice of institutional care over the home care of children.

A conservative alternative to liberal daycare plans has now taken firm shape. The conservative strategy is to recraft federal tax policy to expand parents' choices by leaving them with more of their earned income. In the 100th Congress in 1988, the Holloway bill and the Schulze bill proposed expanding eligibility for the current Child and Dependent Care Credit, extending it to all parents with preschool children. President Bush's plan for a $1,000-a-child tax credit for the working poor would be constructed alongside of the existing Dependent Care Credit. It also derives from the same philosophical thrust: higher net incomes for families achieved through tax policy; and it, too, aims over the long run for universal application.

Critics of this approach have advanced two complaints. First, they say that tax relief for the parents of small children is not a daycare plan. They charge that parents might use the extra money for things other than purchased daycare. This is, of course, exactly true; that's the whole point. This approach pulls us out of the bizarre and narrow world of the alleged "daycare crisis" and into the larger question of what is best for families and children. It leaves the choice between homecare and daycare with parents, not with bureaucrats and those vested interests who have a financial stake in social parenting.

The second, more important criticism is that tax relief of $150 to $400 per child under the Holloway bill, $750 per child under the Schulze bill, or even $1,000 per child under the Bush plan, is not enough to make any real difference. First-class daycare, critics say, costs $4,000 to $20,000 a year; and a measly $1,000 hardly begins to compensate for the loss of income that an employed mother faces if she leaves the labor market and turns toward home.

On the surface, this seems to be a convincing argument: the sums involved don't appear all that large: how can $500, or even $1,000 — the cost of a repair job on an auto transmission — really change anyone's behavior or expand anyone's choices?

In fact, the economics of mothering are far more complex than is usually realized. Changes in financial incentives, on the level of a mere $1,000 annually, can and will make a difference in defining rational economic behavior and in affecting the final choices of women and men. The reality is that very modest shifts in taxes and child care credits can and will encourage many parents to turn toward home.

In this regard, we ought first to look at what I call the paradox of a pro-family income tax. As we look at the impact of the income tax on families, we discover that the levels of general tax rates are less important than the questions of what you tax, and how you treat marriage and children within the tax structure. Oddly, higher tax rates, under some circumstances, can actually work to the advantage of families.

People Respond to Tax Incentives

My central contentions here are that tax policy can play a positive role in strengthening family life, and that people do respond to these incentives.

Take, for example, the favorable tax treatment given to home ownership. In the late 1930s and early 1940s, the Federal Government crafted tax policies designed to encourage Americans to buy rather than to rent their homes. Property taxes and mortgage interest were made deductible. More importantly, imputed rent—the invisible "income" one derives from owning residential property—was excluded from taxation, and remains so today. These were not random actions. Rather, they reflected the high value once placed by our government on widespread property ownership. This can be seen as a modern adaptation of the Jeffersonian dream of a nation of yeoman farm families, each on its own piece of land, and each family with a stake in the maintenance of social order and in the common defense.

This tax policy had results. In 1940, most Americans rented their dwellings; by 1970 America had become a nation of homeowners. Economists Harvey and Kenneth Rosen have calculated that more than 25 percent of the growth in home ownership since 1945 can be explained by tax incentives alone. Similarly, new studies show that the elimination of these tax benefits would sharply reduce home purchases, reweighting incentives in favor of rental units.

Another example of successful pro-family tax policy was the basic restructuring of the tax code that occurred in the Revenue Act of 1948. Crafted by that rarest of modern political phenomena, a Republican-controlled Congress, this reform was strongly pro-marriage in that it adopted for the first time the "married couple," as opposed to the "individual," as the unit of taxation and implemented "income splitting" through the new joint return. This meant that the combined income of a married couple would, in effect, be "split in half" and taxes paid on each half regardless of the real distribution of income between husband and wife. Within a progressive tax structure that reached 70 percent at the highest level, this sharply reduced the net tax paid by married-couple households. It also created a "marriage bonus," or "singles penalty," depending on your point of view.

The 1948 Act was strongly pro-child, too. It raised the personal exemption to $600 per family member (from $200). This was a conscious attempt to relieve the financial burdens of parents with many children.

More important, though, the Revenue Act of 1948 also placed a high marginal tax on market labor — especially on the real or potential labor of a second earner — and so encouraged a focus on what economists call home production. It is important to remember that the choice facing able adults within a family is not simply between marketwork and leisure time spent eating bonbons; rather, it is a three-way choice between marketwork, leisure, and home production. Whether devoted to child care, food preparation, cleaning, sewing, canning, handicrafts or gardening, home labor enjoys at least one clear advantage over marketwork: it is not subject to income tax.

Hence, a progressive income tax with a joint filing provision discourages market employment by a second earner and encourages home labor. This is because the potential second earner in the household faces a tax on initial earnings conditioned by the total income of the first earner. For example, if the family is in a 40 percent tax bracket and the husband earns $40,000, and the wife then goes to work at $20,000 a year, the marginal income tax on her new income is $8,000; when payroll and state and local taxes are added, half of the family's new income is gone.

This often-ignored economic incentive toward work-in-the-home can, in some circumstances, be very powerful. In the early 1970s, for example, Reuben Gronau of Hebrew University calculated that the average value of uncounted home production by a fulltime American wife exceeded 70 percent of the family's money income, after taxes, and was almost equal to the market

income of her husband when the family had at least one child.
Moreover, when a young mother entered the paid labor market,
the value of lost home production — things such as child care,
gardening, and hot meals that she no longer had the time for —
far exceeded the gain in money earnings when at least one preschool child was involved.

In short, under a progressive income tax structure where
home production is not taxed, the entry of the average mother
into the labor force actually brings a net decline in the family's
living standard, although that decline will be hidden because we
never "cash out" the value of lost production in the home.

Nonetheless, human beings almost instinctively know
what's going on. Sociologist Janet Hunt recently has shown that
the net effect of higher marginal tax rates is to encourage the
substitution of home production for market production. Faced
with higher taxes on additional earned cash income, American
families will choose to grow more vegetables at home and eat
less often at McDonald's. She calculates that, with a one point
increase in the marginal tax rate, the average married woman
works 39 fewer hours annually in the marketplace, and devotes
29 more hours to home activities such as child care. In a sense,
the family defends its living standard by a turn toward home
and a defense or reconstruction of the home economy.

In a curious way, then, high marginal taxes under the Revenue
Act of 1948 actually encouraged greater family self-sufficiency,
and heightened domesticity. The evidence even suggests that
this Act may have had a hand in sustaining the baby boom into
the mid-1960s: having babies and devoting one's time to work in
the home both made economic sense.

Critics of home production contend that such home-centered-
ness comes at the price of efficiency. These critics argue that
when market production is specialized, it creates economies of
scale, whereas home labor is that of the generalist. If one looks
at the production of light bulbs or shoes, this is undoubtedly
true. But if one looks at more qualitative types of home-labor
essential to raising brighter, healthier children — what economists call "human capital" formation — it is easy to prove that
the good home care of children is better for them and the nation at large than good institutional care; and that attentive

meal preparation at home is superior nutritionally to the fast-food shop.

Recent decades, though, have witnessed the dismantling of these pro-family aspects of the U.S. tax code. The Tax Reform Act of 1969 responded to complaints about the so-called "singles penalty" under existing law, and slashed tax rates for the unmarried. Inadvertently, this created the notorious "marriage penalty," the situation in which a two-earner married couple, in some circumstances, would pay higher net federal taxes than if both were single. Successive increases in the standard deduction and a high inflation rate also reduced the real value of the personal exemption, exerting a particularly strong negative pressure against families with children.

Taxation of Home Production

Finally, the tax-law writers chose with increasing frequency in the late 1960s and 1970s to tax home production, to the net benefit of market labor. One clear goal at the time was to reduce the disincentive to market work facing women under an income-splitting system. As June O'Neill of the Urban Institute put it, "A system of joint filing is likely to discourage the market employment of married women." Experts also argued that the failure to tax home production encouraged persons to produce their own goods and services, rather than buying them. This in turn reduced the potential tax base. But since the taxation of home production goods and services was impossible to do directly, given the huge difficulties of measuring work within the home, policy architects chose instead to give targeted tax cuts to households with employed wives, which had the same effect.

Specific measures with these intentions were the expansion of the Child Care tax deduction in 1972, and its replacement by the more generous Child and Dependent Care Credit in 1976. We need to remember that this Child and Dependent Care Credit was seen by some tax experts in the IRS and the relevant Congressional committees as a way of indirectly taxing mothers at home. The basic theory behind these policies was to equalize the tax treatment of "purchased" and "home-based" child care by making both kinds of "services" exempt from tax.

Similarly, Congress' attempt to reduce the "marriage penalty" in 1981 tax legislation (through a partial deduction on the second income of a two-earner household) had the same rationale: it was called an indirect way of taxing the extra "imputed income" produced by the homemaker within the one-wage-earner family.

The theory behind this implicit tax on the home was, in fact, badly flawed. To begin with, it assumes that every human action, even the display of tenderness in the home, is potentially subject to federal tax, a horrendous doctrine that strikes at the very foundations of liberty.

More directly, if the Federal Government really wanted to count, and adjust for, the economic benefits that homemakers and mothers give to their husbands and children, then the proper adjustment certainly would not be tax relief for the two-career couple using daycare. Rather, the only rational approach under such a theory of taxing "imputed income" produced in the home would be massive tax relief for persons not married (that is, persons who enjoy no imputed income from a spouse); moderate taxes on childless couples; heavy taxes on two-career marriages with children in daycare; and crushing income taxes on traditional married couples with a mother at home raising children.

This would be, of course, an utterly stupid and idiotic income tax structure, for it would penalize the very people who are renewing the nation through their children. Yet oddly, between 1965 and 1980, this appears to be the very theory that guided our tax policy experts, and it produced the dramatic rise in the income tax burden falling on young families.

Indeed, this theory continues to influence some tax experts. Their private answer to complaints about the Child and Dependent Care Credit is that it's a fair adjustment compensating for the untaxed services of fulltime homemakers. As this argument arises, we need point to the dangerous implications of its logic. Their argument would not produce fairness, but the erosion of the freedom and autonomy of the home. This is such a distressing and weird theory of taxation that, fortunately, only "experts" could believe in it. I don't think any Senator or Representative would go before a crowd of real people to try to explain, let alone defend, the taxation of home production.

Before proceeding to the next point, and lest I be accused of arguing for a great increase in tax rates, let me note that the fate of the family is only one consideration in crafting an income tax. We need also look at the effect of marginal tax rates on capital formation, and on incentives to save and invest. My central point is that, as Congress works for a pro-family income tax, the primary focus should not be on tax rates, but rather on preventing any taxation — direct or indirect — of the value of home production. The existing Child and Dependent Care Credit has precisely that technical effect, which is why this issue is so important. The camel's nose on the taxation of home production has been in the tent since 1972, and it is time we drove it out.

In understanding the powerful economics of mothering, we also ought to look at the new insights of a group of micro-economists studying the incentives facing and the decisions made by individuals and families. They have recently rediscovered and documented the economic logic of the traditional family and of traditional gender roles. Above all, the work of figures such as John Ermisch, Robert Willis, and Michael Ward, points to the crucial economic role of the homemaker. More than a lifestyle option, the homemaker emerges through economic analysis as the very heart and soul of a modern and free society, the absolutely essential profession that secures true social and economic progress.

The New Home Economics

This "new home economics," as it is called, has discovered, for example, that marriage between an employed husband and a wife-at-home makes valuable economic sense, since each partner brings complementary skills to the marital bond. It's a division of labor that makes both of them better off than if they remained single. However, a marriage between economic equals — with both spouses in the labor force — offers little direct economic gain, since the true division of labor in their household is so sacrificed. Indeed, in a regime of pure wage and job equality, individuals avoiding risk will tend to rely more on "trial marriages." The same economic incentives will make existing marriages more fragile, because they make little economic sense, and make divorce increasingly popular.

In analyzing fertility trends, the "new home economists" say that the normative displacement of the homemaker by the career-oriented woman drives birthrates ever downward. In a 1979 study, researchers showed that two variables largely account for fertility trends in the United States since 1945: fathers' income, which varies directly with fertility (that is, more money means more births); and the "opportunity costs" facing women, which vary inversely with fertility (that is, rising real wages and employment opportunities for women mean ever fewer births).

Accordingly, in a society where traditional families of a male wage-earner and a female homemaker predominate, economic growth will stimulate fertility, the desirable and historically common situation. However, the economists also say that, in a society where women's job opportunities are expanding and their potential pay is moving towards equality with men's, economic growth will drive fertility downward, with no apparent stopping point short of zero births.

While some may not like the message, our own recent past seems to confirm the point. The "baby boom" of the 1945-64 era was also a period when cultural norms reinforced the homemaker role, when male wages rose steadily as a "family wage," and the real wages of employed American women rose very slightly. By way of contrast, the "baby bust" of the late 1960s and '70s occurred during a period when the homemaker and the mother were denigrated or attacked, when new "equal opportunity" laws opened numerous career paths for women, when the real wages of young men actually declined, and when the average hourly wage for women soared.

In short, the "new home economics" shows that America has entered a new social-economic era, in which an increase in real per capita Gross National Product results in the depression of fertility. Indeed, the "more equal" that men and women become in job opportunities and wage scales and the more rapid the economic expansion, the more will marital fertility push toward zero.

So it is with astonishment that some micro-economists are discovering that the "homemaker" was not just an arbitrary lifestyle choice imposed by sexist patriarchs on a stupid, passive population, as conventional wisdom would have us believe. Rather, the homemaker can be seen, in a very real sense, as the pivot of industrial society, the central actor, the necessary social role that reconciles a modern economy with the family, that lets us have our cake and eat it too, that allows for human reproduction within a system of sustained economic growth. With the majority of American women in the homemaking role during their child-rearing years, Americans could have both economic growth *and* children.

But if the number of homemakers continues to dwindle, we face a stark choice: either economic growth *or* children in sufficient numbers to sustain the nation. Under current trends, we can no longer have both.

The Powerful Effect of Small Subsidies

The third aspect of the economics of mothering vs. non-mothering that needs our attention is the powerful anti-family effect of a small amount of daycare subsidy.

Why have feminists clamored so intensively for federal support of daycare? The simple fact is that reasonably good daycare is quite expensive, annually costing from $4,000 per child over the age of three, to $20,000 for good infant care. Moreover, an important 1974 study conducted by the University of Wisconsin's Institute for Research on Poverty showed "that most middle- and upper-income families are not willing to cover the full cost of quality group child care." Why? Because it doesn't make economic sense.

Let's see why, in more detail. Take the educated married woman, with one preschooler, who can earn $25,000 a year in a white-collar job. Assume, too, that her husband has a salary of $35,000.

As she looks at her economic situation, she sees that the marginal federal taxes (income and payroll) on her salary total $10,000. State and local taxes gobble up another $2,000. The extra wardrobe needed for her work costs $1,500; her purchased lunches while at work amount to $1,500; additional auto and transport expenses are $2,000 a year. Her costs for daycare— with a preschool, learning component—are $5,000. In sum, the direct costs of her employment are $22,000, leaving her with a net cash gain of $3,000 for her efforts. If she is buying reasonably good infant daycare, even that $3,000 will quickly disappear.

But, if the Federal Government gives her a $480 tax credit for her daycare expenses, and indirectly subsidizes the price of daycare through a grant to her center, her net daycare costs might be cut by over half, and her net income will double from

$3,000 to $6,000 for a year. At lower salaries, the marginal effect of the daycare subsidy would be even greater.

Now it is true that she has not yet calculated the value of her lost home production. But if she looks simply at her cash returns, a modest federal daycare subsidy has doubled her net earnings, a not inconsiderable feat.

Hence, it is only with state subsidy, direct and indirect, that institutional daycare becomes rational economic behavior for many American families. It was only through federal subsidies, such as the Child and Dependent Care Credit worth up to $1,440 annually, that daycare could grow to challenge home care as the dominant form of child rearing in America. Indeed, I believe that it is no coincidence that the most dramatic jump in the employment rate of married mothers with preschoolers—from 30 percent in 1970 to 54 percent today—came only after the introduction of the Child and Dependent Care Credit and the expansion of related subsidies.

In sum, the incentive provided by a federal subsidy or tax credit in the $500 to $2,000 range can, has, and will have a powerful effect on the choices that young parents make. If you accept the principles behind the free market, you have to believe that people make rational responses to economic incentives, at least to some degree.

This means that, if the Federal Government tilts taxes and subsidies to the advantage of marriage and the birth of children, you will see more of both. If the Federal Government taxes home production and subsidizes daycare, you will see fewer mothers-at-home and more institutionalized children. And if the Federal Government stops taxing home production and ceases its covert financial war on traditional families, we will see many more of them.

Again, huge sums and vast programs of income redistribution are not necessary to turn the tide. Nor do we demand an explicit, direct subsidy of "Moms at home." All we need do is to tie tax relief of the size found in the Schulze or Bush proposal to the presence of children, and reject any requirement that the mother be employed in order to qualify for the credit. If we do only these two things—mere shifts in the neighborhood of $1,000 per child—then the natural incentives found in home production and the family economy will again work in favor of home and family.

Chapter 2

RAISING CHILDREN
IN A DIFFICULT AGE

by Karl Zinsmeister

A commentator on current trends in America describes the social, economic, and governmental pressures which have made it harder to raise children. He explains the costly personal and societal consequences, now and for the future.

Karl Zinsmeister is a Washington, D. C.-based writer and Adjunct Research Associate at the American Enterprise Institute for Public Policy Research. His articles have appeared in publications ranging from the Journal of Economic Growth *and* Policy Review *to* Reader's Digest. *He also writes for several national newspapers, including* The Wall Street Journal, The Washington Post, *and* Newsday. *He edited one book with Ben Wattenberg and is currently writing a book called* The Childproof Society: Are Americans Losing Interest in the Next Generation?

Mr. Zinsmeister was educated at Yale University and Trinity College in Dublin, Ireland. He is a former assistant to Senator Daniel Patrick Moynihan, and has been consultant to research and policy groups. He serves on several national advisory boards including one at the Department of Education on Teaching and Schools. He is the originator of a weekly radio commentary on social and economic trends called "Trend Watch," currently syndicated nationally to more than 100 radio stations.

Mr. Zinsmeister works at home so as to help his wife with the rearing of their two young children.

Our subject is the family environment in America today, and the pressures that parents now face in the course of raising children. I will touch on economic pressures, on governmental pressures, on biases in the tax code, on public opinion attitudes, and on psychological barriers. My thesis is that it has become harder to raise children, and that our current system is not even-handed, not value-neutral, with respect to family choices. In fact, our current system is full of inducements to place young children in hired care. I suggest that there will be a price to be paid for that.

The Pressures on Children

I am presently writing a book about how Americans regard their children. That necessarily involves looking closely also at how we regard our childbearers. Unfortunately, I have concluded from my research that national affection for both children and childbearers has declined sharply in the last generation. The material I've gathered is often very sad and sometimes even grim. Most of the problems are quite familiar, but the relevant facts are worth recapping.

The first thing that strikes you when you look at American children today is how many must grow up without the full attention of two, or in some cases even one, adult guardian. Most of us realize the divorce rate has finally leveled off. But that is only because the marriage rate has fallen so low. Divorce has stabilized, if that is the right term, at a level more than double the pre-1970s norm.

People also have a general sense that births out of wedlock are currently a big problem for children, but not many realize the full extent of the decay. In just the first six years of the 1980s, right in the midst of a supposedly calm and conservatizing era, the number of illegitimate births nationwide soared 32 percent. The astonishing result is that about a quarter of all children born in America this year will arrive without benefit of married parents.

There will be demonstrably unhappy consequences for most of these children, and that is what makes birth out of wedlock more than just a private concern. The vast majority of unmarried fathers live apart from their children, and most unwed mothers end up on welfare. (Fifty-five percent of the children born to unmarried parents in 1980 were receiving Aid to Families with Dependent Children payments in 1981.) The average period of dependency for unmarried mothers and their children is nine years. Today 14 percent of all children live in poverty, even after all government assistance is counted, and family decay is far and away the major reason.

The net result of our divorce and illegitimacy trends is that fully one-quarter of all minors in this country presently live with just one parent. That is double the 1970 level. (It compares to just four percent among Japanese children today. Could broken homes be part of our competitiveness problem?) An even more frightening fact is this: at *some* period in their childhood, at least 60 percent of all youngsters born today will spend time in a single-parent home.

There are, of course, many wonderful single-parent homes, and many sad two-parent homes. But starting out with just one parent's love, and one parent's time, and one parent's earning and doing power is a very serious strike against any child, and one he will usually be able to overcome only with difficulty.

Education is obviously another area where American society is not doing particularly well by its children. Despite sharp increases in spending per pupil, the quality of our schools has clearly declined. Today schools do less education, and more social remediation, than ever before. They have been turned into nutrition centers, family planning clinics, instruments of social and racial integration, baby-sitting centers, drug treatment units, driving instructors, job training sites, and reform houses. In the process, we have assured that they will provide little in the way of intellectual instruction. As former Yale President A. Bartlett Giamatti has warned, "Ask the public school to do more than it can and it will not do anything well."

Then there are more basic problems. Shockingly, about two million crimes — thefts, assaults and robberies — are committed in schools every year, and five percent of all secondary school teachers are physically attacked. One-quarter of all school principals reported in 1980 that student possession of weapons was sometimes a problem in their schools. The days are long past when a teacher's worst fear was a well-aimed spitball.

Crime in general has become a serious hazard to American children. Homicide is now the leading cause of death for inner-city youth. In light of this, it seems scandalous that none — not one — of the self-styled "children's defense" groups has focused the maintenance of public order as an issue of preeminent importance to the young. After all, it is vulnerable groups like the young who are most at mercy when public order decays. Why no outcry about crime levels from those who purport to speak for children?

The catalogue of rising risks to American children goes on and on, including problems like high exposure to drug use, early sexual activity, and so forth.

It is clear that growing stresses of this type are felt acutely by children. Many doctors and child psychologists report sharp increases in the number of children exhibiting psychosomatic and stress-related illnesses. Childhood admissions to psychiatric wards are up. Obviously, the most serious manifestation of childhood stress is youth suicide. It is striking to note that, while suicide levels have fallen steadily for adults in recent decades, the teenage suicide rate has tripled in the last 30 years.

One widespread source of childhood stress is the increasing separation of children from their parents at young ages. Rising use of daycare for the very young is the clearest sign of this, but older children are also suffering from a lack of parental time and attention. In 1984, more than seven million children between the ages five and 13 had no parent at home when they got out of school, and more than two million of these "latchkey kids" returned to a house that contained no adult at all.

Declining parental attachment is an extremely serious risk to children today. The verdict of enormous psychological literature is that time spent with a parent is the very clearest correlate of healthy child development. There is nothing better you can do for your children than give them your time.

Unfortunately, a very worrisome pile of research is now accumulating which suggests that when the very young go into extensive non-parental care, many—possibly most of them—will suffer emotional and intellectual harm. As discussed in more detail elsewhere in this volume, symptoms found in recent studies include low self-esteem, sharply increased aggressiveness (kicking and biting, etc.), weak child-parent bonds, poor social skills, and poor academic performance. These things have been found to occur not just where the daycare is of low quality—as most daycare is, and always will be when it is provided on a

mass, institutional scale—but also among children in
best and most expensive forms of hired care, for insta
on-one nannies in the home.

It is only very recently that out-of-family childrearing began
to be practiced on a mass scale, and we really don't know what
the final results of this giant experiment will be. But the gamut
of possibilities suggested by various observers runs from fleeting
emotional disorders and increased violence from a minority of
full-time daycare children, to increased alienation and emotional isolation among many individuals when they become
adults, to the appearance of low-level psychopathic symptoms
in certain of these children when they grow up. It is estimated
that as much as half of one's adult character may be formed by
the age of four. Opportunities squandered in those early years
often cannot be compensated for later.

The Industrialization of the Family

One of my conclusions in the book I am working on is that
what we are seeing in this country today might be thought of as
the final stage of industrialization—namely, the industrialization of the family. After all, from a short-run, purely economic
point of view, it is very inefficient to take talented, educated
adults out of the labor force for years at a time to raise children.
Accommodating our economic structures and social practices to
family demands would require lots of difficult choices. So, instead, we are attempting to redefine the child-parent relationship. Children being the passive agents they are, this produces
less resistance.

As a result, childrearing is gradually being transformed. Instead of a great social imperative, undertaken by individual
adults participating in a long chain of human interdependence
and love, it is becoming a branch of the modern service economy. Just as we pay others to bake our bread and build our
houses, so many Americans have decided they would like to pay
someone else to raise their children.

The question is, can we get away with that? Can we profes-
sionalize parenting, turn it over to an occupational class operat-
ing out of institutions that often resemble hospitals more than
homes, without doing serious harm to our children? The latest

answer of science to that question is increasingly *no*. There is no emotionally adequate substitute for the parent, at any price, for most young children.

But one need not have waited until the latest negative research started coming in to suspect this. One of the dirty little secrets of the current daycare debate—something that comes as a great surprise to persons who have taken their cues only from media reports and daycare activists—is that for many years, pediatricians, psychiatrists and child development experts have been warning that serious risks result when children are separated from their parents for significant blocks of time at a young age.

The roster of authorities who have expressed doubts about daycare has included Penelope Leach, Lee Salk, Benjamin Spock, Urie Bronfenbrenner, Selma Fraiberg, the American Medical Association, the Centers for Disease Control, and many other distinguished groups and individuals. Dr. Burton White, former director of the Harvard Pre-School Project and perhaps the country's leading authority on the first three years of life, has put it bluntly: "After more than 30 years of research on how children develop well," he says, "I would not think of putting an infant or toddler of my own into any substitute care program on a full-time basis, especially a center-based program."

Common sense could have taken us more speedily to much the same place that ponderous research is now leading. To me, it is astonishing, really, that so many of us ever convinced ourselves that it is not necessary to actually talk to, teach, hold and comfort our babies ourselves, that we could leave those things to our housekeepers or sitters all day, that as parents we could just pick out the clothes, toys, schedule and diet, set the *tone* for the child's life, while leaving most of the actual rearing (which of course can often be messy) to strangers. Assuring ourselves that we'll scour the newspapers carefully to find the very best stranger available, because we recognize that child care is one of the most important purchases we'll ever make, just doesn't seem convincing.

Are Parents Replaceable?

How is it, I wonder, that so many parents have come to think of themselves as replaceable? How did they come to have such a low opinion of the importance and difficulty of successfully acculturating a child? How have some of us convinced ourselves that we can buy wisdom and happiness for our children the same way we get our houses cleaned or our cars repaired? How have others of us come to believe that establishing government programs to rear children is no more problematic than setting up programs to pave roads or deliver our mail?

This runs against all credibility. Anyone who denies that time, physical presence and intensive one-on-one nurturing are important to children denies every truism of human development research. Anyone who doubts that prolonged separation from one's central loved one can cause serious human privation doubts literature's oldest theme, the first-hand experience of nearly every person, and all that we know about the workings of the human heart and mind. When it is very young children who are involved, beginning life without a secure and unconditional attachment to the only people who really matter to them — their parents — then the potential for damage is truly worrying.

Warnings about full-time daycare's potential to harm very young children have often been strangled, even literally suppressed. This is primarily because they are viewed as an impediment to careerism — and unbridled careerism is a modern fixation, an unquestioned good for everyone from big-business operators to feminist agitators. Just the same, the ambiguity of the warnings can't fully explain the uncritical enthusiasm which daycare has generated over the last decade. Caution lights have appeared, yet we've chosen to ignore them. We have not wanted to notice.

And why have we not wanted to notice? What is it that has made it so threatening to today's childbearing generation to hear that their children need them? I believe that the personal gratifications of an intimate relationship with one's offspring are no less powerful today than in the past. Apparently, however, some people do find them less compelling in the face of modern life's competing blaze of pleasures. Personal priorities, misplaced values, selfishness — call it what you will, I accept that that is probably part of the problem.

But there is another problem, which I consider even more difficult. This is that social support for childrearing, and social esteem for childraisers, has fallen precipitously in this country in recent decades. We have in large measure washed our hands of the idea of children as a common treasure. Bearing a child today can be a lonely and isolating event, for modern mothers in particular.

Often inadvertently, we've recently kicked some long-standing social supports out from under children and parents. Many of the institutions which used to undergird children and child-raising — things like decent public schools in the cities, stable marriages, strong "backdoor" networks among parents, relatives nearby to help out and offer advice, a safe public environment which allows children to play outdoors without supervision — all these have collapsed. Without a supportive social environment, raising a child can become an exhausting task, too much for some parents to handle alone.

This has been exacerbated by the ongoing loosening of ties between generations. Age groups have segregated themselves: families with children in the suburbs, single adults in fashionable city enclaves, older people living independently in Sunbelt retirement communities. Grandparents and extended family members are less accessible, and less willing to be depended upon by parents looking for occasional relief from child care responsibilities. With fewer load sharers available, some parents give up and resort to daycare centers.

How Taxes Affect the Family

We have also allowed the economic position of parents to deteriorate compared to other groups. Tax changes in particular have penalized family making. It is a remarkable but unappreciated fact that, in the period after World War II, middle-class families with children were almost entirely exempt from federal income tax. A married couple family with the median income, two children and average deductions paid just $9 in federal income tax in 1948. That was less than one-third of one percent of their income.

There were two reasons for this. One was that taxes in general were lower. The other was that the personal exemption for dependents was quite high then — the equivalent of nearly $7,000 today.

Our tax structure used to single out families with children for special protection. A couple without children, or a single person, with the same income as the family of four above would have owed seven percent and ten percent of their income respectively in federal income taxes. The consensus was that families with childraising responsibilities were making social contributions, and that they had special needs and vulnerabilities, and so ought not bear any heavy tax burden.

Today, on the other hand, children are viewed as a kind of private consumption item, and tax burdens don't vary much by family responsibility. Parents and young bachelors are treated much the same. Families with median income and two children pay lots of federal tax these days. Indeed, it's quite interesting: employed wives are earning 28 percent of total family income at present. That's just about the size of the average family's total federal tax bill. In other words, the average employed wife is working just to pay off Uncle Sam, no more.

I am very enthusiastic about President George Bush's "child tax credit" proposal, partly because it represents a small reversal of this trend of increasing federal burden on childraisers. There is an even more exciting aspect to the plan. It is one of the very few new social programs put forth in the last three decades which would be absolutely evenhanded and fair to parents who stay home to raise their own children.

There is an illusion in some quarters that our current tax and spending system is balanced, that it is neutral about various family types, and that any new measures to aid traditional families would be unfair favoritism. The point needs to be made very strongly that the Bush child tax credit, and other proposals which would extend help for the first time to stay-at-home parents as well as to employed parents, are not special breaks for special interests at all. All they would do is begin to *even up* the current incentive structure, which is badly skewed toward dual-earner, daycare-using couples.

Most egregiously, we currently have the Child and Dependent Care Credit which costs the U.S. Treasury more than $3 billion a year and is available only to parents who pay others to raise their youngsters. Nothing can be claimed by parents who provide the care themselves. Employed parents have also been allowed to shelter more income in Individual Retirement Accounts (IRAs) than stay-at-home parents. And so forth.

This bias in favor of employed parents makes no sense whatever from the point of view of equity. Two-wage-earner couples have substantially higher average incomes than stay-at-home parents, so the government is effectively redistributing money from poorer to richer families. Even more, such measures are indefensible from a child welfare perspective. If one is trying to create the most hospitable possible environment for child development, one ought to be trying to link parents as closely as possible to their children when they are young, not subsidizing their separation.

Home As a Social Center

One other factor which has increased the isolation of parents in recent decades is the transformation of the American home. At one time, particularly in farm settings which used to be much more common in this country, the home served not only as a family base but also as a social and economic center. It was a place where valuable things were produced, where interesting people could be met, and where society's work got done. Most homes were occupied all day long. Men and women often labored side by side, and in immediate proximity to their children. Family making and work were much better integrated, and children were not considered incompatible with productivity or social life.

Today, however, home, social center and workplace have been radically separated, flung to separate ends of our society. In typical suburban communities, the home is often a lifeless backwater, a place far out of the working mainstream, sometimes little more than a place to sleep. Most of the productive undertakings through which citizens earn their bread and establish their self-worth take place far away.

There is no reason this need be true, however. Over time, with some determination to end the brutal artificiality of the bedroom community, secluding suburbs and alienating city apartment blocks alike can be shaped into something more closely resembling true communities, which of course would make life at home with young children infinitely more agreeable. With new technology and services, vast societal wealth, all sorts of newly accessible communication and information sources,

and a very serious long-term labor shortage looming (this conference is taking place in one of a number of metro areas around
the country with unemployment rates below three percent), the
rebirth and refinement of domestic industry is also both possible
and desirable.

There is much useful work — whether in business for oneself,
doing manual piecework by contract, or connected to an office
by computer modem — which can now be decentralized, and
transacted at home by people who want or need to keep a hand
in the world of paid employment while devoting substantial
energies to family responsibilities. If homes are no longer viewed
as evening and weekend "crash pads," but rather as private
sanctuaries with fluid boundaries to the larger world, then life
as a home-based parent becomes much less frightening.

This, however, is not happening as fast as it should. A host
of zoning laws, labor regulations, union objections, and just
simple conventions are dampening the trend toward home-
based work. Doctors, architects, attorneys, psychologists, and
others who would like to work part-time at home are often dis-
couraged by municipal rules. Individuals in non-professional
occupations, such as hairdressing and tailoring, have long faced
very serious regulatory obstacles to home-based work.

Of course, economic and occupational pressures are only
part of the problem facing stay-at-home parents. The psychological environment may be even more unbalanced. Public
opinion polls show a tremendous decline since the 1950s in the
prestige accorded by our society to parents. Americans who
give precedence to their children are often denied the same level
of esteem and psychic rewards accorded to those who favor their
careers. Women in particular are more likely to be admired and
appreciated for, say, launching a catchy new ad campaign for
toothpaste than they are for nurturing and shaping an original
personality. It's a truly perverse set of priorities.

Surely the private satisfactions of raising children are as immediate, tangible, and even overwhelming, as ever. But there is
now much less collective approval and far fewer cultural ratifi-
cations to being a parent than there once were. It can be psychologically very difficult to be "just" a mother today. And like it
or not, those collective images matter to all of us. Even the strong-

est individual can be worn down by a steady stream of subtle and not-so-subtle messages telling us that, if we were really talented, or really ambitious, we would be in the paid labor force rather than home raising children.

This has been especially true, given that American parents have been getting terrible advice from some of the experts on whom they've relied. Many prominent child advocates have been intimidated out of saying anything critical about daycare. And no wonder! Anyone who expresses reservations about a world of mass daycare will inevitably be accused of harboring a secret desire to keep women barefoot and pregnant in the kitchen. As a result, a broad spectrum of informed opposition to daycare based solely on children's interests has been bullied into silence.

The Feminist Message

So parents have gotten the message that there is no reason not to hand their very young children over to hired custodians. Betty Friedan says daycare is "good" for children. Kate Millett insists that "the care of the young is infinitely better left to trained professionals rather than to harried amateurs with little time nor taste for the education of young minds." Women's magazines are chock full of similar advice.

Young women have often been made to feel that they would be dupes, weaklings and dullards if they didn't jump into the workplace and leave their kids to "less ambitious, less career-capable" hands. It has almost seemed foolish not to hire a substitute parent.

Increasingly, women are finding the courage to protest against this unfair caricature in which maternalism — as complex and humane an impulse as exists within the human breast — is reduced to a kind of penal servitude, whose essence is to debate soap powders. But the protesters swim against a very strong flow. Psychologist Marjorie Hansen Shaevitz concludes from her studies of female roles that "right now there is real prejudice against women who don't work."

I believe one of the tragic ironies of feminism's utter failure to put forth a scheme for meaningful family life and childraising is that it has made worse many of the problems it originally proposed to solve. For instance, in my view one of the most cogent longstanding criticisms of American sex roles and economic arrangements has been the argument that many fathers get so wrapped up in earning and doing at the workplace that they become ground down, dehumanized, losing interest and energy for the intimate joys of family life, and failing to participate fairly in domestic responsibilities. But now, with a large assist from feminist ideology, it appears that workaholism and family dereliction have become equal opportunity diseases, striking mothers as much as fathers. That's not progress.

I spoke at a conference on children some time ago at which daycare campaigner Sylvia Hewlett told an anecdote about her efforts to convince the national accounting firm of Arthur Andersen to institute a company daycare policy, because 40 percent of Andersen's professionals are women. Nearly all of these women, Hewlett pointed out proudly, work "60 hours a week." It was essential, she argued, that programs be put into place so that, after delivering their babies, these hard working employees would keep on in their jobs just as before.

Apparently, Arthur Andersen's executives saw the business value in the plan and accepted her proposal—which is no surprise. Keeping those new parents grinding away is great for business. But I asked myself: what kind of human society urgently encourages its new parents to hold 60-hour-a-week jobs, as if nothing changed when their child was born? What kind of life are we giving those youngsters? Is tax preparation and figure juggling (or any other paid occupation) really so urgent and noble an undertaking as to justify sacrificing the welfare of our children?

Germaine Greer, in her revisionist incarnation, has written that, "In order to compete with men, Western woman has joined the masculine hierarchy and cultivated a masculine sense of self." And, "the closer women draw in social and economic status to the male level, the more disruptive childbirth becomes." I believe the female role defined in strict feminist terms—that is to say, as this mirror image of maleness—simply cannot be reconciled with the maternal role. Something must give. When society denies that childbearers have special talents and special vulnerabilities, it is women who suffer. To deny the existence of womanliness and sexual exceptionalism is to rule out motherhood.

The daycare center is so valuable to feminists because it allows them to tell women that they can avoid squarely facing that monumental, and frightening, choice. You don't have to choose, they say, you can live your life by our principles without giving up anything. If daycare worked as advertised, it would indeed be the ideal palliative — allowing modern Americans to have children without ever fully accepting the life changes, including necessary limitations, that that decision entails.

But, of course, that is an illusion. And, the bill for all this self-deception comes due in the worst possible place: in our cribs and nurseries, where children are blighted by some parents' infantile insistence upon "having it all" — upon enjoying all the benefits of gender without obeying any of gender's urgent commands. In the very saddest cases, daycare becomes a pitiful stopgap for fathers and mothers who have produced children but refuse to become parents.

Relatively few Americans are attracted to the more radical versions of feminist rhetoric, where open hostility to family values is common. But even sophisticated and subtle feminist arguments have sometimes had the inadvertent effect of damaging American family-making, for instance, by contributing to the de-legitimization of self-sacrifice. Subordinating one's strivings to those of another — child or adult — is the same as being taken advantage of in much feminist theory. It is a sign of weakness, to be avoided by liberated thinkers. Without question, Americans have become less "other" oriented in recent years, and American women in particular have moved from their long-standing role of heroic abstainer to one much closer to the traditional self-absorbed position of males.

The Shift Toward Self-Interest

Of course, feminism is by no means the only culprit in this area. It has operated in overlapping fashion with a variety of other extreme individualist heresies. The shift toward self-interest has particularly been encouraged by a rising materialism. Since this country's beginnings we have struggled to reconcile the materialistic indulgence that capitalism allows, and sometimes even requires, with the forbearing Puritan values of deferred gratification, investment in the future, and good neighborliness. But the balance seems to me to have tipped a bit toward consumerism in the last generation.

This affects childrearing in two ways. First, the minimum essentials of childhood have been redefined in such a way as to make starting a family a frightening financial prospect. Under prevailing standards, it costs about $200,000 to raise a child to adulthood. You don't have to spend that much, but most parents will. The accepted standard of what constitutes a materially adequate childhood has risen very high, putting heavy economic pressure on parents.

The second effect of rising American materialism is that many young adults have become accustomed to such a high standard of living — foreign vacations, restaurant meals, charge cards, and so forth — that any life change which requires the couple to exist with just one income feels like a hardship.

In fact, this is the case that is most often made in defense of daycare. It is said that both parents "have to work" in order to make ends meet. This clearly is true in some cases. But it is hard for me to take seriously the generalized argument that most American families can't afford to take some time out of the labor force when their children are young. After all, per capita income in this country — adjusted for inflation — has doubled in the last 22 years. Our houses are 30 percent larger, on the average, than our parents' were. And so forth. You'd have a hard time convincing me that this country can't afford to take care of its children in their vulnerable years.

There is strong evidence that most parents agree with me. Though you rarely hear this in the current daycare debate, the fact is that today three out of four mothers with young children (under age three) either are not employed at all or are employed only part-time or seasonally. Despite the economic social pressures, most Americans still prefer to arrange their lives so they can be with their children when they are very young. This is changing, but we haven't gone fully off the deep end, yet.

What many of those parents who say they can't afford *not* to take paid employment really mean is that they would find it difficult to change their living standards to accommodate the shift. Health club memberships, video tapes, rented summer cottages, $30 haircuts — these kinds of things are being widely accepted as normal middle-class expectations. In themselves, rising living standards are perfectly healthy. But when they begin to distort vital human relations, there is reason for worry.

The fact is, these appetites are stoked shamelessly by marketers of red convertibles, by have-it-all popular magazines, by retailers of all sorts for whom dual-earner couples are an economic gold mine. Let me say as an aside that one ought not expect business people to be particularly friendly to the pro-family agenda in this area. In any case, so long as consumption standards remain as high as ours have become, one can see why many parents feel pressure to keep their full-time jobs even when their young children need them.

In the combined face of economic seductions, enormous social pressures, and the false promise of a costless liberation from serious responsibilities, it is in some ways little wonder that parenting-by-proxy has grown so much in the last two decades. But our society may pay a very stiff price for that shift. Less-well-adjusted children and less-happy parents are likely.

There are larger hazards as well. If it is true, as Edmund Burke said, that "we begin our public affections in our families" and proceed from there toward "a love of mankind," then we begin to see what might be at stake if ever the natural parental devotion to children breaks down.

Chapter 3

COLLECTIVIZED CHILD CARE IN OTHER COUNTRIES
by Eric Brodin

A scholar from Sweden describes, from first-hand experience, the conditions in his native country where the universal institutionalization of infants and preschool children is a national objective, and where the labor-force employment of women is compelled in order to pay the taxes needed to finance the socialist welfare state.

For the last eight years, Eric Brodin has been the Lundy Professor of the Philosophy of Business at Campbell University in North Carolina. A native of Gothenburg, Sweden, from 1972 to 1980 he was director of the Foundation for International Studies in Malmö, Sweden. Since immigrating to the United States, Dr. Brodin has spoken and written extensively about life in Sweden and other European countries based on his first-hand experience and as an international traveler. His booklets on Sweden's family policies have had a wide circulation.

Those who deal in public policy issues are constantly told that the United States is lagging behind Western European nations in general, and Sweden in particular, in providing government social services and regulations. It, therefore, is important to hear from one who has personally observed the effects of European governmental policies on the family.

Dr. Eric Brodin received his undergraduate education at San Francisco State University, his M.A. at the University of California at Berkeley, and his Ph.D. in Political Science and International Relations at the Graduate Institute of International Studies of the University of Geneva in Switzerland.

The proposed federal (as well as state) legislation on child care presents us with a problem that needs to be addressed which has nothing to do with the posturings on this issue by various politicians. In my remarks, I shall deal with some international comparisons and especially address whether we can learn some lessons from my native country, Sweden, which in so many ways has been a pioneer in the trappings of a welfare state, as well as in family and child care legislation.

A recent article in *U. S. News and World Report*[1] reported on the growing tendency in Europe to provide governmental care, even for the smallest children. The 12 member states of the European Community (E.C.) and its 322 million citizens are dealing with child care in a number of different ways. These range from tax credits to government funded *écoles maternelles* in France, so-called "baby nests" in Italy, and "peuterspeelzalen" in the progressive-minded Netherlands. The costs of many of these programs have become such a large burden that some of the governments can no longer afford the vast and expensive programs, as the demands for these services are increasing. Denmark, Belgium, Great Britain and the Federal Republic of Germany have actually been forced to curtail some of the daycare programs already provided. In other places, the funding and responsibility for child care has moved from the central to local government.

The *U. S. News and World Report* article, written by Robin Knight in London, clearly indicates a preference for governmental daycare which is illustrated by the following paragraph: "Many Europeans remain tradition-bound in their thinking about women's roles. An E.C.-wide poll in April [1988] found that 54 percent believed the ideal family still is one where the wife is at home or employed part time. Attitudes count as much as resources in determining the scale of child care provisions. Historically the Dutch, the Irish, the British and the Germans have been most hostile to the idea of working mothers; today this aversion is reinforced by center-right governments." The article criticizes the Federal Republic of Germany because, after promising daycare places for 60 percent of their three- to five-year-olds, "funds are kept short" and "30 percent of the under-three with working mothers are left alone or minded by siblings."

One wonders whether in Germany there are no more grand-parents or older relatives, who in so many cultures worldwide, serve honorably and importantly as the minders of small children whose parents are employed. It is no accident that the nations with the least government-provided care for the very young, such as Spain, Portugal and Italy, are also the nations with the "extended family," that is, a family unit consisting not only of the core family of parents and children, but also including grandparents, unmarried aunts, cousins and the like. Any discussion of child care which fails to consider this natural and important aspect of child care in an extended family is not a balanced one.

The Greed of the Welfare State

In Denmark which, together with Sweden, has the world's highest per capita tax burden, governmental social welfare spending has had to be cut back considerably because there is no way the country can afford to continue its vast panoply of social welfare provisions without increasing taxes. But income taxes already average 50 percent and go as high as 68 percent. Part of the problem is inherent in the welfare state itself.

Sweden, where income taxes are 78 percent, has reached the point, according to Jürgen Habermas, an East German Marxist theoretician, "where the dislocation in the social structure caused by the free play of the market forces becomes so great that the people are no longer willing to pay the price of the necessary remedies. The demands for security remain, but the desire of each person to contribute to the cost of this security diminishes. The welfare society then faces a crisis of confidence."[2] It is obvious to any observer of Europe's welfare states that the condition of crisis has touched a number of them already.

The welfare society — whether you call it cradle to grave, or womb to tomb — can be financed only by the taxes from a labor market in which almost everyone is working and paying taxes. The policy in Sweden of giving the unemployed more than 90 percent of their regular earnings in unemployment compensation provides a disincentive to look for employment, and that is exactly what is happening.

The head of a rehabilitation center in Copenhagen, Denmark, Jens Aage Bjoerkoe, says: "If we fail to carry out major social reforms and alter our social policies, we could end up in the absurd situation where a third of the population produces goods and services, another third are social workers, and the last third are welfare cases and pensioners. The price of our material welfare is that we have made each other weaker in many other areas."[3]

Even so ardent an admirer of the Swedish welfare state as Paul Samuelson recently sounded a voice of warning: "Once societies like Sweden, Norway and the Netherlands pushed the scale of taxation and redistributive expenditures well past 50 percent of GNP, the law of diminishing returns seemed to set in."[4]

Sweden's Anti-Family Policies

As in so much of family legislation, Sweden was among the first countries to introduce sex education. The governmental involvement was taken for granted from the outset. Alva and Gunnar Myrdal, who were at that time highly complimentary of Hitler's eugenic and family policies, laid the foundation of Sweden's modern welfare state when they published their book in 1934 on *Crisis in Swedish Population Policy.*[5] The Myrdals (who later both, but in separate categories, received a Nobel Prize) had presumed that a post-World War II Sweden would see an explosion in population figures. It didn't turn out that way, but the assumption that the central government had an important role to play in the shaping of family policies nevertheless remained part of the *raison d'être* of the welfare state. Alva Myrdal laid it on the line: "The doctrine that women's place is in the home is traditional thinking enmeshed in an accumulation of vague interests, confused emotions and pure nonsense."[6]

The Reverend Dr. Paul Marx, OBE, president of Human Life International, recently visited Scandinavia. In his newsletter, he wrote about Sweden: "Only about 90,000 babies are born each year in this dying nation of 8.4 million people, 15 percent of whom are foreigners. Counting the births of foreigners, the family size in Sweden is 1.6 children. In 1985 Sweden had the oldest population in the world, with 16.9 percent over the age of 65."[7]

That the views enunciated by the Myrdals as early as the 1930s are still the orthodoxy in Sweden's welfare state today was eminently confirmed in a newsletter from the Swedish Information Service, released by the Swedish Royal Consulate General in New York City. Rita Ann Reimer, with an M.A. in Liberal Studies from George Washington University, spent six weeks in

Sweden in 1985 studying Swedish family law. She began her paper, titled "Work and Family Life in Sweden,"[8] with this significant observation:

> "Swedish laws and social policy reflect fundamental assumptions that are not widely accepted in the United States. The most important of these in the context of work and family life is that each non-handicapped adult is responsible for his or her own economic well-being. This means, among other things, that both parents, including mothers of young children, are expected to work for pay usually outside the home. Two necessary corollaries to this assumption are that both parents are equally responsible for the economic support of their children; and that children function best when their emotional needs are satisfied outside the family unit as well as within."

Dr. Reimer also points out, "The Swedish government would also like to shape how the leisure time is utilized. It views the ideal marriage as consisting of two equal wage earners; two equal citizens; two equal parents; and most importantly in this context, two people with equal amounts of leisure time." To bring this about, it is possible, for example, for a man to be paid to stay at home, providing the mother goes away to an all-paid vacation without her husband or children.

With virtual monopoly control of the electronic media (two television channels and three radio stations), the government can ensure that its policies receive wide diffusion. In fact, the law requires that 40 percent of air time be devoted to explaining and demonstrating the virtues of the welfare state. Programs may, for example, be documentaries that ridicule the mother at home. In 1970 the Minister of Finance Gunnar Straeng said: "We don't want to force the woman into the labor market; she should have a right of choice. If she wants to stay home and have a lower living standard, she should be allowed to do so."

Radical voices in Sweden, and especially in the last few years the shrill voices of the feminists, like to characterize the mother at home as living an "unworthy parasitic life." The feminists assert that her isolated life at home makes her into a "spiritual cripple."

The radical proposals were to become central government legislation during the 1960s. This coincided with the radical Olof Palme becoming the Minister of Education (and later, Prime Minister). The *Report to the United Nations About the Status of Women in Sweden* in 1968 admitted that its radical proposals might seem revolutionary and unrealistic to other countries, but claimed that "an ever increasing opinion in Sweden supports these demands."

Yet only one year earlier in a book entitled *The Woman in Sweden in Statistics*, it was shown that, of married women with children under age ten, only seven percent wished to be employed full time and 33 percent wished to be employed part time, whereas more than half, 53 percent, did not want to be employed at all. The situation is very different today. Today more women between 16 and 65 are employed in Sweden than in any other country within the Organization for Economic Cooperation and Development.

The entire taxation system relies upon both parents working full-time in the paid labor force and contributing payroll taxes to support the welfare state. To elect to stay home is actually viewed as a disloyal act. For years the Social Democratic housing policy encouraged the building of very small apartment units. Owning one's own home was ridiculed as bourgeois middle class. Small apartments helped to reduce family size, as well as to exclude grandparents and other relatives, thus creating one-generation households. This policy upset tradition so that the people could be much more readily manipulated to fulfill the objectives of the socialist welfare state.

Sweden's Daycare Policies

In order to provide for everyone's employment it was, of course, necessary for the government to initiate the building of government daycare facilities. In 1971 the so-called daycare facility investigation report was issued. The new provisions for children from six months to seven years were to include facilities for 52 children. Twelve children were to be under two-and-a-half years; the others were in two so-called sibling groups, each with about 20 children between the ages two-and-a-half to six years. The legislated dictates called for four children per adult and a play area of five square meters per child.

The testimonies of physicians, psychologists and parents alike were ignored in the formation of this and later legislation. Studies pointed out that children under three years of age should preferably not be in daycare centers. One investigation showed that children under three years of age were ill four months out of 12 when they were cared for in such centers. Nor had the creators of Swedish family legislation learned anything (if they even attended) from the international symposium on "Fostering the Role of the Family in Today's World," held in Warsaw, Poland in 1970. Professor Antonina Kloskowska summarized the findings of the Warsaw symposium in these words: "The facts presented during the symposium supported the conclusion that the psychological development of the child in its initial years is better in an ordinary home environment than at any state child care facility regardless of how excellent it is."[9]

The radicalization of Swedish sex education, child care and family legislation has been carried out successively through four main avenues. One has been the vast network of special interest organizations utilized by the socialists for propagandistic indoctrination. These organizations include a type of socialist boy scout movement called Young Eagles. This network has a wide program of adult education courses in tax-supported education centers. It has a special organization to attract Christians into socialism called the Brotherhood movement. It can reach out to millions of people who rent their dwellings because the government-allied organization has the exclusive right to negotiate for all who rent in Sweden. Finally it has a very large and ideologically honed organization for Sweden's growing number of pensioners.

Combine this network with Sweden's largest party, which has the right to appoint two-thirds of the bishops of the Swedish State (Lutheran) Church, and a compulsory affiliation with unions, and it's obvious that the socialists have vast propaganda powers. And that is not all.

The ruling party in Sweden appoints the majority of the boards which decide the content of radio and television programming. It has also decided that the whole judicial system is to be used to transform society. In 1969 the then Swedish Minister of Justice (Kling), in the directives for a new family law system, said: "The legal system is one of the most important instruments

which the state can use in order to meet peoples' expectations
and to link these up to developments into new channels."[10]

Schools "Liberate" Children from the Family

Finally, the school, the educational system, was one of the
most important means of changing Swedish society into new and
radical patterns. This is how one of Sweden's pedagogic experts,
Stellan Arvidsson, characterized the family in a handbook given
out by the socialist "temperance organization" Verdandi:

> "One of the difficulties which the school has to face is that
> the homes do not respect the principle of the freedom of religion
> and the child's human rights. In many homes the parents seem
> to think it is their duty to bring up their children in the Chris-
> tian faith. . . . The children are inveigled into the conception
> that there is a personal, omnipotent God, that personal salva-
> tion can only be obtained through Jesus, and that there exists
> a personal life after death. With these peculiar notions the
> child arrives at school and gradually discovers that there are
> other views than those of his parents, conceptions which may
> even have more validity than those the parents taught. The
> children may refuse to listen to these new views and thereby
> be hindered in their free development. The children may also
> absorb the new views resulting in an inner conflict which the
> authority-bound education of the home is responsible for."[11]

This liberation which the school was to complete is a "liberation" from the family, a process which is to substitute the state
for the family. The family is seen as a narrow, restrictive, inhibi-
tory unit contrasted with the wider and more free collectivity of
the state. In 1968 the former chairman of the People's Party's
youth group (ostensibly a non-socialist party) put it in even
clearer terms. In his book *Child in Sweden*, Pehr Garton declaimed:
"The parental monopoly cannot be broken solely by indirect
measures — the State must intervene directly by, for example,
taking the children from the parents during part of their growing-
up years, perhaps a few hours each day, so that a balance of
power is more clearly expressed. . . . It is for the best for the
children and society that a universal and compulsory preschool
program become clearly indoctrinating, thus enabling society to

intervene more directly when it comes to the children's values and attitudes."[12] With anti-family views such as these by Sweden's leading intellectuals, is it any wonder that the moral bankruptcy of Sweden is evidently almost complete?

It is the policy of Sweden's Social Democratic party (which has ruled for 50 years, with only one inter-regnum of six years) to provide institutionalized daycare for all children. They hope that by 1991 they will have built up a network of daycare institutions which are almost exclusively municipal or governmental centers. It is very doubtful that this can be accomplished. The cost is simply prohibitive. In 1959 there were only 1,104 daycare centers in Sweden. By 1980 there were 8,618. By 1991 the Social Democratic government hopes to be able to provide for 430,000 children whose parents are employed.

The estimated current cost of daycare in Sweden today is $10,000 per child per year. Of this, 90 percent comes from tax revenues and only ten percent from the parents. Some statistics are given which indicate that "only" 46 percent of the "need" has been met. There is a basic inability of the governing Socialist party to recognize that there are actually alternatives to the governmental program. Some 30,000 children of employed parents today receive private care paid for by their parents. This private care will gradually be squeezed out, condemned by the Socialists as "profiteering in human needs."

Sweden's unions have strongly propagated for the "professionalizing" of the daycare industry. One spokesperson said in a debate article: "The gain which the state makes from the taxes paid by the working woman would be greater than the cost of building out the daycare system."[13]

But not only is this not correct, the whole principle of choice has been nullified. In the last election, the three non-socialist parties united around a program to benefit the mother at home with a voucher-like compensation which would have cost the Swedish taxpayers about $750 million. With the re-election victory of the Socialists last September, such care will now amount to $1 billion as they intend to build out collective child care centers by 1991.

Aside from the costs, what is the quality of care received in these institutionalized centers? Anna Wahlgren, a journalist and an employed mother, reported in the Swedish newsweekly *Reportage* in 1980: "Children are drugged. Infants are given nerve medicines. Healthy, normal, ordinary children are given tranquilizers so that they will sleep. There are four-year-olds who have developed dependency syndromes. There are child daycare centers where half the children are given sleeping pills and others where pre-written, ready-made prescriptions are available without a doctor giving as much as five minutes of his time to either child or parent."[14]

"Being Young in Sweden"

Professor Sven Rydenfelt, of the University of Lund in southern Sweden, tells in his book, *The Decline of the Welfare State*, about the problems of "being young in Sweden": "Has there ever in time and place been a society whose young people are treated so badly and felt themselves so unhappy as in today's Sweden? Of Swedish mothers with children under the age of seven, 70 percent are in the work force. Altogether too many preschool children have reasons to feel abandoned and unfortunate. In the schools of this welfare state — nine years' obligatory schooling — altogether too many children are ill at ease and so unhappy that they are incapable of learning anything. Too many pupils are experiencing school as some kind of prison — forced labor institution — and feel so suppressed and ill treated that they must revolt. Since 1950 the cases of vandalism reported to the police have increased 12 times.

"Too many of the school children attempt to flee a painful reality by the means of alcohol and narcotics and before long will end up in uncontrollable situations. As a consequence the suicide rate among the seven- to 16-year-olds has doubled since 1960. . . . Badly treated and emotionally undernourished, they become aggressive youths whose accumulated aggressions are expressed, not only in violence and vandalization in the schools, but also result in criminal acts against the established society, a society from which they feel they have been expelled. Since 1950 criminal acts by the 15- to 17-year-olds have increased by seven times. The Swedish suicide statistics are relatively high, but the official reports do not tell the whole truth. The mortality rate among young criminals and drug addicts is 15 times higher than the average, and the Swedish hospitals are increasingly filled with youthful addicts. Many deaths among the young are in reality disguised suicides—they drug themselves to death because they can't stand living in Sweden's welfare state."[15]

Collective and increasingly compulsory daycare is only one step in the gradual break-up of families. Families provide the most basic—and therefore conservative—element in our society. Individuals can be easily manipulated by the state. Not so with families which tend to preserve that independence from which a successfully cooperating society can be built. Brita Sundberg-Weitman, a highly-placed judicial representative in Sweden, says in a book published in 1981: "There is one country in Europe where authorities are exposing children to physical harm and psychological torture. In this country social welfare agents are breaking constitutionally protected laws and have committed clearly illegal acts. There, government authorities can separate a child from his or her parents in order to prevent the parents from giving the child a privileged education. In that country it is possible to place a social welfare agent in the home for 20 hours within one week in order to teach the parents to show proper respect for the state."

No, this distinguished jurist is not speaking about Stalinist Eastern Europe. She is speaking about Sweden.

Will someone be able, before long, to describe the situation in the United States in similar words? That is one of the reasons why this conference on child care is so important. We must continue our commitment to traditional and family-related values. We are here to raise a standard of liberty for all to see. On that standard (as well as within our hearts) should be inscribed: "For our God, our religion, our freedom, our peace, and our children."

I am one among millions who have been privileged to find refuge in this land of freedom after usurpation by corrupt governmental power in our native lands prevented truth from making itself believed. I pledge with you today that I will redouble my efforts because eternal vigilance is the price of liberty, without which we cannot have a vision for the future. I have left the ancestral homeland of my family because I am convinced that America is "the last, best hope for mankind."

Our tasks are clear. We must learn the lessons which history teaches us, lest we repeat its costly mistakes. Let us pledge our efforts so that freedom will not be extinguished from this land, realizing, in the words of a great man of God, that "No success in life can compensate for failure in the home."

Notes

1. August 22, 1988.
2. Legitimationsproblem im Spätkapitalismus.
3. *Los Angeles Times* (August 23, 1987).
4. *New York Times* (November 1, 1987).
5. Reprinted by the M.I.T. Press (1968) under the title *Nation and Family: The Swedish Experiment in Democratic Family and Population Policy.*
6. *Ibid.*, p. 398.
7. Special Report #45, p. 4.
8. *Social Change in Sweden*, 34 (April, 1986).
9. *Rädda Familjen/Save the Family* (1972), p. 36.
10. *Ibid.*, p. 22.
11. *The Atheist's Handbook* (Stockholm: Prisma, 1963), p. 59.
12. pp. 130, 135.
13. *Svenska Dagbladet* (April 27, 1988).
14. *Reportage*, Stockholm, 8 (1980).
15. *The Decline of the Welfare State* (Stockholm: Timbro publishers, 1983), pp. 57-59.

Chapter 4

A CHILD PSYCHIATRIST
LOOKS AT CHILD CARE

by Donald B. Rinsley, M.D., F.R.S.H.

An authority on child development and personality disorders describes how a baby discovers the world around him during the first years of life, and how there is no real substitute for the presence of a caring mother and father. He urges — for the sake of the children — that society choose quality care for children, which is family care.

Donald B. Rinsley, M.D., F.R.S.H., is Clinical Professor of Psychiatry at the University of Kansas School of Medicine, and Senior Faculty Member in Adult and Child Psychiatry at the Karl Menninger School of Psychiatry and Mental Health Sciences. He is an internationally recognized authority on child and adolescent development and personality disorders and has published more than 50 scientific papers and two books devoted to these subjects.

Dr. Rinsley holds fellowships in the American Psychiatric Association, the American College of Psychoanalysts, the American Society for Adolescent Psychiatry, the American Association of Children's Residential Centers, the American Association for the Advancement of Science, the New York Academy of Sciences, and the Royal Society of Health of London. He is certified as a Diplomate of the American Board of Psychiatry and Neurology and the American Board of Medical Psychotherapists.

Dr. Rinsley is an honor graduate of Harvard University (A.B.) and Washington University School of Medicine (M.D.). He was formerly a resident in Pediatrics at the St. Louis Children's Hospital and trained in Psychiatry, Child Psychiatry and Psychoanalysis at the Menninger Foundation. He was the 1968 winner of the Strecker Award of the Institute of Pennsylvania Hospital for contributions to the care and treatment of severely mentally ill children. He is married and the father of one daughter.

Daycare may be defined as the outplacement of children below age three years in some form of supervised child care facility other than the child's natural home. The term nursery school is used by some for such outplacement of children above the age of three years and generally below six years of age. In this country at the present time, daycare facilities are largely unregulated and range from neighbors', friends' and relatives' homes to group care operations supervised by strangers who may or may not have had child care training or been parents themselves.

There is growing evidence that infants and toddlers placed in for-profit daycare facilities do not grow and develop as well as those raised in natural two-parent families. Accumulating studies indicate that outplaced young children do not thrive as well, suffer more infectious diseases, and display more learning and behavior problems when compared with home-reared children. Clinical data based upon psychoanalytic child development studies have helped to explain to some extent the reasons for these negative effects of daycare placement.

During the first three or four years of life, the child undergoes an enormous expansion of intellectual, emotional and neuromuscular development. From the very beginning of life outside the mother's body, the infant seeks to relate to, and to bond with, the mother by means of reflex actions of contact-seeking, rooting and sucking. This bonding relationship is essential for the later development of the child's capacity to form human relationships, thereby to become a socialized human being. It forms the basis for the individual's ability to think clearly, to develop a sense of property ("what is yours, what is mine"), to respect others, and to learn.

The mother's capacity to nurture her baby, to enjoy her relationship to it, is maximized by the loving care and support she receives from her husband, the child's father. Additional studies show that the child is very early able to distinguish between the mother and the father in terms of attitude, tone of voice and general behavior. Nature has provided that, for full and complete development, the growing infant and child requires both parents from the beginning. There is evidence that the child's intellectual development is maximized by the presence of a caring, involved father who takes a strong interest in and intimately interacts with and relates to his youngster. The mother-infant bonding relationship, healthily supported by a loving, caring father, is the most important influence that shapes the child's future relationships and capacity for social living throughout his future life.

How is this so? We know that the newborn infant comes into the world unable to regulate its own body processes to any great degree. Indeed, for some hours after delivery, the baby is unable to maintain its own body temperature and needs to be warmed by close contact with the mother's body or, in her absence, in a temperature-regulated isolette. The baby's heart and blood-circulating systems, its feeding and digestive system, its breathing system, its sense organs, and its nerves and muscles begin to function to maintain its life as a result of intimate contact with the mother.

In the nursing-feeding situation, the baby "takes in" much more than milk or formula. It takes in, as well, the features and characteristics of the mother's breast, face and body and her attitudes toward the baby as she sings, coos and talks to him. By so doing, she puts to rest the baby's natural storminess and irritability, which in turn strengthens the baby's natural urge to "take her in," to make her image a part of his inner world. Thus are the foundations of the baby's later personality laid down during this very early bonding period—this first year of life.

During that period, the infant utilizes this early bonding with the mother to develop the beginning of a sense of self. He or she takes great interest in the mother, looking intently at her, touching and feeling her face, her body, her hair, her necklaces and earrings, forming an inner image of her as she holds him close while feeding and playing with him or her. At about six months, the baby suddenly seems to "come alive" to the world, appearing alert to things and events outside the mother-infant relationship and now more able to maintain sustained attention to them.

Soon the baby begins to crawl away from mother, to assert his natural drive for independence, but only with the mother's ongoing support and nurturance. At about ten months he stands up and takes the first hesitant steps toward walking and exploring the world "outside," toward the far-off goal of becoming an independent human person.

At about 18 months, the toddler has "taken in" mother to the extent that he begins to have the ability to form an inner image of her when she is not present. Over the next one-and-a-half to two years, the toddler will be more and more able to call up that inner image of mother in order to ease and put to rest his storminess and irritability when she is not there. At the same time, the toddler begins to realize that people and things outside himself or herself have an existence of their own, apart from and independent of him or her. They are real, and—wonderful to behold—so is he or she!

When the Child Starts to Separate

Thus begins the child's effort to begin to separate from mother, to find himself or herself as a person in relation to, but yet apart from her. At this time, the father plays a very important role in the youngster's drive to "be oneself," both by continuing to support his wife's healthy need to help the baby to launch himself on the way toward eventual independence and accomplishment, and by furthering that launching by increasing personal involvement with his youngster.

As healthy separation proceeds, the "inner images" that the child has of both father and mother become increasingly available to the child to strengthen the child's need to regulate his inner experiences when the parents are not immediately available. But these images are not yet stable and reliable enough to allow for such inner regulation, and it will take another several years before they are. In the meantime, the child will be prone to experience feelings of abandonment, accompanied by some degree of anxiety and even panic, when the parents are not available and the inner images he has of them cannot be summoned up to ease the youngster's inner tension. For the average child, these stable, reliable, tension-relieving inner images are not in place much before 36 to 45 months of age, and even then, they will need frequent strengthening, reinforcement, by the parents' nurturant and disciplinary presence.

The stability and availability of the child's inner parent-images make an indispensable contribution to the development of the child's self-image. Between one-and-a-half and three years of age, the child begins to experience himself or herself *as a person* in relation to those images. As noted, the child now begins the exceedingly important process of distinguishing between self and non-self, between "me" and "not-me," between what is "inside" and what is "outside." This is called developing *a sense of reality*, of distinguishing what is real from what is imaginary.

Associated with this important development, there occurs a great leap forward in the child's ability to think and reason, which occurs around age two. As a result, the child now begins the long process of intellectual development which underlies his ability to "make sense" of the world and of his relationship to himself and to things, people and events encountered in everyday life. All this will require many more years of intellectual, emotional and social growth and development as the child proceeds through the school years, ultimately preparing him or her for the eventual attainment of mature adulthood. Throughout these years, the child will continue to rely on the presence of a stable two-parent family to sustain him or her in this important effort.

Of course, this is not to say that substitute parenting cannot serve an otherwise well-endowed young child's natural, inborn drive to grow and mature with reasonable effectiveness. Thus, parental illness or even death will require that other caretakers be brought in to look after the infant or toddler, and the pressure of economic necessity may unfortunately force an otherwise well-motivated mother to turn her child over to others during the working day.

But evidence suggests that the mother-infant bond, which actually begins to form during the mother's pregnancy, is unique and cannot be fully substituted for by even the most sensitive and caring surrogate mother figures. Much less can it be substituted for by even the best-trained day caretakers, who may also be responsible for several or more other outplaced children who make time-consuming and often enervating demands. As all good mothers know, and no man needs to tell them, meeting a young child's needs for contact and nurturance during the first half year following delivery is a full-time proposition. Nor can the child be left out of sight for even brief periods for several years thereafter, lest his enormous curiosity and physical activity propel him into dangerous situations inside and outside the home with which he is as yet too immature to cope.

As is well known, the human being requires the longest period of parental guidance, discipline and nurturance among living organisms before the young one is capable of mature, independent life. No substitute has been found, nor is ever likely to be found, for the natural two-parent family to serve as the vehicle for the optimal training and socialization of the human child. It follows that whatever serves to strengthen the family serves also to strengthen the society of which it is so important a part. By the same token, whatever weakens, impairs or damages the family ultimately serves to weaken, impair or damage society as a whole.

Transmitting Societal and Family Traditions

The most important factors that underlie and strengthen the family's role in producing healthy, socialized children are the collective beliefs, rules, customs and cultural standards and norms that govern and regulate their behavior. Together, these constitute society's *traditions*, whether secular or religious. Some of these undergo evolutionary change over time, while others remain unaltered in the wake of changing social conditions. Together with society's extra-familial institutions — its laws and statutes, its schools and its religious institutions — the family transmits these traditions to its children from generation to generation, to impart to them the ethical and moral codes and standards by which to govern themselves, and by which society as a whole governs itself.

Thus, the childrearing process, for which the family has the primary and major responsibility, consists of the countless ways in which the child learns to "take in," to internalize these traditions, to make them a basic part of himself or herself, hence to utilize them to become a contributing member of the next generation.

To recapitulate, the basis for the young child's intellectual, emotional and social growth and development is derived from the infant-toddler's capacity to "take in" the parents, as it were, to identify with them, thereby to generate stable inner images of them in relation to which the child proceeds to form a stable inner image of himself or herself, leading eventually to the formation of his later identity as a person. As I have mentioned, these images should be in place by the time the average child reaches three-and-a-half to four years of age.

Throughout the remaining childhood years, the child continues to "take in," to internalize and to further elaborate and remodel the parents' attitudes, values and rules of conduct as these are supplemented by what he learns from his ever-growing experience outside the home from contacts with peers, other children and adults, the school, the church or temple, and the written and broadcast media. As his intellectual and emotional horizons continue to widen, the child becomes more and more his "own person" as this is furthered by his increasing capacity to think, reason and make judgments about oneself and the world in which one lives. Throughout this enormously fertile period of development, the child must rely on the stability and support of his family and home environment as the reassuring nest from which he will one day launch himself into the world as an emancipated adult.

Based on these facts, the use of multiple or substitute caretakers for the young child must be looked upon with a most critical eye. If they are necessary for whatever reasons, the best substitute parents are extended family members — grandparents, uncles and aunts, for example — who have a genuine emotional interest in the child. The use of such extended family members typifies the more tightly knit, traditional families in which the relatives, including those who may serve as substitute or proxy caretakers for the child, share similar attitudes and points of view, including those concerning how to raise children. As a result, children raised in such an extended family atmosphere tend to receive relatively consistent parenting, and hence are not subject to changing and competing attitudes and values before they have developed the intellectual and emotional capacity to evaluate and effectively deal with them.

In the United States in particular, both the basic and the extended family have become seriously weakened in recent decades, as we all know. The latter, which has long served as the essential support for the former, has suffered as a result of widespread social mobility, with countless families moving away, far distant from their brothers, sisters, parents, aunts, uncles and loved ones. Even worse, the growing divorce rate and the vast increase in the number of one-parent families, usually without a father, have deprived large and increasing numbers of children of the optimal two-parent childrearing experience. It has been estimated that, by the year 2000, a majority of people will have been brought up in such one-parent families.

The Growth of Daycare

As expected, one result of these changes has been the relatively enormous growth of substitute daycare for children under age three and of nursery-school care for older preschool children. Daycare facilities vary from relatively good small groups with interested, caring adult supervisors to large, poorly run groups conducted by poorly trained and ill motivated individuals with little or no interest in the children other than to control their behavior, leading in not a few cases to actual child neglect and abuse on a scale which is greater than that portrayed by the generally understood statistics on the subject. In both situations, however, the adult caretakers lack the emotional bonding with the children that only the natural family's parents can provide.

Of course, we must remember that not every natural, two-parent family raises healthy children. Natural parents suffering from mental and personality disorders, sexual perversions or criminal anti-social tendencies can and do seriously damage their children's potential for healthy growth and development. Again, there are always some children raised under such conditions who can and do emerge as successful and even creative adult citizens. As I have mentioned, however, the evidence strongly suggests that the outplacement of young children in daycare with adult strangers, no matter how caring they may be, has negative long-term effects on their overall growth and development.

There is also growing evidence that too-early placement of young children in school may place limits on their ability to make full use of their developmental potential. By the same token, these studies indicate that keeping the child at home with caring parents through age seven to nine appears to maximize that potential. Most children are unable to discipline themselves much before that age, even with adult guidance, to long hours of regimented classroom attendance, rigid schedules and sustained concentration. The result of forcing them into such a situation is often to provoke a distaste for school and for learning, even of a life-long nature. There is further evidence that excessive early peer socialization tends to promote undue aggressiveness, and it certainly increases the risk of acquired infectious diseases. More and more parents have come to realize that too-early enrollment of the young child in formal school is not in the child's best interest.

Some of the reasons for this are to be found in the young child's natural absorption in fantasy and in the play that accompanies it. Play has been described as the child's work, and he needs a good deal of time for it. He needs to draw and mold, rub and smear, run and jump, manipulate and invent, stick his nose into everything he can, create a world of imaginative "make-believe," both when playing with peers and friends and when playing alone under his parents' watchful eyes. He needs to explore the real world around him, looking, touching, poking, smelling — discovering. In his play and fantasy, he acts and re-enacts his daily experiences in his world and the satisfactions, frustrations and conflicts it brings to him. The make-believe persons, figures and situations he creates out of these experiences serve as important stimulants for his intellectual and emotional development. The fantasies associated with them form the necessary basis for his increasing ability to think and to plan effectively and creatively.

It has rightly been said that the healthily developing child who is raised in a healthy two-parent family learns three fundamental things about himself or herself at least: "I am myself, a person"; "I can do things and I am capable"; and "I am a boy" or "I am a girl." The third of these has to do with what is called sex or gender identity. It means that the child born as a boy comes to view and consider himself as a male, and the child born as a girl comes to view and consider herself as a female. Thus, the child's natural biological or physical identity as male or female comes into line with his or her psychological identity as such. By the time the healthily developing child has graduated from toddlerhood, he or she has identified with the parent of the same sex: the boy naturally desires to imitate, to be and to become like his dad, and the girl like her mom. The parent of the opposite sex is essential to strengthen, to reinforce the child's sexual or gender identity, by providing a role model for the child's later selection of a mate when he or she has become an adult, ready for the choice of a marriage partner.

One need not be a genius to understand that a child raised in a healthy two-parent family, with a mother and a father who are committed to and love one another, will very likely "take in" and develop a positive view of marriage and family life that will equip him or her for a healthy home and family life in the future. The opposite is also painfully true. A child raised in a broken, one-parent, abusive, or neglectful family, or a family characterized by parental illness, violence or infidelity, will "take in" and develop a dim, negative view of family life. The result will be to set the stage for a repetition of a similar situation in the child's later years. It has truly been said that, as the twig is bent, the tree's inclined. Thus do violence, neglect, abuse and misery breed violence, neglect, abuse and misery in the next generation's families.

A Weakened Society Weakens the Family

As noted before, whatever weakens the family ultimately weakens society. In turn, a weakened society weakens the family, and even the healthiest family will find it difficult to raise its youngsters in a greatly troubled society or nation. Many have come to believe that the United States in particular, and Western society in general, have become increasingly troubled. Traditional cultural norms and values have become increasingly eroded. Drugs, violence, crime and delinquency, juvenile suicide, illegitimate pregnancies, abortions and sexually transmitted diseases, including AIDS, have skyrocketed. Violence and pornography have reached epidemic proportions in the media. Drugs, medications and household preparations are widely advertised as a means to achieve health, happiness, physical beauty and sexual potency. The public schools in many places have become a national disgrace, with huge numbers of overworked, poorly paid, and often poorly educated teachers serving as glorified baby-sitters in classrooms unworthy of the title *learning environments*.

Traditional standards of good and bad, right and wrong, healthy and sick have given way to a form of valueless, situational ethics, typified by the so-called Playboy philosophy in which anything goes and whatever you want to do is fine as long as it pleases you to do it. Popular music has long since degenerated into dissonant, non-melodic and often ear-splitting noises performed by far-out, wildly gyrating, ill-clad shouters and screamers, themselves immersed in illicit drugs, who serve as youth idols for the young. Sexual perversion, including "committed" homosexuality and lesbianism, are portrayed as "liberated alternate lifestyles." And the law forbids a moment of prayerful silence in the classrooms of a nation whose motto is "In God We Trust."

More and more parents, themselves the products of broken, often abusive homes, find themselves confused and perplexed in such a social atmosphere and unable to serve as healthy role models for their increasingly confused and perplexed children. A 50 percent divorce rate reflects an increasingly common view of civil and ecclesiastical marriage, not as a lifelong commitment to homebuilding and childrearing, but rather as a sort of easily terminated way station on the road to that shibboleth of the 1950s, 1960s and 1970s called "self-actualization." Does it come as a surprise, then, that large numbers of parents view their children as irritating impediments, to be shunted aside in the pursuit of the parents' egocentric personal goals? And ready at hand are the daycare facility and the nursery school to serve as dumping grounds for the unfortunate offspring of these self-serving parents.

Happily, however, it is also evident that a majority of mothers, otherwise driven into the work force by economic necessity, would much prefer to remain at home full-time with their young children. That preference reflects their natural biological need to fulfill their nurturant parental responsibility to their youngsters well beyond the moment at which they brought them into the world. They know that parenthood is their most important occupation, and they would postpone entering full-time work or educational self-advancement until their youngsters are mature enough to grow and develop healthily without round-the-clock attention and care.

The solution for a majority of working mothers, in my view, is to provide them with adequate financial support so that they need not be employed outside the home, at least during the first three to five years following their children's births, and hopefully beyond that. In these economic times, and in view of what is known of child development, it would be far wiser to provide government funds to keep mothers at home, than to pour billions of dollars into substitute daycare and nursery school facilities that inevitably serve as inferior, and not rarely dangerous, alternatives to natural parental care.

It is a truism that our children are our most precious natural assets. They are the coming generations' adults whose individual and collective efforts will determine whether and how our nation and our way of life will survive in an immensely troubled world. That survival will be guaranteed by an enlightened pro-family social policy which fully supports and strengthens the parents' overwhelmingly important tasks as guides, caregivers and instructors of the nation's children. It will be endangered by anything, including widespread substitute child care, that detracts from and ultimately weakens the natural family's capacity to perform that task.

Chapter 5

ATTACHMENT AND
INFANT DAYCARE
by Brenda Hunter

A scholar who has examined the up-to-date evidence on day-care explains the Attachment Theory, the Strange Situation, and the power of mother love. She challenges some of our current cultural attitudes about the role of motherhood.

Brenda Hunter is the author of Beyond Divorce *and* Where Have All the Mothers Gone? *She holds a Master's degree in English and has taught at several colleges and universities.*

Mrs. Hunter is currently working on her doctorate in psychology at Georgetown University. Her dissertation (for which she has already collected her data) is a study of educated, employed mothers' attitudes toward separation from their first-born infants.

Because of her concern for the American family, Brenda Hunter founded, and is president of, a national organization for mothers who elect to stay home called Home by Choice. She is the wife of Don Hunter, an attorney, and the mother of two grown daughters.

The year is 1780 and Lieutenant Lenoir of the Paris police notes with some bitterness and regret that, of the 21,000 babies born in Paris that year, only 1,000 were breastfed by their mothers. Another 1,000 were lucky enough to be breastfed at home by live-in wet nurses. As for the rest, they were deported to the countryside and handed to "illiterate child peddlers who thronged to the capital's street corners and marketplaces."[1] Once these deported babies arrived at their foster homes, often rural hovels, they were fed winesoaked bread and mashed chestnuts. As a consequence, they suffered from scurvy, dysentery and other diseases which killed half of them by the age of two. When they died, their indifferent parents seldom inquired about the causes of death. One survivor, Charles Maurice de Talleyrand, a famous French diplomat who was described as "cynical, immoral, and self-seeking," spent his first four years with a wet nurse in the country. As a result of her negligence, he fell off a chest of drawers and returned home dragging a clubfoot, lame for life.

This account of maternal solicitude comes from the 1981 book, *Mother Love*, by French feminist Elizabeth Badinter. Badinter, whose book has caused a greater stir in France in this decade than any other feminist document, has impeccable credentials. A Ph.D. in philosophy, Badinter is the first female professor at Paris' prestigious Ecole Polytechnique.

Her book's theme is that maternal instinct does not exist. Badinter believes that, when mother love is evident, it is culturally induced. If no cultural pressure exists for women to love and nurture their children, then, writes Badinter, women will act according to their own nature, which is selfish and self-centered.

To better understand the rejection of motherhood in 18th century France, we need to realize, says Badinter, that during this time mother's work in the home was not valued by society. "At best it was considered normal; at worst, vulgar." Women received no applause for nurturing their children and they knew that, to feel any sense of self-worth, they "had to choose a path other than motherhood."[2]

Does this sound familiar? Whether we believe in maternal instinct or not, Badinter's words have a ring of truth. It sounds as if she is describing cultural attitudes in America during the past two decades. Whereas upper-middle-class women in 18th century France went to the salons, modern mothers are encouraged to head for the marketplace.

An intriguing sub-theme in Badinter's book, and one that is highly relevant to our discussion, is the absence of feeling that existed between 18th century parents and their returning children. Badinter notes that the parents were not particularly joyful when their children, sometimes sick or maimed, returned from the countryside. Keep in mind that these children were seldom visited by their parents during their sojourn in the country. Talleyrand's mother visited him only twice in four years, and this was considered normal. Badinter writes that the relationships between French parents and their children during the 18th century were marked by emotional distance.

What caused this absence of feeling, this lack of an emotional bond, between the parents and their children? From a psychological perspective, this can be explained as a lack of attachment. Attachment refers to the emotional bond or tie that forms between a baby and his parents during the first year of life, which colors the whole of life.

"The Foundation Stone of Personality"

According to British psychiatrist John Bowlby, well-known for his theory of attachment, the attachment relationship that a young child forges with his mother "forms the foundation stone of personality." Bowlby writes in his book *Attachment and Loss* that "the young child's hunger for his mother's presence is as great as his hunger for food," and that "her absence inevitably generates a powerful sense of loss and anger."[3]

The formation of this attachment relationship between the baby and his mother, then, is a critical developmental issue during the first year of life. Psychologists Sroufe and Waters (1977) describe attachment as a "psychological tether which binds infant and caregiver together,"[4] allowing the baby to explore his environment while using his mother or caregiver as a secure base.

I need to point out at this juncture that babies form an attachment relationship with their fathers, also. Bowlby, however, believes in a hierarchy of attachment figures with one functioning as a "touchstone."[5] It is to this primary attachment figure that the child turns when he is frightened, ill, or distressed. Researcher Michael Lamb, who has written extensively about the father's role in child development, is careful to point out that the research shows that the baby attaches to both parents during the first 12 to 18 months of life; but when the child is tired or hungry or distressed, and both mother and father are in the room, the unhappy baby makes a beeline for his mother.[6]

In my thinking, Lamb's research review underscores Bowlby's belief in the central importance of the mother during the child's earliest years. Even though society has tried to draft fathers, baby-sitters, nannies, and corporations to serve as "mothers" in recent years, mother, it seems, is not off the hook. She is still a central figure in her child's emotional development.

Bowlby notes further that all babies attach to their parents, even abused babies. What varies from child to child is the quality of that attachment relationship which he has with his parents. Is it secure or insecure? The research shows that a young child forms a different attachment relationship with each parent. He can have a secure attachment to one and an insecure attachment to the other. Fortunate, indeed, is the child who is securely attached to both. Psychologist Mary Main believes, however, that as we mature into adulthood we merge these two relationships into one composite view of our own attachment history.[7]

If the child forms a secure attachment relationship with his parents, he will, according to Bowlby, form an internal working model (or an inner representation) of himself, his world, and his parents that is positive. He will be a cooperative individual as he grows up, possessing high self-esteem. He will be able to trust others. He will be capable of establishing intimate relationships with his spouse and his children later in life.[8]

If, on the other hand, the attachment relationships the child forges with his parents are insecure, what then? Then, according to Bowlby, the child will come to view the world and others through the lens of mistrust. He will also feel unworthy in his core and will possess low self-esteem. Later in life he will have difficulty establishing intimacy with those people who matter most—his spouse and his children.[9]

Bowlby further suggests that, once a young child has formed these internal working models of self, the world, and his primary attachment figures, they will be difficult to change. Our internal working models (or our inner representations) exist outside of conscious human awareness, and thus they resist change. We are, says Bowlby, like computers that have programmed and stored certain information. We will automatically respond to new situations and other people based on the information derived from past experiences. Bowlby does believe that it is possible to reappraise our internal working models later in life, but he states that this is no easy task.[10]

The Strange Situation

Thus far, we have discussed attachment theory. How can we determine whether any attachment relationship is secure or insecure? To date, most of the research in the attachment area has focused on infants and young children.

The primary way of measuring an infant's attachment relationship with his mother or father is a laboratory experiment called the "Strange Situation." Created in the late 1960s by psychologist Mary Ainsworth, this experiment consists of 8 three-minute episodes involving mother, stranger and baby in a laboratory setting.[11] The most important part of this experiment consists of two reunion episodes when the mother comes back into the room, having left her baby, first with a stranger, then alone. Now that is a strange situation for most babies, wouldn't you agree?

What do babies do when their mothers leave them and then return after a brief absence? Remember that the baby does not know that Mom waits just outside the door. Some babies go slightly berserk; others appear not to notice. Having spent three days at the University of Virginia viewing videotapes of the Strange Situation, let me tell you that this experiment is a little drama. I was amazed at the differences in the babies.

The first type is the securely-attached baby. This baby has had sensitive, consistent and responsive mothering. He has, thus, learned to trust his mother. He is usually quite upset when his mother leaves, and no stranger can comfort him. When his mother returns, this baby crawls or runs to her, wanting to be picked up. He is easily comforted by his mother and is soon happily playing with toys.

How different the behavior of the insecure babies. Ainsworth found two groups of these — the "anxious-resistant" and the "anxious-avoidant." First, the anxious-resistant. These babies usually head for their mothers after the brief separation, but they are angry and ambivalent. They have had unpredictable mothering. Sometimes their mothers have been loving and dependable; sometimes they have not. So these babies have learned that mother cannot be depended upon consistently to meet their needs. Hence, their anger. Also, these babies tend to be inconsolable. They do not stop crying when their mothers try to comfort them. Nor do they become happily engaged with the world around them.

Then there are those babies whom Ainsworth calls anxious-avoidant. These intrigue me most because they look great in any setting. They seem to personify the American virtues of independence and individualism, except as Ainsworth has said, it is not normal for babies this young to be so independent.[12] These anxious-avoidant babies do not appear to need their mothers. When the mother leaves the room, this baby usually does not cry. He continues to play happily in her absence, unlike the distracted, distressed securely-attached baby. And when mother returns? This baby avoids his mother. I saw babies actually crawl or walk away from their mothers.

If this baby is picked up, he invariably squirms, wanting to be put down. Moreover, this baby seems to like the stranger as much as his mother. If the baby is distressed, any warm body will do. Interestingly, Ainsworth found that the mothers of anxious-avoidant babies did not like physical contact with their babies. These mothers often repulsed their baby's bids for physical comfort.

I have given you this much detail on the Strange Situation because it is the chief instrument used in infant daycare research today and it is often referred to in the media. I wish I could show you a videotape of babies and their mothers in the Strange Situation because the behavior by the babies is so different.

When I got home after those days of seeing and hearing distressed babies, I was exhausted. I was also profoundly moved. I realized that even as young as 12 months we know (albeit in a primitive way) if our mothers are trustworthy or not. That's a pretty young age to begin grappling with the knowledge that some people can be counted on while others cannot.

Another important reason for understanding the Strange Situation is that studies since 1980 which have used this experiment have found that when babies are placed in "other than mother" care during the first year of life — even good quality care — about 50 percent are insecurely attached to their mothers. This is an important statistic because, when Ainsworth first started her research, a third of the babies were insecurely attached. Thus, the number of insecurely attached babies in day-care is definitely on the rise.

New Evidence on Daycare

The psychologist who is sounding the alarm today in the area of infant daycare is Jay Belsky of Penn State University. Belsky, who has been a daycare researcher for more than ten years, said in 1977 that he found little evidence of any negative effects of infant daycare. Belsky has since come to believe that infant daycare may, in fact, erode a young child's sense of trust, security, and order in the world.

Belsky, whose two sons were raised at home in the care of their mother, believes that the research since 1980 which has used the Strange Situation indicates that infant daycare has harmful results. Writing in the publication *Zero to Three*, Belsky mentions several studies that show the harmful effects of infant daycare.[13]

A study by Schwartz of daycare and home-reared infants found that those babies who began daycare during the first year of life were more likely to avoid their mothers during the re-union episodes of the Strange Situation than those babies raised at home by their mothers.[14] Another study by Wille and Jacobsen found that, among 18-month-old children who avoided their mothers upon reunion, those who were anxious-avoidant had experienced more than three times as much "other than mother" care as those found to be securely attached (15.9 hours per week vs. 4.5 hours per week).[15]

Another study by Chase-Lansdale and Owen found that boys were more likely to be insecurely attached to their fathers when their mothers were employed.[16] This is interesting since some psychologists feel that boys are more vulnerable psychologically from birth than are girls. In this study the children were from stable, middle-class families.

Finally, another study by Barglow et al. of affluent families in the Chicago area found that, when babies were placed in out-of-home care during the first year of life for 20 + hours per week, they displayed more avoidance of their mothers than those babies cared for by their mothers at home. Barglow suggests that, when mother goes back to her job during the baby's first year of life, the baby comes to view the daily separations as rejection.[17] In other words, while the mother herself may not be rejecting her baby and thereby producing avoidance, the baby interprets her absence as rejection.

What about the long-term development of those children placed in daycare during the first year of life? A study by Schwarz et al. found that three- and four-year-olds who had been in daycare since the early months of life were more physically and verbally abusive with adults and peers than their home-reared counterparts.[18] A Bermuda study of two-year-olds found that all those who had started group care in infancy were later rated as more maladjusted when studied at three to five years of age than those cared for at home or those who started group care later.[19]

A longitudinal study of kindergartners and first graders conducted at the University of North Carolina found that children placed in center-based care during the first year of life were more likely to hit, kick and push other children than children reared by their mothers at home. These same children were also more likely to "threaten, swear and argue."[20]

What can we conclude from this evidence? Belsky has concluded that early infant daycare may be associated with avoidance of mother and may indicate greater insecurity of attachment. (Psychologists, I have discovered during my years as a psychology graduate student, love to use the equivocal word "may.") This early avoidance, says Belsky, has been associated with diminished cooperation with adults as well as social maladjustment in preschool and the early elementary school years.

Belsky believes that this evidence is highly consistent with Bowlby's attachment theory. He suggests that those repeated daily separations from mother create avoidance. They also create mistrust in mother. And this avoidance later places the child at risk emotionally, particularly in his social relationships.

Some time ago I interviewed psychologist Byrna Siegel at Stanford University for a magazine article I was writing. Siegel has spent more than 1,000 hours observing children in daycare. Less equivocal than some other psychologists, Siegel said that she believes "we are altering the cultural fabric" in this society with the mass exodus of children into daycare. Siegel feels that children who are growing up without a close maternal bond will someday engage in fewer marriages and incur more divorces.

I have spoken with others in the mental health profession who wonder if we are not foolishly experimenting with a generation of children when we, in this country, advocate daycare for the very young. One, who teaches at Harvard Medical School, told me that he predicts that many hospital beds in psychiatric wards of the future will be filled with those currently growing up without a close bond to parents.

We just don't know what the long-term effects of daycare will be. As I have indicated, most of the research to date has focused on infants and young children. What about the effects of early daycare on adolescents and adults? Because we do not know what the long-term effects will be, some, including Belsky, suggest that we proceed with caution. Even Harvard's Jerome Kagan, himself an advocate of daycare, has said of daycare children, "I know they will be different, but I can't say how."[21]

So this is the news from the front in the area of infant daycare research. Just as the attachment theory predicts, babies are at risk psychologically if separated from their mothers for 20 + hours per week during the first year of life. This shows up as avoidance of the mother after brief separations. As the number of infants in daycare increases, so too does the number of insecurely attached babies.

Our Current Cultural Climate

But what about the mothers of these babies? Harking back to French philosopher Elizabeth Badinter, have we created a cultural climate in America that wars against mother love? Is this partly responsible for the fact that infant daycare is the fastest growing segment of the daycare population?

I believe we have created a cultural climate that makes it hard for women to elect to rear their children themselves. Just the other day, I received a letter from a mother at home who said that people often ask, "and what do you do?" Said this mother, "The mother at home is continually intimidated and devalued by others. I find myself vacillating and wondering about my worth due to the pressures placed on me by the world's value system."

If the mother at home is constantly challenged, devalued and intimidated, what about the mother in the marketplace? During this past summer, I have been doing my own research in the Washington area, interviewing more than 100 educated employed mothers of first-borns. Although I have not yet analyzed my data, I have formed some impressions from these hours of interviewing mothers.

I would like to suggest that, when a mother feels she cannot take time out in her life to nurture her baby, she pays a high price internally. I believe that she detaches to some extent from her baby. Many feel enormous internal pressure arising from guilt. Let me share two examples. These young women, by the way, were not ones interviewed for my study.

When I met Leslie (not her real name), she planned to return to work when her baby was eight months old. Uneasy and guilt-ridden, Leslie later made the decision that she should stay home. Leslie told me months afterward, "I am now relaxed with my baby. Before—when I planned to return to work—I felt I had to do all my mothering in the first eight months. I was tense with my baby. When he had a bad day, I felt like a bad mother. After I decided to stay home, whenever my son had a bad day, I could say, 'He'll get over it. He's just having a bad day, not a bad life.'"

The mother who returns to her career within weeks and months after her baby's birth may, like Leslie, feel enormous internal pressure to do her mothering all at once (or in the hours of "quality time" at the end of the day), or she may distance herself from her baby and miss the joy of those early months.

As I stood in the hospital corridor this past summer, waiting to go into the room to interview a mother, I overheard another woman yelling at a subordinate in her office over the telephone. I knew this woman had delivered her second child only the day before. I could feel her anxiety rippling through the air. She continued to demand, berate, and command as I made my way across the room to talk to her roommate. I learned later that this careerist, who worked until the day of the delivery on Monday, had returned to the office on Friday.

What is happening in this country when we have stressed careerism for women above all else? What is wrong with a nation where it is a status symbol to take as little time off work to have a baby as possible?

The Power of Mother Love

As I leave those questions for you to ponder, I would like to illustrate the power of mother love by sharing with you a story that highlights the importance of mother love during the early years of life. Some of you are familiar with the story of John Merrick, having seen the play or the movie entitled *The Elephant Man*. Anthropologist Ashley Montagu has written an account of this man's tragic life. In the book entitled, *The Elephant Man*,[22] Montagu writes of this hideously deformed man who died in his early twenties.

John Merrick lived as a freak in the carnival world, tormented by his keepers, until he was discovered by the English surgeon, Sir Frederick Treves. Treves, who thought Merrick "the most disgusting specimen of humanity that he had ever seen," hoped that Merrick was retarded so that his awareness of his condition, and his subsequent psychological pain, might be less. Treves discovered, however, that Merrick was a highly intelligent, romantic soul who was fully aware of his sufferings. Moreover, Merrick worshiped women from afar. Women, by the way, invariably screamed when they saw Merrick's deformed head draped with its cauliflower flesh. This changed at the end of Merrick's life when Treves encouraged aristocratic women to visit the shy Merrick at the hospital where he spent his last days.

Treves expected Merrick to be a malignant human, having suffered so much at the hands of others. Instead, Treves wrote, "he had passed through the fire and come out unscathed. His troubles had ennobled him. He showed himself to be a gentle, affectionate, and lovable creature . . . free from any trace of cynicism or resentment."

Apparently Merrick never complained. He didn't even have a home until the last years of his life when Treves secured quarters for him at the London Hospital. In addition, Merrick had no real possessions, save for his clothes, some books, and a photograph of his mother. Merrick's mother, a Baptist school teacher, herself a cripple, died when Merrick was 12. But the evidence is that she cared for him in his early years — after Merrick's father had abandoned both. In speaking of his mother, Merrick always said that she was beautiful. And he remembered that she was kind.

So why was John Merrick, a man who knew the Bible and the psalter intimately, a noble and magnanimous man? Montagu believes that the love Merrick received from his mother during his earliest years inoculated him against personality deformity later on. Montagu did not think it insignificant that Merrick always carried the picture of his mother at all times. Writes Montagu, "Unloved children do not carry portraits of their mothers about with them."

Thus, Merrick may have had a deformed and hideous body, but his was no deformed personality. Over 37 years ago, a British psychiatrist wrote a monograph for the World Health Organization in which he said, "What is believed to be essential for mental health is that the infant and young child should experience a warm, intimate, and continuous relationship with his mother (or permanent mother-substitute) in which both find satisfaction and enjoyment."[23]

John Merrick, according to Montagu, apparently had this "warm, intimate and continuous relationship" with his mother that Bowlby wrote about. Countless others have experienced this as well. Yet there are many, and their number is legion, who go through the days of their lives with a terrible pain, a yearning for mother love never known.

While there have always been mothers who were psychologically unable to provide their young with sufficient nurture, these are not my concern today. I am concerned for those mothers and young children living in a culture that devalues mothering. Today, many babies in this country are being denied sufficient mother love because our culture has made it too costly in terms of psychological pain for some women to elect to stay home during their child's tender months and years. Their self-esteem is based on career, not motherhood. And even those mothers who choose to stay home, and they are the majority, sometimes pay a high price in terms of self-worth.

This should not be. We must work to change cultural attitudes toward mothering in this country. We must speak up for those inarticulate babies who enter daycare in the first months of life. We must, in the words of the prophet Malachi, turn the hearts of the fathers (and the mothers) toward their children.

Notes

1. E. Badinter, *Mother Love* (New York: MacMillan Publishing Co., 1981).
2. *Ibid.*, p. 73.
3. J. Bowlby, *Attachment and Loss*, Vol. 1, *Attachment* (New York: Basic Books, 1969), p. xiii.
4. L. A. Sroufe and E. Waters, "Attachment as an Organizational Construct," *Child Development*, 48 (1977), pp. 1185-1199.
5. J. Bowlby, Lecture at the American Psychiatric Association Convention, Washington, D.C. (1986).
6. M. E. Lamb, "The Development of Parent-Infant Attachments in the First Two Years of Life," in F. A. Pederson (ed.), *The Father-Infant Relationship* (New York: Praeger, 1980).
7. C. Eichberg, "Quality of Infant-Parent Attachment: Related to Mother's Representation of Her Own Relationship History and Child Care Attitudes," unpublished dissertation (1987).
8. J. Bowlby, *Attachment and Loss*, Vol. 2, *Separation Anxiety and Anger* (New York: Basic Books, 1973).
9. *Ibid.*
10. *Ibid.*
11. M. D. S. Ainsworth, M. Blehar, E. Waters, and S. Wall, *Patterns of Attachment* (Hillsdale, N.J.: Erlbaum, 1978).
12. Conversation (1987).
13. J. Belsky, "Day Care: A Cause for Concern," *Zero to Three* (Washington, D.C.: National Center for Clinical Infant Programs, 1986).
14. P. Schwartz, "Length of Day Care Attendance and Attachment Behavior in Eighteen Month Old Infants," *Child Development*, 54 (1983), pp. 1073-1078.
15. D. Wille and J. Jacobson, "The Influence of Maternal Employment, Attachment Pattern, Extrafamilial Child Care, and Previous Experience with Peers on Early Peer Interaction," presented at the meetings of the International Conference on Infant Studies, New York (April, 1984).
16. L. Chase-Lansdale and M. T. Owen, "Maternal Employment in a Family Context: Effects on Infant-Mother and Infant-Father Attachments," *Child Development*, 58 (1987), pp. 1505-1512.
17. P. Barglow, B. E. Vaughn and N. Molitor, "Effects of Maternal Absence Due to Employment on the Quality of the Infant-Mother Attachment in a Low-Risk Sample," *Child Development*, 58 (1987), pp. 945-954.

18. J. C. Schwarz, R. G. Strickland and G. Krolick, "Infant Daycare: Behavioral Effects at Pre-School Age," *Developmental Psychology*, 10 (1974), pp. 502-506.
19. K. McCartney, S. Scarr, D. Phillips, S. Grajek, and J. C. Schwarz, "Environmental Differences Among Day Care Centers and Their Effects on Children's Development," in E. Zigler and E. Gordon (eds.), *Day Care: Scientific and Social Policy Issues* (1982).
20. R. Haskins, "Public School Aggression Among Children With Varying Day Care Experience," *Child Development*, 56 (1985), pp. 689-703.
21. *Fortune* (November 1983).
22. A. Montagu, *The Elephant Man* (New York: E. P. Dutton, 1979).
23. Quoted in Bowlby (1969), *op. cit.*

Chapter 6

NEW LIGHT ON
DAYCARE RESEARCH

by Barbara Hattemer

A researcher synthesizes the great volume of research on daycare conducted by specialists at universities in the United States and England which shows the crucial importance of bonding and attachment of mother and child, and the psychological risks to infants from a daycare experience during the first three years of life.

Barbara Hattemer is the founder and president of the International Foundation for the Preservation of the Family, of Naples, Florida, a new foundation of scholars, academics, and physicians exploring links between family, character, culture and media. She has assembled experts from the United States and Europe who, in an International Symposium on Family Breakdown, have been presenting new research on addiction, perversion, violence and denial in relation to the family.

Mrs. Hattemer is a graduate of Smith College and the Harvard-Radcliffe Management Training Program, and worked for five years for a major management consulting firm. In recent years, she has done research on the impact of media violence and pornography on children. She organized local, state and national coalitions to educate citizens and public officials on the need to retain a national standard of decency in broadcasting. She serves on the Advisory Board of the National Task Force on Families in Crisis, which seeks ways to strengthen families and to prevent domestic violence. Mrs. Hattemer is the mother of four children.

Mothers today are caught in a vise—between peer pressure to accomplish; husband pressure to help provide; their own desire to maintain a professional career; and their equally strong desire to enjoy their babies and to give them the best possible care. Many anguish over what is best for their families. Grandmothers ask, "How can I help my daughter make the right decision about daycare?"

The International Foundation for the Preservation of the Family has sought to answer this question by systematically gathering the existing daycare research, and combining it with the best developmental conceptualizations of the last 25 years. Our goal is to help both families and policymakers make better-informed decisions — decisions based not on political rhetoric and ideology, but on the best scientific research and medical evidence that exists today.

Child psychiatrist and researcher, John Bowlby, at London's Tavistock Clinic, captures the essence of sensitive parenting in the title of his new book: *A Secure Base.* "The primary goal of parenting," says Bowlby, "should be to give a child a lifelong sense of security — a secure base from which he can explore the world, and to which he can return, knowing he will be welcomed, nourished, comforted and reassured." (Bowlby, 1988)

Bowlby argues that the child's ability to establish intimate emotional bonds throughout life will depend on the strength and quality of his attachment to his parents. He states that the integrity and cohesiveness of the bond will influence, in large measure, that individual's mental health and effective functioning throughout life.

Bonding and Attachment

Bowlby explains the mother-child relationship in terms of "attachment theory." The meaning of attachment is readily visualized in the image of a baby rhesus monkey clinging to its mother as she moves about performing her daily routines. The baby appears to be physically attached to the mother. In fact, the baby monkey's intimate physical contact with its mother provides the foundation for its growth and development. Conversely, research with monkeys shows that babies deprived of extensive physical contact grow into adults who are unable to mate and unable to care for their young.

For human babies, the bonding which results in secure emotional attachment to the mother begins at birth. Both bonding and attachment are dependent on continuous, sustained, stable physical and emotional contact between mother and child.

Peterson and Mehl in 1978 found "the most significant variable predicting differences in successful maternal bonding was the length of time a mother had been separated from her baby during the hours and days after his birth." (p.15) Mary Ainsworth (1978) found that the children who develop a secure attachment to mother are those who, during early infancy, are held longest in a tender and loving way.

Systematic research by Mary Ainsworth at the University of Virginia, Mary Main at the University of California, and Alan Sroufe at the University of Minnesota has clearly and consistently shown that the pattern of attachment developed in infancy and early childhood is profoundly influenced by the mother's ready availability, her sensitivity to her child's signals, and her responsiveness to his need for comfort and protection. (Ainsworth et al., 1978; Main et al., 1988; Sroufe et al., 1985)

When a child is confident that his mother is available, responsive and helpful, he develops a pattern of *secure attachment*. When a child is chronically uncertain about his parent's responses to him, he will develop a pattern of *anxious-resistant attachment*. This parent is sometimes helpful, sometimes not, sometimes there, sometimes not. Such inconsistency produces anxious and clinging behavior in the child. Finally, the child whose needs are rarely met and who has little confidence his parents will respond to his call, develops a pattern of *anxious-avoidant attachment*. As he grows older, he may expect to be rebuffed, and often tries to live without seeking love and support from others.

Important Research Often Ignored

This extensive body of research (often downplayed or ignored in the daycare debate) illustrates how patterns of attachment that have been developed by 12 months of age are not only highly indicative of how the child will act in nursery school, but how he will act as an adolescent, as a young adult, and as a parent. (Bowlby, 1988, p.12)

Bowlby expresses concern that, by the end of their first year, some children have already given up trying to communicate with their mothers. (1988, p.132) This failure of communication, alternatively described as a failure to develop the capacity for intimacy or empathy, is one of the most important side-effects, or by-products, of non-maternal child care.

Bowlby has studied these patterns of attachment into the third generation. He has found they not only tend to persist throughout life, but are passed on to the next generation. A study by Main, Kaplan and Cassidy in 1985 found that many mothers describe the same pattern of attachment with their children that they had with their own parents. Main (1988) also found this intergenerational pattern to be true with fathers.

However, the same Main studies also produced encouraging evidence that this negative cycle can be broken. A number of the mothers studied had been able to work through their unhappy memories of rejection by their parents and then go on to achieve a secure attachment to their children. These mothers were able to describe their early experiences accurately, thoughtfully and with balance. In contrast, the mothers with unhappy childhoods, who had insecure attachments with their children, and had not worked through these experiences, had difficulty recalling their childhood and could speak of it only brokenly.

The late pediatrician and psychoanalyst Donald Winnicott — who was as influential in England as Dr. Benjamin Spock was in America — described the conditions for secure attachment as "good-enough mothering" and "holding." He said that a baby does not exist alone; that the mother and baby are a single entity which cannot be separated. The inherited potential of the infant, he said, cannot be realized without an adequate environment provided by "good-enough mothering," a term he hoped would relieve mothers from the strain of trying to be perfect. He used the single word "holding" to capture the essence of providing a good-enough environment. (Winnicott, 1978)

Winnicott said that adequate "holding" is both indispensable to emotional development, and essential for developing a capacity for empathy in the child. During the normal, loving interaction of a child and its mother, the child experiences mother as a "good and happy" person, and, in turn, the child experiences her as seeing him as a "good and happy" person. The infant, and later the child, then internalizes and draws upon these images to comfort himself when the mother is not present. These images become the reservoir the child will draw from as he comforts others in his adult life. (Winnicott, 1978)

The Critical Importance of Empathy

It is now well established that empathy—the degree to which a person is able to aid and comfort others in distress—is influenced by the pattern of caring which he received as a baby. Winnicott found the capacity for empathy to develop between 15 and 18 months of age. (Winnicott)

The capacity for intimacy, the twin of empathy, is a complex phenomenon that is also learned and must be nurtured. University of Virginia psychiatrist and psychoanalyst Vamik Volkan identifies the capacities for several different kinds of intimacy that develop during early maternal-infant interaction: the capacities for body intimacy, for emotional intimacy, for intellectual intimacy and for social intimacy. (personal communication, 1988)

Volkan notes that the infant's thoughts, feelings and knowledge are diffuse and undifferentiated at birth. Over the first weeks, months and years of life, these become more integrated. The role of mothering is crucial. The stable and continuous presence of the mother is vitally important for the child's developing cohesion, integration and differentiation—not only in infancy and toddlerhood, but throughout childhood. (Volkan, 1988)

Understanding the development of the capacity for empathy, intimacy and intimate behavior in early childhood is of particular importance because it later defines the capacity to establish an intimate and committed heterosexual relationship in adolescence and adulthood.

Risks and difficulties are obviously present at all stages of growth and development. But if this is so when both parents are present and able to provide full-time care, what risks are associated with child care that must be supplemented by non-parental (primarily non-maternal) figures? This brings us to the question of daycare.

Penn State University psychologist Jay Belsky agrees with most daycare researchers that more long-term studies are needed before we can be certain of all the effects of daycare on young children. However, after carefully reviewing the growing body of available data, Belsky has concluded that we know enough now to be genuinely concerned. He states, "There is sufficient evidence to regard infant daycare, as we routinely know it and have it in this nation, as a risk factor for the development of insecure infant-parent attachment, noncompliance and aggression." (1988, p. 4)

While he does not conclude that all "infant daycare is bad" or that "only mothers can care for babies," he asserts that the research reveals that non-maternal daycare of more than 20 hours per week, initiated in the first year of life, is a risk condition. Fifty percent of the daycare children he studied (approximately 500 cases) developed insecure attachments to their mothers and a wide range of negative behaviors. In addition, a wealth of data now documents the consistent relationship between evaluations of the security of the infant-mother attachment at 12 to 18 months and negative preschool and grade school behaviors. (Main et al., 1985, 1987, 1988 in press)

Early daycare research studied the degree to which infants became distressed upon separation from their mothers, and their willingness to approach strangers. These studies were typically carried out in high quality, university-affiliated daycare centers which are, in fact, quite atypical of daycare in general. The variables most often examined were intellectual, social and emotional development. (Belsky, 1978)

On the whole, early researchers found little difference between home-reared and daycare-reared infants. Some daycare children showed gains in intellectual development, particularly children from lower socio-economic groups. Emotional and social behaviors seemed to be unaffected. (Belsky et al., 1978)

However, these children consistently showed less interest in their mothers than home-reared children. This finding was interpreted by some researchers as showing precocity in peer relationships. Others, however, warned that this might reflect a failure of attachment to the mother which could foreshadow impaired relationships as an adult. (Weininger, 1986)

The Second Wave of Research

The development of more sensitive research instruments, as well as a greater pool of children who had experienced daycare, produced a second wave of research that showed quite different outcomes. Studies by Matas, Arend and Sroufe, for example, in 1978, and by Waters and Sroufe in 1983, initiated research which focused on the reunion behavior of the child after separation with the parent — a much more sensitive indicator of the quality of mother-child bonding.

In these studies, children who greeted mother positively, or allowed her to comfort them when distressed, were judged to be securely attached to the mother. Babies who either avoided contact with the mother or angrily pushed away from her were judged to be insecurely attached. (Ainsworth, 1978)

This second wave of data indicated that, while intellectual development continued to be either helped or unaffected, the findings began to reveal patterns of conflict in social and emotional development. This was particularly true for children who had experienced full-time, non-maternal daycare started before their twelfth month. (Belsky, 1986)

These children showed more negative social behavior. They were less cooperative with adults, more easily influenced by peers, more aggressive in their play, and less likely to pursue tasks to completion. Emotionally, they tended to cry more, seek more attention, be more clinging, or be more rebellious and antagonistic. Numerous follow-up studies found that anxiously attached infants were more at risk for developing later behavior problems. (Belsky, 1988; Weininger, 1988)

The following studies, cited and reviewed by both Belsky and Weininger in 1986, 1987 and 1988, correlate the behaviors of nursery and grade school children with early daycare history. A 1974 study by Schwartz, Strickland and Krolick of three- and four-year-olds from impoverished backgrounds found youngsters with extensive infant daycare experience more aggressive, both physically and verbally, with adults and peers; less cooperative with grownups; and excessively physically active.

In 1981, Main described how children who received non-maternal care as infants showed reduced toleration for frustration.

That same year, Barton and Schwartz studied three- and four-year-olds who had been placed in daycare before the twelfth month. These children were rated by their peers and teachers as "more likely to cry," "more likely to be troublemakers," "more likely to withdraw and internalize," and "more likely to be loners."

Carolee Howes and her colleagues at UCLA have studied several groups of infants who started in early daycare in the mid and late 1970s. At five and six years old, one group of children had more fears, were more "active" or agitated, and engaged in "throwing more frequent and intense temper tantrums" than children reared at home. (Rubenstein and Howes, 1983)

In 1988, Deborah Vandell and her colleague Mary Anne Corasanti at the University of Texas found that third grade children who had received more than 30 hours per week of infant daycare were more likely to have poorer study skills, lower grades, and diminished self-esteem.

Another recent study by Howes in 1988 found that the quality of early child care made a significant difference in the behavior of kindergartners, and that those in the lowest quality care were the most hostile.

Other research by Farber and Egeland in 1982 indicates that the negative effects of infant non-maternal care include "less persistence" in dealing with difficult problems, less compliance in following their mother's instructions, and significantly less enthusiasm than children who had received predominantly home care.

Time does not permit a detailed discussion of all of these studies. However, some things are particularly noteworthy. One study of children from affluent homes cared for on a one-to-one basis by nannies (often considered an ideal situation) showed significant attachment insecurity. (Barglow, Vaughn and Molitor, 1987) A study of children cared for by fathers found 100 percent of these infants established secure attachments to their mothers. (Belsky and Rovine, 1988) This suggests the crucial role of the father in child care.

Vaughn, Deane and Waters (1985) also found that children in non-maternal care who were classified as securely attached to their mothers at 18 months "showed a deterioration in the quality of adaptation over the period from 18 to 24 months (p. 133) and were indistinguishable from formerly insecure children." Belsky suggested "the possibility that one consequence of early care may be heightened vulnerability to subsequent stress, irrespective of early attachment history." (1988, p. 37)

Belsky has gone to great lengths to identify and describe what he calls the "ecology" of daycare. He means by this that the daycare setting is only one factor in a complex system which includes the mother's and father's emotional attitudes and skills; the family's socio-economic circumstances; the behavior of the mother upon reunion with the child; and the presence or absence of conflict in the family or mother-infant relationship.

A Third Wave of Research Is Needed

A third wave of research is required for the future. We need to know more about the actual factors that contribute to insecure attachment. While 50 percent of children exposed to full-time, non-maternal care develop an insecure attachment, the other 50 percent do not. What is there about these children, about their daycare settings, and about their mothers, fathers or families that enables them to experience risk conditions without negative consequences? And, if no consequences appear in the childhood years, will they appear later when the individual marries and raises a family of his own?

The physical and psychosomatic implications of early child care have been carefully studied by physicians, psychologists, and psychosomatic and psychoanalytic researchers for more than 50 years. The mother-infant relationship is now understood, among other things, as a "regulatory system."

In his important 1987 book, *Psychosomatic Medicine and Contemporary Psychoanalysis*, psychiatrist Graeme Taylor, of Mt. Sinai Hospital in Toronto, states that "infant researchers now conceptualize the mother-infant relationship as an interactional system that organizes and regulates the infant's behavior and physiology from birth." (p.124)

Taylor explains that "although this regulatory system begins at a biological-neurophysiological-behavioral level of organization, it gradually shifts to a more psychological level as the infant's mind develops the capacity to form symbols, to think, and to use language, and as the infant becomes increasingly aware of being separate from the mother." (p.125) This maternal-infant "regulatory system" facilitates the emergence of self-regulatory mechanisms.

Taylor states that there are many hidden regulatory processes in the mother-infant relationship. He systematically describes the intricate nutritional, tactile, thermal, and vestibular mechanisms involved, and how this highly significant mother-infant relationship defines the regulation of heart rate, sleep-wake states, enzyme levels of growth hormone, thermoregulation, and vestibular balance. It also helps define the responsiveness of the immune system to later infection and subsequent susceptibility to diseases such as heart disease, liver disease, cancer and diabetes. (p.133)

Taylor's study highlights the physiological effects of maternal-infant contact and separation, and how the mother, through her tactile stimulation (holding, touching and caressing) of her child, serves as an external regulator of internal bodily processes.

Psychological regulatory effects are equally important and complex. In the simplest terms, each child is born with a psyche and a soma — a mind and a body — that are not fully integrated. Just as many of the child's bodily functions are externally regulated by the mother, so too are important psychological functions — in particular, the external soothing of states of emotional distress. In the adequately parented child, at the end of the first year, an integration of the mind and the body takes place. Successful psychosomatic integration enables the child to regulate himself.

Taylor warns that a failure of external regulation may result in a failure in psychosomatic integration at the end of the first year, with the potential for consequent alterations in immunocompetence — the ability of the immune system to function normally. One of several potential outcomes of such regulatory failure is the development of what is termed a "disease-prone personality."

One example of this is the work of endocrinologist Joseph Calabrese at the Cleveland Clinic Foundation. After extensive review of both animal and human studies of mother-child attachment, Calabrese described how maternal deprivation can lead to "immuno-compromise" (a weakening of the immune system), in which the individual is less able to defend himself against childhood and adult diseases.

In his recent study of AIDS patients, for example, Calabrese found a pattern of insecure attachment and lack of "good-enough mothering" in early childhood to be a common factor in their life histories. This appears to have affected their capacity to regulate stress and develop immunological competence. (Calabrese, 1987)

In summary: existing research indicates that the greatest risks in non-maternal care center around the insecurity and instability which occur in failures of mother-infant attachment due to frequent and prolonged separations. Failures in maternal-infant attachment can result in disturbed social relations, disturbed personality formation, psychosomatic vulnerability, thought disorders, and distortions in gender identity.

Secure attachment serves as a basis for self-reliance, self-regulation, self-containment (the development of internal controls), independence, and ultimately the capacity for mature interdependence. Insecure attachment is frequently found in the history of individuals who remain dependent on others — both other people, and other things such as drugs, alcohol, or deviant and violent behavior patterns.

It is important to remember that the care of the child under three is the care of the developing personality, not the formed personality. It is the ongoing emotional relationship and bond established between the infant and mother — and later between the infant, mother and father — that becomes the basis of the formation of the whole personality. Secure children are much more able to establish themselves as unique individuals than insecure children.

Do We Want to Restructure Society?

By restructuring the mother-infant relationship through widespread daycare, we are changing the institution that forms personality. Eventually, society itself will be restructured. If daycare produces large numbers of insecure, anxious and angry individuals, we must expect to see these traits reflected in the personality of the culture. We must guard against raising a generation of disturbed, lonely children who cannot relate well to other people, who are without internalized values and controls, and who are more susceptible to disease.

While it would be quite wrong to imply that daycare will result in pathological personality formation, the research does indicate that daycare can add a significant level of extra distress and conflict to the all-important infant-mother-father relationship. Trauma, conflict and deprivation introduced during this period affect the ultimate fate of the personality in profound and radical ways.

We also know that the basic patterns established in early childhood remain relatively fixed and constant. Though they are reworked during adolescence and again in early adulthood, they are extremely difficult to alter. Failures in early childhood are the most damaging and, in many cases, the most irreparable of all suffered by an individual.

Parents have only one opportunity to mold the personality traits that their child will bring to every situation he faces in life. Society must rediscover the importance of parenting.

The "mothering process" needs to be re-valued to counteract the serious devaluation of women, children and families that has occurred during the past two decades. This renewed value must be communicated to women so that they feel supported in fulfilling the demands and requirements necessary for effective and successful mothering. To appreciate the importance, complexity and skill implicit in the mothering function is to take an important step in restoring the prestige and importance that have receded from mothering in the last decades.

Beyond that, what can we conclude? What do these facts mean as each family grapples with its own decisions? Speaking now, as a mother and grandmother, becoming acquainted with this body of knowledge has opened my eyes to things I didn't know before. I can see generational continuity in my own family. I realize, for example, that leaving each of my two younger children when they were four months of age for a three-week trip was poor timing. I wish I had known then how such a separation would affect each child.

We must inform parents, industry and government of these facts. We must encourage mothers who have a choice to stay home with their babies as long as possible. We must help mothers who must use non-maternal care to learn about the developmental needs of their babies and how they can minimize the effect of daily separations. We must encourage business to be flexible and innovative in employment practices for women of child bearing age, and to realize the enormous gain in future productivity for the nation if our children are spared the trauma of too many early separations. We must encourage government to value mother care of babies.

And we must not forget father. Common sense, as well as important recent research, confirms that he must play a much more important role in child care than he has in the past. Including the father in a much more active and central way in the "parenting partnership" would do much to alleviate the isolation, stress and alienation that many women feel.

The child care choices of families, business and government must be based on the needs of all three partners in the relationship — mother, father and child — and on the knowledge of psychological science about how to form and develop healthy personalities in our children.

References

Ainsworth, M., M. Blehar, E. Waters, and S. Wall. *Patterns of Attachment: Assessed in the Strange Situation and at Home.* Hillsdale, New Jersey: Lawrence Erlbaum, 1978.

Ashbach, C., B. Hattemer and D. Scott. *Daycare: Hard Realities, Tough Choices — A Preview.* Naples, Florida: IFPF Monograph Series, 1988.

Ashbach, C. and D. Scott. The long shadow of childhood: the impact of daycare on the developing personality. *Restoration*, September-October 1988, 1(5), 28-32.

Barglow, P., B. Vaughn and N. Molitor. Effects of maternal absence due to employment on the quality of infant-mother attachment in a low-risk sample. *Child Development*, 1987.

Barton, M. and J. Schwartz. Day care in the middle class: effects in the elementary school. Paper presented at the American Psychological Association's Annual Convention, Los Angeles, August, 1981.

Belsky, J. and L. Steinberg. The effects of day care: a critical review. *Child Development*, 1978, 49, 929-949.

Belsky, J. Infant day care: a cause for concern. *Zero To Three*, 1986, 6, 1-7.

Belsky, J. Two waves of daycare research: developmental effects and conditions of quality. In R. Ainslie (ed.). *The Child and the Day Care Setting.* New York: Praeger, 1984, 1-34.

Belsky, J. Developmental risks associated with infant daycare: attachment insecurity, noncompliance and aggression. In S. Chehrazi (ed.). *Balancing Working and Parenting: Psychological and Developmental Implications of Daycare.* New York: American Psychiatric Press, Inc., 1988.

Belsky, J. and M. Rovine. Nonmaternal care in the first year of life and the security of infant-parent attachment. *Child Development*, 1988, in press.

Bowlby, J. *A Secure Base: Clinical Applications of Attachment Theory.* London: Routledge & Kegan Paul, 1988.

Calabrese, J., M. Kling and P. Gold. Alterations in immunocompetence during stress, bereavement, and depression: focus on neuroendocrine regulation. *American Journal of Psychiatry,* September 1987, 144, 9.

Calabrese, J. Maternal deprivation and immuno-competence. Paper presented at the IFPF Conference on Child Care, Philadelphia, February, 1988.

Emde, R. The prerepresentational self and its affective core. *The Psychoanalytic Study of the Child,* 1983, 38, 165-192.

Farber, E. and B. Egeland. Developmental consequences of out-of-home care for infants in a low income population. In E. Zigler and E. Gorden (eds.). *Day Care.* Boston: Auburn House, 1982, 102-125.

Harlow, H. and M. Harlow. The affectional systems. In A. Schrier, H. Harlow, and F. Stollnitz (eds.). *Behavior of Non-Human Primates.* New York: Academic Press, 1965, Vol. 2.

Howes, C. Relations between early child care and schooling. *Developmental Psychology,* 1988, 24(1), 53-57.

Mahler, M., F. Pine and A. Bergman. *The Psychological Birth of the Human Infant.* New York: Basic Books, 1975.

Main, M. and D. Weston. Quality of attachment to mother and to father. Related to conflict behavior and the readiness for establishing new relationships. *Child Development,* 1981, 52, 932-940.

Main, M., N. Kaplan and J. Cassidy. Security in infancy, childhood and adulthood: a move to the level of representation. In I. Bretherton and E. Waters (eds.). *Growing Points in Attachment: Theory and Research.* Monographs for the Society for Research in Child Development, Serial 209, Chicago: University of Chicago Press, 1985, 66-104.

Main, M. Analysis of a peculiar form of reunion behavior in some day care children: its history and sequelae in children who are home-reared. In R. Webb (ed.). *Social Development in Childhood: Day Care Programs and Research.* Baltimore: Johns Hopkins University, 1977.

Main, M. Personal Communication. Cited in J. Bowlby. *A Secure Base: Clinical Applications of Attachment Theory.* London: Routledge & Kegan Paul, 1988, 134.

Main, M. and J. Cassidy. Categories of response with the parent at age six: predicted from infant attachment classifications and stable over a one month period. *Developmental Psychology,* 1988, in press.

Matas, L., R. Arend and L. A. Sroufe. Continuity of adaption in the second year: the relationship between quality of attachment and later competence, *Child Development,* 1978, 49, 47-56.

Osofsky, J. (ed.). *Handbook of Infant Development* (2nd edition), New York: Wiley, 1987.

Peterson, G. and L. Mehl. Some determinants of maternal attachment. *American Journal of Psychiatry,* 1978, 135, 1168-1173.

Phillips, D., K. McCartney, S. Scarr and C. Howes. Selective review of infant day care research: a cause for concern, *Zero to Three*, 1987, 7(3), 18-21.

Pine, F. *Developmental Theory and Clinical Process*, New Haven: Yale U. Press, 1985.

Rubenstein, J. The effects of maternal employment on young children. *Applied Developmental Psychology*, 1985, 2, 99-128.

Rubenstein, J. and C. Howes. Adaption to toddler day care. In S. Kilmer (ed.). *Advances in Early Education and Day Care*. Greenwich, Connecticut: JAI Press, 1983, 39-62.

Rubenstein, J., C. Howes and P. Boyle. A two year followup of infants in community-based day care. *Journal of Child Psychology & Psychiatry & Allied Disciplines*, 1981, 22(3), 209-218.

Schwartz, J., R. Strickland and G. Krolick. Infant day care: behavioral effects at preschool age. *Developmental Psychology*, 1974, 10, 502-506.

Sroufe, L. A. Attachment classification from the perspective of infant-caregiver relationships and infant temperament. *Child Development*, 1985, 56, 1-14.

Stern, D. *The First Relationship: Infant and Mother*. London: Fontana, 1977.

Stern, D. *The Interpersonal World of the Infant*. New York: Basic Books, 1985.

Taylor, G. *Psychosomatic Medicine & Contemporary Psychoanalysis*. New York: International Universities Press, 1987.

Vandell, D. and M. Corasanti. The effects of early daycare on lower school behavior patterns. Paper presented at the International Conference on Infant Studies, Washington, D.C., 1988.

Vaughn, B., K. Deane, and E. Waters. The impact of out-of-home care on child-mother attachment quality: another look at some enduring questions. In I. Bretherton and E. Waters (eds.), *Growing Points in Attachment: Theory and Research*. Chicago: University of Chicago Press, Monographs for the Society for Research in Child Development, 1985, 50(1-2), 110-123.

Volkan, V. Personal Communication, 1988.

Volkan, V. *The Need for Enemies*. New York: Jacob Aaronson, 1988.

Waters, E. and L. A. Sroufe. Social competence as a developmental construct. *Developmental Review*, 1983, 3, 79-87.

Weininger, O. The daycare dilemma. *Journal of Family & Culture*, 1986, 1(2).

Weininger, O. Paper presented at the IFPF Conference on Child Care, Philadelphia, February, 1988.

Winnicott, D. *From Pediatrics to Psychoanalysis*. London: Hogarth, 1978.

Chapter 7

HOME GROWN CHILDREN
HAVE THE ADVANTAGE
by Raymond S. Moore

An authority on home education explains that early institutionalization of young children is a physical, academic, and psychological handicap to normal children. He describes some of the extensive research which proves that children educated at home until at least seven or eight years of age are academically superior, socially better adjusted, and more resistant to peer pressure.

Raymond S. Moore is a developmental psychologist, former teacher, principal and city school superintendent, university professor, college dean and president, and U. S. Office of Education official. He is internationally known for his pioneer research, experimentation and writings on work-study and on the age at which children should enter school. His research has been commended by noted psychologists and educators and has appeared in professional and popular journals in the United States and abroad.

Dr. Moore has testified in cases in dozens of states in defense of parents who are homeschooling their children. He is the author of many best-selling books including School Can Wait, Better Late Than Early, Home Grown Kids, Home-Spun Schools, Home Built Discipline, Home Made Health, *and* Home School Burnout.

Dr. Moore is the founder and director of the Moore Foundation of Camas, Washington, and also of the Hewitt Research Foundation and Hewitt-Moore Child Development Center. He has a master's and doctorate in education from the University of Southern California. He works professionally with his wife Dorothy. They have two children of their own and shared the rearing of five more.

For more than three centuries, American children spent most of their time with their families rather than in school. Those 300 years of creative ideas gave birth to the Industrial Revolution. Then we began to set up public institutions, ostensibly to teach immigrant children the English language and to keep them out of sweatshops. By the end of World War I, America's plan for tax-paid education was maturing. By the end of World War II, 90 percent of our children were institutionalized in tax-paid government schools. The family was put in the back seat for most of the school day, and the state became the driver.

About the end of World War I, America's literacy began to decline. By World War II, illiteracy was already growing. After the Soviets launched *Sputnik* in 1957, we began rushing our little ones into school, and our adult "survival literacy" sank from an estimated 80 to 90 percent in the 19th century to 50 percent today. By survival literacy I mean the ability to make out an application for a driver's license or a job.

This appalling rate of functional illiteracy is often blamed on bad teaching or television. Most Americans have little idea of what *we*, the parents, are doing to destroy the self-worth of our children. When they are grouped with their age-mates in institutions more than they are with us—until about junior high school—they become peer dependent. They knuckle under to peer habits, manners, drugs, sex, and various addictions. Some schoolmen call this "education."

"Education" is not synonymous with "schooling." True education involves parental precepts, example and leadership *at least* as much as the child receives in school. We believe youngsters should be educated from birth and their parents helped to understand their likely needs even before conception. Our chief concern here is about the relative accountability and skills of the family and of the state in rearing and educating children.

We are particularly interested in a correct interpretation and application of early child education (ECE) research which (a) stands the test of replicability and selfless interpretation and (b) is cross-fertilized with reliable findings in ECE-related disciplines. I will first illustrate these two points to show how and why ECE research must be carefully examined and interpreted lest families plunge even deeper into confusion. Then I will present impressive research evidence for delaying school entrance and early formal schooling. Finally, I will show how the home fits best into the educational pattern as it seeks a harmonious balance of the mental, physical, moral, and social powers in children.

Examining and Interpreting Research

Take Head Start as a prime object of ECE research. For more than 20 years, the U.S. Department of Health and Human Services (HHS) and the old Department of Health, Education and Welfare (HEW) have depended primarily on one unreplicated study in Ypsilanti, Michigan to justify spending billions of taxpayer dollars.

Was the research sound? Was it properly used? HHS staffers privately declare that, because it reaps the votes of the underprivileged, Head Start has become a political football in a costly Congressional game. Somehow, early on, HHS discarded Home Start—the program some researchers thought was HHS's most productive child care arm. Despite its productive service to homes and close similarity to the present highly successful Ypsilanti experiment, Congressmen somehow found Home Start less politically viable than Head Start.

Head Start money not only gets votes, but also puts butter on researchers' bread and gives comfort to vested interests such as the National Education Association (NEA) which want mandatory all-day kindergarten and all children in school by ages 3 or 4. Similar interests have been carried so far that in 1972 California State School Superintendent Wilson Riles declared readiness "outmoded."[1] He greased the legislative skids to authorize schooling for all California children down to age two and a half.[2] Fortunately, alert citizens saw its dangers and wise legislators voted down this plan.

We speak of "vested interests" because such educators and educational groups have hardly a research leg to stand on. They seem less concerned with children than dollars and jobs. In our analysis of more than 8,000 ECE studies under federal grants, we could not find one replicable study which suggests that daycare or kindergarten is desirable for a child who can have a normal home.[3]

Nevertheless, the Ypsilanti study was well done. Its researchers began by studying "store front" Head Start operations under the direction of skilled professionals and well-trained para-professionals. Yet in a few years it became apparent to these perceptive specialists that they would serve children and families far better if they spent more of their time with target children and families in their homes instead of in institutional settings.[4] Thus they became parent educators in a fuller sense, teaching home management and ensuring that their influence spread out to other children in each family — along lines pioneered by Phyllis Levenstein[5] in New York, L. G. Daugherty[6] in Chicago, Mildred Smith[7] in Flint, Michigan, and Susan Gray[8] and Barbrack and Horton[9] in the South where results were unusually cost effective and consistently satisfying.

There are wide differences between typical lay-oriented Head Start operations and the sophisticated, highly professional Ypsilanti program that has prospered in well-financed continuity for more than 20 years. In fact it has been so well financed that to replicate it nationally would break the government bank. HHS and Congress have either deliberately ignored or astonishingly overlooked this vast difference between the highly-professional, home-oriented Ypsilanti Head Start and the typical Head Start. For years they were at least as diverse as a Rolls Royce and a Yugo.

The unique Ypsilanti study rightly reported positive results, especially after centering its efforts more in the home. Typical Head Start has never consistently survived similar scrutiny. University of Chicago's Benjamin Bloom, Head Start's "father,"[10] along with Westinghouse Learning Corporation[11] and others, have long considered Head Start a failure.

Yet HHS uses Ypsilanti data to justify standard Head Start operations. HHS apparently pays little heed to its critics, including some of its own staffers who dare not press the matter. HHS promotional literature and appeals to Congress have been largely based on deliberately or ignorantly skewed rationales, *i.e.*, on expensive and unique Ypsilanti rather than typical Head Start.

The sequel here is as interesting and perhaps even more potentially damaging than the main feature. HHS stands by while education associations and other vested ECE interests use the Ypsilanti data on disadvantaged children to suggest that Head Start should be applied in principle to all normal children. This is much like saying that, if hospitals help ill children, all healthy youngsters should be hospitalized, too. In all these plans, no consideration is given to possible damage to families.

So much for misinterpretation and misapplication of ECE research. Another striking example demonstrates the lack of cross-disciplinary interest and activity among researchers themselves which ultimately ensures that only a skewed or partial picture will be offered to those on educational frontiers.

Outstanding researchers such as David Elkind correctly determine that we are rushing our children into school and burning them out.[12] Yet Elkind, president of the National Association for the Education of Young Children (NAEYC), appears to be unaware of the findings of Urie Bronfenbrenner and others that parents are more positive socializers of children than are peers,[13] or of Stanford's Albert Bandura that peer dependency (and its social contagion) is pervasive among preschoolers.[14] Nor that there is 15 times the likelihood of communicable disease[15] and 15 times the incidence of negative aggressive acts[16] among daycare children as in a normal home.

American educators in general demonstrate an indifference to sound research when it's uncomfortable, inconvenient, or challenges their vested interests. Nor are they alone. Our studies in Japan and Northern and Central Europe have found educators there also set in their ways.[17] Among the few exceptions we have seen are in Alaska when that state found that early schooling endangered the vision of Eskimos; in Norway when its kindergarten experiment did not turn out as expected; and in the Philippines when educators learned the value of work education.

Speaking specifically of ECE research, University of North Carolina Professor Earl Schaefer, former head of ECE research for the National Institutes of Health, lamented that "Although much [ECE] research data has been generated . . . they have as yet had minimal impact on educational planning . . . ."[18] When I was graduate research and programs officer for the U.S. Office of Education, Morvin Wirz, the head of our Division of

Handicapped and Rehabilitation, insisted that "So many of our programs . . . operate from the gut level—without basis in research. Drawers are full of research, but they are ignored."[19]

Such indifference to the mental and emotional health of children is not new. The pages of history outline great cycles—*e.g.*, Chaldean, Medo-Persian, Greek and Roman—that began with vigorous cultures awake to the needs of children, and ended with families surrendering to the state—on the advice of Plato, Aristotle and others. Stronger familial societies inevitably won.[20]

Research provides links from past to present and offers moving perspectives on children today, like Greece and Rome and their persuasive examples of the reasons for declining literacy, academic failure, widespread delinquency, and rampant peer dependency. These four problems act in concert to deny our goal of happy, confident children—healthy in body, mind and spirit.

Whether or not we can be conclusive about causes, America's decline from an estimated 90 percent literate population in the last century, to only 50 percent today who have survival literacy or better, parallels our scramble to institutionalize children earlier.[21]

Formal Schooling Can Wait

Instead of studying how best to meet their needs, we often put our little ones out of the home, away from environments which best produce secure, outgoing, healthy, happy, creative children. Both in our research analyses and our basic studies at Stanford[22] and the University of Colorado Medical School,[23] we were forced to conclude that America is rushing its little ones out of the home and into school long before most, particularly boys, are ready,[24] and that no children should be confined in formal, structured classrooms before age eight or ten, and for some, even 12.

The effect on mental and emotional health is deeply disturbing, so much so that boys, whose maturity lags behind girls about a year at normal school entry, outnumber girls 13 to one in learning failure classes and 8 to 1 among the emotionally disturbed.[25] It is apparent that most educators have little understanding of the depression, sense of failure and disaster bred by forcing youngsters to repeat a grade. Yet our Stanford team found that no state in America makes provision in its school laws for this late maturing of boys![26]

University of California, Berkeley learning psychologist William Rohwer, basing his conclusions in part on investigations in 12 countries by Sweden's Torsten Husen,[27] offers a solution much like what thousands of home-teaching parents have found:

> "All of the learning necessary for success in high school can be accomplished in only two or three years of formal skill study. Delaying mandatory instruction in the basic skills until the junior high school years could mean academic success for millions of school children who are doomed to failure under the traditional school system."[28]

Dr. James T. Fisher, who in his prime was considered by many to be the dean of American psychiatrists, would also agree.[29] At age eight, instead of school, his wealthy father sent him west to learn how to punch cattle and work with his hands. He returned home to Boston at 13, unable to read or write and "the most bowlegged boy in Boston." He graduated from a Boston high school three years later, convinced that he was something of a genius, until he found that any normal child could do the same if he "could be assured of a wholesome home life and proper physical development." Dr. Fisher added that such a plan "might provide the answer to . . . a shortage of qualified teachers."

Rohwer's and Fisher's solution would delay school entrance at least until the child is 11 or 12 — ages which in our research picture become critical. Urie Bronfenbrenner and his Cornell University team, for instance, found that children who spend more of their time with their peers than their parents until at least the fifth or sixth grades (about ages 11 or 12) become peer dependent.[30] They knuckle under to peer values which Bronfenbrenner calls "social contagion." Listed here could be almost any habit, manner, obscenity, finger sign, rivalry, ridicule, drug or alcohol use, or sexual practice, and even kinds of music, dress and haircuts that conflict with normal family values.

Such peer dependency brings losses of self-worth, optimism, respect for parents, and even trust in peers. Surprisingly, attractiveness of peers does less to force this dependency and these losses than children's feelings of parental indifference or rejection.

No wonder, then, that consistent, warm parental responsiveness leads the Smithsonian Institution's formula for genius and leadership.[31] Harold McCurdy, the study's chief investigator, adds two other ingredients to the recipe: very little time spent with peers and much free exploration in which parents encourage the child's interests, motivation and creative bent in working out his own fantasies (in contrast to adult-contrived videos, comic characters, and other learning crutches). McCurdy noted that

". . . the mass education of our public school system is, in its way, a vast experiment on reducing . . . all three factors to a minimum; accordingly, it should tend to suppress the occurrence of genius."

Another reference to the 11-13 year age range is the Bar Mitzvah transition for Jewish children—when they are considered to reach the age of responsibility at about 12 for girls and 13 for boys. This is particularly interesting not only in terms of Bible references to the age of Christ when He first went to Jerusalem and reportedly outwitted the rabbis at age 12, but also in terms of current cognition research at Oklahoma University.[32]

There David Quine, until recently a counselor and math and science specialist from the Richardson, Texas public schools, is studying the differences between conventionally-schooled children and youngsters taught at home—primarily through informal methods with a great deal of warm parental responsiveness and considerable freedom to explore and create on their own. Working with Professors Ed Merrick and Jack Renner, Quine is confirming Jean Piaget's findings that the average conventionally-educated child reaches the period of "formal operations" (consistent, adult-level reasoning) about ages 15-20. But home-taught children who are taught informally, responsively and given freedom to explore, develop adult-level cognition between 10 and 11 or 12.

Here we have a sound guide for parents who are willing to make the effort to build truly thoughtful children. When mothers and fathers respond often and warmly, using more and more "whys" and "hows" in their conversations as their children mature, when they identify their offspring's interests and capitalize on them, when they lay down consistent precepts and set sound examples in values and manners, they build children of great mental, physical and spiritual stability and power. Parents are badly needed in this role for a much longer period of their children's lives.

Is Socialization of Children Desirable?

It is well known that children are generally not sound role models, particularly in groups outside the family. Little wonder that the Smithsonian found that the history of genius is largely a history of children who were reared at home.

The average owner of a fine dog is more careful in giving him obedience training than most parents are of their children. The owner would laugh you to scorn or answer angrily if you suggested that he send his young dog down to the kennel or pound daily in a yellow group cage to receive some socializing by his peers. He knows that a dog's manners and normal restraint go out the window the moment he moves in with the pack. Yet that is precisely the exercise most American early schoolers go through each school morning, beginning on the school bus.

The sociability developed via peers, which is so prominently hailed by most school officials and parents, is in fact an undesirable, negative quality, embracing *narcissism* — the "me-first" ethic — instead of the more positive trait of golden-rule *altruism*. It builds *age-segregation*, as children are virtually caged with their peers, instead of the far more desirable quality of *age-integration* where children get along well with all ages, colors and creeds. Bronfenbrenner and colleagues lay the blame for this social contagion primarily at the door of our schools.

Whether or not the child is desirably socialized, top learning psychologists warn that early formal schooling is burning out our children. Many teachers who attempt to cope with these youngsters are also burning out. The learning tools of the average child who enrolls today between the ages of four and six or seven are neither tempered nor sharp enough to cope with the academic litter that increasingly is tossed at them.

During the 1950s and 1960s, Paul Mawhinney, Director of Pupil Personnel, and other psychologists in Michigan's elite Grosse Pointe School District decided on an experiment to enroll 4- and 5-year-olds in school.[33] Money was never a problem in this wealthy suburb. For 14 summers a testing program was carried out to select early entrants for kindergarten. Parents fought to have their children accepted and were often angered if rejected. Yet after 14 years, Mawhinney found that: (1) Nearly one-third of the entrants became poorly adjusted. (2) Only about one out of 20 was judged to be an outstanding leader at the end of the experiment. (3) Nearly three out of four were lacking in leadership. (4) About one in four of the very bright entrants was either below average in school or had to repeat a grade. (5) The experiment was a failure—and for many a personal experience in failure, destroying their self respect.

After only five or six years of this experiment, Grosse Pointe psychologists had misgivings. Yet they were forced to continue the experiment for nearly nine more years because of pressures from the parents, who insisted on the superiority of their young children. Sadly, these children felt incapable of doing what was expected of them; if they had been allowed to develop normally, their prospects were in virtually every case outstanding. Even worse for many, they appeared to sense that they had not lived up to parents' expectations and had disappointed them in a significant way.

Similarly in Montclair, New Jersey, Principal John Forester studied 500 children from kindergarten through high school.[34] He found that those pupils who were very bright but very young at the time of school entrance did not realize their potential. They tended also to be physically less mature, emotionally less stable, and less likely to exercise leadership than those who were not rushed. Forester feared that early school entry and formal kindergarten—as demanded by the NEA, other vested interests and uninformed laymen today—not only may result in maladjustment in school, but that it may have "an adverse effect on adult life."

The Child's Senses

Thus far, enough research evidence has been offered to satisfy the average objective thinker about delaying formal studies. Yet there is much of a specific nature to be told, for regardless of the overwhelming evidence, unobjective thinkers daily demonstrate political power and ability to lead us down education's primrose path. They may need more evidence.

We risk national survival when we accept what we ignore. All replicable evidence, as far as we can tell, points in one direction, namely toward letting little children grow naturally and in balance mentally, physically, spiritually and socially, so that their values are established before they are institutionalized. All developmental aspects in children's lives point in this natural direction, *e.g.*, their senses, cognition, neurophysiology, maternal attachment, and other readiness factors.

The children's senses are tools they use to convey facts and acts into their mental mixers—their brains. Whether we speak of vision, hearing, taste, touch or smell, the senses generally mature on an intersensory basis. That is, they average out in maturity for most children between the ages of eight and ten, with some stabilizing later, but few if any earlier.

More than 3,000 studies have been made along these lines by the Optometric Extension program of the American Optometric Association, with consistent findings that young children's eyes should not be put upon with much reading at least for the first six to eight years.[35] During the first eight to ten years, their reading should be limited to 15 or 20 minutes at a time, for they need rest through refocusing their eyes on distant objects—which are much more natural activities for those ages than closeup reading or drawing.

Vision is a broad-based neuropsychological process; that is, it involves the brain as well as the eye.[36] Even though a single, clear visual image may be received by the eye, a child still may not be able to decode printed material because of deficiencies in organization and interpretation in the central nervous system (CNS) due to lack of maturation. Though it is generally accepted that the human eye is as fully functional as the adult's at birth, other factors affect overall vision—from the differences in plasticity due to age and the developmental advancement of the visual cortex and related CNS factors.

Development of the eye itself corresponds somewhat with that of the nervous system as a whole. During the first three years of life, the eye increases in size.[37] Yet there is no drastic change in refraction.[38] Then, there is a clear visual progression from three to seven and a half years of age, on the average, with visual perception disabilities virtually disappearing after age 10 in the normal child.[39]

By the age of 13 or 14 the eye usually reaches its maximum growth.[40] At the time when most children enter school, the visual-perceptive mechanisms are still incomplete, compared to the development of adult mechanisms.[41] So myopia is frequently the result of prolonged looking at near objects at an early age.[42]

Two Texas ophthalmologists, Henry Hilgartner, M.D.[43] of Austin and Frank Newton, M.D.[44] of Dallas independently reached the same conclusions. They found that, as school entrance ages moved from a relatively unpressured eight around 1908 to a strictly-enforced six in the early 1930s, the incidence of myopia (abnormal near-sightedness) changed from one in seven or eight in 1910 to five out of six by 1962.

Similar reports came from Francis Young of Washington State University, who evaluated older Eskimos who had little or no formal schooling before Alaska became a state.[45] He then examined Barrow, Alaska preteen children who had been in school since age 6. He found, depending on their ages, that 58 percent to 68 percent of all the children were already visually crippled. He later told us personally that, by late teens, the figure rose to 88 percent.

Ludlam supports Young's findings, suggesting that, while the cornea is fully developed at birth, growth of other parts of the human eye continues to the ages of nine to 11.[46] He warned against formal reading programs or any extended voluntary reading by children earlier than ages six or seven. A few years ago, Dr. Hilgartner told us that he seldom sees a 12-year-old with normal vision anymore.

Auditory acuity and perception is similarly a broad-based neuropsychological process and is also a function of age, although most children seem to achieve it somewhat earlier than visual maturity.[47] Fairly satisfactory auditory perception is generally achieved by age 8.[48] This follows consistent increase in auditory perceptual ability from age five, so that there is a clear difference between the interpreting and ordering of auditory stimuli in the average third grader and the first grade child.[49]

Nearly every family has "hearing" experiences which create consternation, impatience or trouble because parents don't understand. Others are often comical. For example, Saralee Rhoades of Missouri found her children pledging allegiance to the American flag, then throwing themselves down in great hilarity and commotion. When she investigated, she found that they heard "fall" instead of "for all" at the end of the pledge, so they thought they were simply following orders. Others have been heard to pray, "Our Father, who art in heaven, Howard [instead of "hallowed"] be thy name." Many never do overcome these early auditory discrimination errors — such as saying, "I axed him" for "I asked him" or "keep tract" for "keep track." President Carter always said "new-kew-ler" when he meant "nuclear."

Learning to Read

When integrating vision and hearing with taste, touch and smell, none of which are mature in most children before ages 8 to 10, you can understand why many children under classroom teachers and peer pressures, do poorly in reading. Add to this the failure of many teachers to understand that there is no special reason why immature children should not see letters backward (mirror-imaging), nor that they should naturally read in any particular direction. Japanese script, for example, runs from left to right or right to left, or very often from top to bottom.

We know a lot about reading, but no one knows exactly how we read. We agree with the Michigan Reading Association's bumper sticker that proclaims, "The child who reads is the child who was read to." But, we repeat, no one knows exactly how this all happens. We do know, however, that when children's learning tools are not yet sharp and tempered by maturity, there will be delays in reading and other skills.

Now put yourself in the place of this otherwise bright and creative 5-year-old, faced as he is with pressures to perform, and his "shovel" still in the tinfoil stage. It may not turn into sharpened steel for a year to five or six years. Yet you give him a task as hard as shoveling snow or gravel from your driveway. Richard and Penny Barker's Britt learned to read at 4 and her sister, Maggie, at 11. Yet by the time Maggie was 12, she was

reading at least as skillfully as Britt did when she was 12. Early
reading doesn't necessarily suggest greater brilliance!

On the other hand, this all does suggest that our mandating
little kids into formal, scheduled, structured work before they
have had a chance to grow up naturally, can from one perspective be considered a form of child abuse. The emotional lashing
they take from their peers and often from teachers while trying
to lift an unbearable load is akin to ancient torture, only it
might be much more damaging than the lashes once given to
village sluggards. The sheer dereliction of states that mandate
little boys into school, and subject them to the same constraints
as they lay on the more mature little girls, says something about
the ignorance or selfishness of those who make laws. Are we
afflicted with madness? What do we have against our children?

It has been clearly demonstrated that a late-starting child,
given time to mature, will quickly catch up and usually pass
children who have entered school earlier, and do so with much
less likelihood of insecurity, depression, neurosis, failure, and
failure's twin—delinquency. This freedom to grow in the family
nest is particularly crucial to handicapped or "exceptional" children, who usually suffer from the cruelty of which groups of
children are capable—as sure as a pack of dogs will mercilessly
humiliate a young newcomer and quickly destroy the obedience
training and manners so carefully trained into him. Rivalry and
ridicule become shafts of barbed steel in the hearts of children
who are immature, slow, or otherwise exceptional.

The practice of "special education" which has flowered in the
last generation is often one of the cruelest jokes of all. Many, if
not most of those exiled to what many children consider the gar-
bage pile, are basically bright and creative youngsters who
haven't been given time to grow up. We have found that so-
called dyslexia is in at least 99 out of 100 cases *not* true dyslexia
at all. Dyslexia, by definition, is "an impairment of the ability to
read due to a brain defect."[50] True dyslexia is actually rare. But
misdiagnosis of learning disability is rampant. We seem somehow compelled to fill up our "special ed" classes. Honest educators lay that "somehow" to a greed for additional dollars and
jobs, including federal subsidies, which has no relationship
whatsoever to the true professionalism which holds the develop-

mental needs and welfare of the child paramount to all other considerations. Some are frank to say that, if they don't go after their share of federal dollars, they may lose their jobs.

We have already referred to the Quine studies and to Piaget. Suffice it to say, Piaget called the rushing of little children "the American thing." When some of us spent time with him and his assistant, Barbel Inhelder, at Geneva in the 1970s, he seemed neither alarmed nor desperate about the American rush. He simply seemed dismayed, stoical, rather helpless at Americans' disregard for sound research. This has also been noted by Piagetian authority John L. Phillips.[51]

Children's Thought Processes

If Americans want thoughtful children, they must be concerned about their thought processes. The Quine study should be a warning here. Piaget pointed out that decisions involving a combination of several ideas ". . . are not easily made until 11 or 12 years of age."[52] Hans Furth adds that, "These general concepts of the developing intelligence evolve whether the child goes to school or not."[53]

It is popular these days to point to Japan's educational system as a model. Having lived there for a number of years and having been close to many of Japan's leading educators, we know well of their lament at their historic lack of creativity. They readily admit that they can pick up others' inventions and improve on them. They consider themselves a rigidly disciplined society, but do not claim to be a creative people. Their astonishing success may well derive more from their self-discipline and their close family ties — two areas in which America pretty well trails the industrial world. Yet despite its strong family closeness, Japan's educational pressures are felt by many Japanese leaders to be responsible for the highest child suicide rate in the world.

The child's various maturity levels — senses, cognition, brain development, sociability, etc. — come together or integrate roughly between the ages of eight to 12. We call this the children's IML or "integrated maturity level" — the approximate time they are ready for formal, structured learning.[54] One child, even a twin, may develop rapidly in vision, and his sibling more rapidly in auditory discrimination, but most children will level out in these maturational levels and be far more ready for institutional life by ages ten to 12 than by five or six. The IML may be as important—or more so—for school readiness as IQ and other inventories have been for school counseling; it offers a clear and impressive planning base for parents and teachers.

If children appear to have no physical sensory deficiencies, educators often assume that their senses are ready to accomplish the usual school tasks. However, Morency and Wepman found that the child who enters school perceptually unready (visually, auditorily, intersensorily, etc.) will have difficulty in school achievement and will unlikely be able to catch up even after his perceptual processing ability is fully developed.[55] When academic pressures are imposed before the IML, there is genuine risk that the sensory avenues may be damaged or closed when still immature, and the child will be learning handicapped. This is one explanation why astonishing increases in "special education" enrollments have paralleled the lowering of school entrance ages.

Jensen, McCarthy, Kohlberg, Olson, and Brenner and Stott are among the many researchers who insist that readiness involves experience as well as sensory readiness, and/or that children may differ 4 or 5 years or more in reaching both sensory and cognitive maturity.[56] Brenner and Stott's 15-year study on children's readiness led them to generalize that, the older a child is, the better he will function and structure his environment, and the more he will have in experience and understanding of the world. The greater his body of knowledge before he goes to school, the more successful he will be at the beginning and in subsequent school years. Joseph Halliwell's examination of all the available studies comparing early and late school entrants brought the same conclusions.[57] This is also a clear reason why children who start later, and usually in a higher grade, will shortly be well ahead of early starters in achievement and leadership.

The brain is far too vast an area to treat fairly here, but a synopsis may be found in our book *School Can Wait* or, for lay reading, in *Better Late Than Early*.[58] Brain development (neurophysiological readiness—reasonable maturity of the central nervous system, including the ability to coordinate perceptual processes) is a variable frequently overlooked in evaluating school readiness.

The central nervous system is not structured to mature as a single unit or organ, but rather as a complex interworking of many highly sophisticated lesser elements. Each separate functional area has its own timing and sequence of development. We speak here of myelination (sheathing of nerve fibers), lateralization (melding of the hemispheres of the brain), brain weight, etc.

Furthermore, and importantly, the structure and the function of the human brain appear to move along together in the learning process.[59] Yet we are cautious about specifically limiting any of these and about relating one to another. At birth the brain is about one-quarter of the adult weight, possessing virtually all its brain cells and all major brain regions. By six months its weight has doubled, but thereafter growth slows down; from two years until adolescence it is relatively uniform. The brain continues to grow in mass until about age 25, but CNS maturation is not necessarily uniform. It is generally useless, even dangerous, to presume upon or toy with this process in the young child by overloading the CNS.

While we are only at the threshold of understanding brain growth and maturation, we repeat neurophysiologists' findings that the function of the central nervous system becomes possible as structure develops. There are qualitative breaks in the unfolding of intelligence and conscious experience. From our current understanding of brain development, these also follow the growing capacity to process multisensory information simultaneously. Replicated research evidence suggests this capacity is not fully accomplished until ages eight to ten or even later.[60]

This helps us to understand the conclusions of Elkind, Rohwer, and of Husen — who (with Rohwer's help) found from his studies of 12 or 13 foreign countries that, the earlier children enter school, the more likely they are to hate it.[61] Once again we use the analogy of tempering and sharpening of tools: Young children's tasks often become as frustrating to them as being told to cut down a good-sized tree with a dull ax or knife.

Attachment to the Mother

If there is any area of child development on which researchers agree, it is on the crucial importance of maternal attachment. This does not deny the need for paternal attachment, but recognizes the mother as generally closest to the child in the early years. Leading students such as Mary Ainsworth, Sylvia Bell, John Bowlby, Marcelle Gerber, J. L. Gewirtz, R. A. Spitz, L. J. Yarrow, F. A. Pedersen and others are alarmed at the movement away from mother and the home.[62] Dr. Bowlby, then ECE head of the World Health Organization and the acknowledged dean in the maternal attachment arena, suggests that a home must be very bad before it is bettered by a good institution.[63] He was particularly concerned about breaks in maternal attachment before age eight.

The sum of the thinking of these authorities is that attachments and quality of care influence learning from birth into the school years. The strength and quality of attachment is principally determined by the amount and kind of care given by the mother or mother figure. For those mothers who suggest that they give "quality time" in lieu of quantity of time, we feel constrained to ask if they or their husbands may do that at the office. The affectional bond gives stability to children's uncertain world and contributes to a healthy independence.

An attachment is an affectional bond that gives stability in a world full of uncertainties. The mother or mother figure to which the child has become attached affords a safe base from which to explore the unknown, a place to which one can return when things "out there" become too threatening. An emotional stability develops that builds a desirable independence and makes possible a child's persevering in spite of frustrations — to stay with a task until a goal is reached.[64]

Anxiety, fear and stress generated by separation from parents may move beyond the creation of emotional problems or neuroses to develop serious learning and behavior problems. When anxiety becomes acute or chronic, as it does with children who are given jobs for which they do not have adequate tools, it may result in low performance, erratic conduct and personality disorders as a result of what Ruebush calls "disorganization of cognitive responses."[65]

Parental attitudes are powerful in this process. Children are quick to discern parental indifference, as previously noted from Bronfenbrenner. Martin Engel, director of America's National Day Care Demonstration Center in Washington, D.C., observed:

> "The motive to rid ourselves of our children, even if it is partial, is transmitted more vividly to the child than all our rationalizations about how good it is for that child to have good interpersonal peer group activities, a good learning experience, a good foundation for school, life, etc., etc. And even the best, most humane and personalized daycare environment cannot compensate for the feeling of rejection which the young child unconsciously senses."[66]

Yet educator demands for earlier schooling largely ignore the child's need for parental attachment.

The standard rebuttal here, of course, is that these days women must be employed so the family can financially survive. There are at least two appropriate questions for this rationale (bearing in mind that we do not condemn those mothers whose circumstances compel them to take a paid job or whose psychological makeup makes mothering difficult or impossible): (1) Who works harder than a good mother at home, many of whom have home industries in which their children share responsibility and rewards? (2) What do we do with *Fortune* magazine's recent questioning of the trendy assumption that times are harder on today's families, moneywise, than a generation ago?

> "Are American families today really under more economic pressure to generate two incomes than they were in, say, the Fifties? No way. Women today may be under new social pressures to get out there and work; they are also looking at job opportunities not available to their counterparts 30 years ago. But America's Daddies today are on average more able to support the Mommies than they were in the Fifties. In 1956 the average male head of household with a nonworking wife earned $4,833. Adjusting for 30 years of inflation, that's $22,000. The equivalent figure for 1986 was $25,803."[67]

The conventional wisdom seems to the editors of *Fortune* to be neither good reasoning nor common sense. It is logical that families should decide — and society must acknowledge their constitutional right to decide — whether to give credence on the one hand to conventional wisdom and extra family "needs" or to the welfare of their children on the other.

The Homeschooling Alternative

At least 45 of the 50 United States have changed policies or laws to accommodate those parents who wish to delay schooling, and there is optimism in the remaining five that they will fall in line.[68]

For the first three centuries or more of American history, the homeschool dominated the educational scene. There were of course church, private and "common" schools, but many or most of those institutions operated for only eight to twelve weeks or so out of the year. Children remained at home for most of the time. Even while in school, the school days were usually short enough to let children out early to do real home work — their chores. Until the public school became dominant in American education, there were no education confrontations between parents and the state.

As public education has become dominant and the family influence has decreased in education, illiteracy and delinquency have increased. We have earlier presented reasons for this dilemma from the research of Bandura, Bronfenbrenner, McCurdy and others. Throughout history the home has excelled in achievement, behavior, sociability and creativity. And for good reasons.

First, we must concede that homeschools are advantaged by concerned parents. Public and other schools would not be in as deep perplexity today if the parents of *their* children were as concerned as home-teaching parents.

Second, homeschools provide many times more responses per day than are heard in the average classroom. John Goodlad found that classroom teachers average about seven minutes altogether all day in personal dialogue with their students.[69] There is also the chance that those receiving most attention are the misbehaving ones. This seldom allows more than a response or two per child daily unless he is naughty, while in an average homeschool a youngster receives upwards of a hundred responses a day. Great educational power lies in adult example and response.

Third, the tutorial situation has proven in virtually every study on this topic to be far more effective than the classroom.

Fourth, the application of the Smithsonian formula or findings for informal instruction in the "Eight-Year Study" (to which I will refer later) are far more likely to be applied at home than in a conventional school. When combined with the Hewitt-Moore plan for balancing study with entrepreneurial work and service for the less fortunate neighbor, this builds strong children.

Every state that has made comparative studies of its homeschools and public schools has found that home-taught children excelled (*e.g.*, Alaska, Arkansas, Oregon, Tennessee and Washington). That this was even true in Alaska, where parents were teaching the same curricula at home as teachers used in classrooms, is of special interest. The only possible exception might be math teaching in Tennessee, where the two tests given showed a toss-up between home and classroom teaching.[70] Yet when we reported this in our seminar, Tennessee teachers told us that they were given advance copies of tests and told to teach from them. In reading, the homeschoolers' scores ranged to the 93rd percentile on Stanford tests, 31 points higher than Tennessee public schoolers' score of 62 — itself 12 points higher than the national norm.

Although we do not have a national sampling of achievement figures, we did study 31 families taken to court across the nation and found that the average child scored in the 81.1 percentile on standardized tests. Among the Hewitt-Moore Child Development Center's more than 5,000 students, the current average is well above the 80th percentile, including students transferring from public schools.

We give much credit here to the Smithsonian formula and lessons learned from the famed "Eight-Year Study" undertaken in the twenties and thirties, in which it was found that informally-taught children excelled those in conventional classrooms, and those with no formal teaching at all excelled above all.[71] Although we don't suggest license, we remember conclusions such as Rohwer's that suggest waiting for formal education until about junior high age, and studies such as Mermelstein's and Shulman's which demonstrate that, at least until age nine, unschooled children do at least as well as those in classrooms.[72]

Additional credit must go to experimental techniques and materials which are now available to conventional schools as well as homeschools through the Hewitt Research Foundation, including *Math-It* and *Winston Grammar*, which have proven respectively that they can turn a math failure around usually within a week, and can make most students enjoy grammar.[73] Such programs do rely on readiness. For instance, Basic *Math-It*'s readiness measure asks a concentration level which ensures that students be mature enough to count from 20 to one, with eyes closed while tying a bow knot.

Credit also is due to the work-study balance in which children become entrepreneurs and helpers to those less fortunate than they. This can also help conventionally-schooled children by making them officers in a family industry — making and selling bread, muffins, cookies and wooden toys, or performing lawn services, baby-sitting, old-folk care, or any of hundreds of goods and services. Children can take over the responsibility for writing checks for monthly bills and otherwise, as part of their math, become involved in contriving to save on utilities and food. Self-worth and creative achievement flourish here.

We have no recorded evidence of delinquency among children who have been exclusively home taught. Generally they are considered model citizens. In one Arkansas trial we witnessed, the judge said he wished that we could have many more such models as the student who stood before him. This scene has been repeated many times in courts and legislatures.

The same principles and evidence apply in the home as we cited earlier. Additionally, John W. Taylor V completed a national sampling of homeschooled youngsters based on the Piers-Harris Children's Self-Concept Scale in cooperation with several universities.[74] Among the findings: 77.7 percent of the children ranked in the top quartile, with over half of them in the top 10 percent. Only 10.3 percent of the homeschoolers scored below the norm. Parents' educational level seemed to make no difference in the children's performance.[75]

Those who are prejudiced because of groupthink or vested interests may argue against the home and for the school as a sanctuary for young children. But even in the harassed family nests of our troubled times, the proof of the pudding is delicious in the eating. Not only do home-taught children average significantly higher than those classroom taught, but they are producing disproportionate numbers of geniuses of classical quality from Virginia and Florida to Washington and California, from Mississippi and Texas to Michigan, Wisconsin and Idaho.

These include top GED, SAT and Merit Scholars and entrepreneurs from ages six to 18 who make and sell everything from lemonade to computer ROMs, and make from 25 cents an hour to more than $20,000 yearly. They range from full-scholarship Ph.D. candidates to a 14-year-old middle child of a family of 11 children who is whizzing on a $10,000 consultancy at his state's largest chemical corporation, potentially saving the company millions of dollars a year. Some of these youngsters operate several successful businesses before age 18. Others are already successful free-lance writers and editors of articles and books. If the all-American goal is good citizenship and the ability to make a living, family schools on the average are excellent laboratories and showcases for education.

These are citizens whose children know many warm responses and have a great deal of freedom to explore. The most productive of them do not know what it is to have their brains squashed into the conventional lecture-textbook-test extrusion process dumbed down for the "average student," whoever he may be. The textbook becomes a resource more than a prison; he reads directly from great biographies instead of swallowing predigested, second-hand textbook food. This may be necessary in college, but not in basic education. They do not need parental confrontation or drill after they have learned their basic skills. They dwell more on whys and hows than on whats, wheres and whens. They become thinkers rather than mere reflectors of others' thoughts, creators rather than peer dependents.

Every study which has faced the issue of parent teaching ability has concluded that home education flourishes regardless of parent education level. Interestingly, home teachers who are certified teachers generally admit they have more trouble than those who don't—probably because they have more to forget and have no place to pass the blame if students don't achieve. Nor should this be surprising, for every authority or study we can find on certification suggests that it's a doubtful, unproductive demand in basic education.[76]

One of the most important factors of all is the integrity of the family. If we are to take our research seriously (and we invite anyone who can provide replicable data to the contrary, to produce it), and if we are interested in the survival of our culture, it is time to take seriously Zimmerman's challenge that something radical must be done.[77] Our educational system is already considered totalitarian by some overseas authorities.[78]

One of the principal problems, as we have noted, is that we have plenty of research but don't apply it when (a) it confronts our vested interests or traditional practices and (b) when a very strong personality or powerful group makes it embarrassing for us to disagree. On this second factor, Irving Janis observes that this is precisely what obtained at some of America's greatest failures, *e.g.*, the Bay of Pigs, Pearl Harbor and Vietnam.[79] He declares that, however fine a group we have (scientists, educators, or politicians, etc.), and assuming "its humanitarianism and its high-minded principles, [it] might be capable of adopting a course of action that is inhumane and immoral." He concludes poignantly, in the spirit of Parkinson's law:

> "The more amiability and esprit de corps there is among the members of a policy-making ingroup, the greater the danger that independent critical thinking will be replaced by groupthink, which is likely to result in irrational and dehumanizing actions directed against outgroups."

These days many families find themselves to be in the outgroup, facing with trepidation the ingroup of school officials and social workers who frequently are haling parents into court for teaching at home, and in some cases are taking their children. Fortunately the ingroup constitutes only a small percentage of these officials, but they are ominous enough to scare many parents out of the family tranquility they cherish. Delay in school entry is not procrastination, but rather the disciplined view.

We conclude that our only reasonable chance for survival as a free democratic society is to educate parents on the value of cherishing their children longer in their homes. As we look at modern trends, with millions both in daycare and in nursing homes, we are compelled to conclude that, the earlier you institutionalize your children, the earlier they will institutionalize you.[80]

Notes

1. "Getting Smarter Sooner," *Time*, 98:4 (July 26, 1971), p. 38.
2. Raymond S. Moore, Robert D. Moon, and Dennis R. Moore, "The California Report: Early Schooling for All?", *Phi Delta Kappan*, LIII:10 (June 1972).
3. Raymond S. Moore and Dorothy N. Moore, *School Can Wait* (Provo, Utah: Brigham Young University Press, 1979); Raymond S. Moore and Dorothy N. Moore, *Better Late Than Early* (New York: Reader's Digest Press, 1975); both now published by the Hewitt Research Foundation, P.O. Box 9, Washougal, Washington 98671.
4. L. J. Schweinhart, personal letters to Raymond Moore, Ypsilanti, Michigan (April 28, 1981 and May, 1988); L. J. Schweinhart and David P. Weikart, "Preschool Experiences Affect Juvenile Delinquency Rate, 15-Year Study Finds," High/Scope Educational Research Foundation, Ypsilanti, Michigan (April 22, 1986).
5. Phyllis Levenstein, "Learning Through (and From) Mothers," *Childhood Education*, 48:3 (December 1971).
6. L. G. Daugherty, "Working With Disadvantaged Parents," *NEA Journal*, 52 (1963), p. 18-20.
7. Mildred B. Smith, "School and Home: Focus on Achievement," in A. Harry Pasow (ed.), *Developing Programs for the Educationally Disadvantaged* (New York: Teachers College, Columbia University, 1968).
8. Susan W. Gray, "Children from Three to Ten: The Early Training Project," in Sally Ryan (ed.), *Longitudinal Evaluations of Preschool Programs* (Washington, D.C.: Office of Child Development, 1974); "The Child's First Teacher," *Childhood Education* (December 1971); *Selected Longitudinal Studies of Compensatory Education—A Look from the Inside* (Nashville, Tennessee: George Peabody College, 1969).
9. Christopher R. Barbrack and Della M. Horton, *Educational Intervention in the Home and Paraprofessional Career Development*, DARCEE Papers and Reports, 4:4 (Nashville, Tennessee: Peabody College, July 1970).
10. Benjamin S. Bloom, *All Our Children Learning* (Washington, D.C.: McGraw-Hill, 1980).
11. Westinghouse Learning Corporation/Ohio University, "The Impact of Head Start: An Evaluation of the Effects of Head Start on Children's Cognitive and Affective Development," in J. L. Frost and G. R. Hawkes (eds.), *The Disadvantaged Child*, 2nd ed. (Boston, Massachusetts: Houghton Mifflin, 1970), pp. 197-201.

12. David Elkind, "The Case for the Academic Preschool: Fact or Fiction?", *Young Child*, 25 (1970), pp. 180-188; D. Elkind, *The Hurried Child* (Reading, Massachusetts: Addison-Wesley, 1981); D. Elkind, *Miseducation: Preschoolers at Risk* (New York: Knopf, a subsidiary of Random House, 1987).

13. Urie Bronfenbrenner, *Two Worlds of Childhood: U.S. and U.S.S.R.* (New York: Simon and Schuster, 1970).

14. Albert Bandura and Aletha C. Huston, "Identification as a Process of Incidental Learning," *Journal of Abnormal and Social Psychology*, LXIII (1961), pp. 311-318; Albert Bandura, Dorothea Ross, and Sheila A. Ross, "Transmission of Aggression Through Limitation of Aggressive Models," *Journal of Abnormal Psychology and Social Psychiatry*, LXII (1961), pp. 575-582; Albert Bandura and Richard H. Walters, *Social Learning and Personality Development* (New York: Holt, Rinehart & Winston, 1963).

15. U.S. Communicable Disease Control Center, Atlanta, reported in *The Wall Street Journal* (September 5, 1984).

16. Dale Farran, "Now for the Bad News . . . ," *Parents Magazine*, 80 (September 1982).

17. Dennis R. Moore, D. Kathleen Kordenbrock, and Raymond S. Moore, "Lessons from Europe," *Childhood Education* (November-December, 1976).

18. Earl S.Schaefer, "Learning from Each Other," *Childhood Education* (October 1971).

19. Morvin A. Wirz, letter to R. S. Moore (July 19, 1972).

20. Carle Zimmerman, *Family and Civilization* (New York: Harper and Brothers, 1947); also Walter Lippmann in an address to Phi Beta Kappa and the American Association for the Advancement of Science (1940) at the University of Pennsylvania: "Education vs. Western Civilization," *The American Scholar* (Spring 1941), pp. 184-193.

21. *The Adult Performance Level Project* (Austin, Texas: University of Texas, 1983).

22. P. D. Forgione and R. S. Moore, "The Rationales for Early Childhood Policy Making," prepared for the U.S. Office of Economic Opportunity at Stanford University under Research Grant No. 50079-G/73/01 to the Hewitt Research Foundation, then of Berrien Springs, Michigan, but now at P.O. Box 9, Washougal, Washington 98671.

23. D. R. Metcalf, letter to R. S. Moore, March 22, 1974; D. R. Metcalf, *An Investigation of Cerebral Lateral Functioning and the EEG*, report of a study made for the U.S. Office of Economic Opportunity under Research Grant No. 50079-G-73-02-1 to Hewitt Research Foundation, Berrien Springs, Michigan, 1975.

24. R. S. Moore, *op. cit.*

25. Anne K. Soderman, Commentary, "Schooling all 4-Year-Olds: An Idea Full of Promise, Fraught with Pitfalls," *Education Week* (March 4, 1984).

26. P. D. Forgione and R. S. Moore, *op. cit.*

27. T. Husen (ed.), *International Study of Achievement in Mathematics: A Comparison of Twelve Countries*, I, II (New York: John Wiley & Sons, 1967); letter to R. S. Moore (November 23, 1972).

28. W. D. Rohwer, Jr., "Prime Time for Education: Early Childhood or Adolescence?", *Harvard Education Review*, 41 (1971), pp. 316-341.

29. J. T. Fisher and L. S. Hawley, *A Few Buttons Missing* (Philadelphia: J. B. Lippincott, 1951), p.14.

30. Bronfenbrenner, *op. cit.*

31. H. G. McCurdy, "The Childhood Pattern of Genius," *Horizon*, 2 (1960), pp. 33-38.

32. David Quine, "The Intellectual Development of Home Taught Children," an unpublished exploratory study, 2006 Flat Creek Place, Richardson, Texas 75080.

33. Paul E. Mawhinney, "We Gave Up On Early Entrance," *Michigan Education Journal* (May 1964).

34. John J. Forester, "At What Age Should Children Start School?", *School Executive*, 74 (March 1955).

35. R. S. Moore, *op. cit.*

36. S. Krippner, "On Research in Visual Training and Reading Disability," *Journal of Learning Disabilities*, 4 (1971), pp. 65-76.

37. R. J. Robinson and J. P. M. Tizard, "The Central Nervous System in the Newborn," *British Medical Journal*, 22 (1966), pp. 49-55.

38. F. A. Young, "Development of Optical Characteristics for Seeing," in F. A. Young and D. B. Lindsley (eds.), *Early Experience and Visual Information Processing in Perceptual and Reading Disorders* (Washington, D.C.: National Academy of Sciences, 1970), pp. 35-61.

39. M. Frostig, W. Lefever and J. Whittlesey, "Disturbances in Visual Perception," *Journal of Educational Research*, 57 (1963), pp. 160-162.

40. F. A. Young, *op. cit.*

41. D. W. Dyer and E. R. Harcum, "Visual Perception of Binary Pattern by Preschool Children and by School Children," *Journal of Educational Psychology*, 52 (1961), pp. 161-165.

42. F. A. Young, *op. cit.*

43. H. Hilgartner, "The Frequency of Myopia Found in Individuals Under 21 Years of Age," unpublished manuscript, Austin, Texas (1962).

44. Frank H. Newton, letter to R. S. Moore (October 24, 1972).

45. F. A. Young *et al.*, "The Transmission of Refractive Errors Within Eskimo Families," *American Journal of Optometry and Archives of American Academy of Optometry*, 46 (1969), pp. 676-685.

46. W. Ludlam, "Young Readers May Harm Eyes," *South Bend Tribune* (December 12, 1974), p. 34.
47. R. Marty and J. Scherer, "Criteres de maturation des systemes afferents corticaux," *Progressive Brain Research*, 4 (1964), pp. 222-236; H. W. Stevenson and A. Siegel, "Effects of Instructions and Age on Retention of Filmed Content," *Journal of Educational Psychology*, 60 (1969), pp. 71-74.
48. J. M. Wepman, "Auditory Discrimination, Speech, and Reading," *Elementary School Journal*, 60 (1960), pp. 325-333; J. M. Wepman, "The Modality Concept," in H.K. Smith (ed.), *Perception and Reading* (Newark, Delaware: International Reading Association, 1968), pp. 1-6.
49. I. H. Impellizzeri, "Auditory Perceptual Ability of Normal Children Aged Five Through Eight," *Journal of Genetic Psychology*, 111 (1967), pp. 289-294; D. A. Riley, J. P. McKee and R. W. Hadley, "Prediction of Auditory Discrimination Learning and Transposition From Children's Auditory Ordering Ability," *Journal of Experimental Psychology*, 67 (1964), pp. 324-329.
50. *Random House Dictionary of the English Language* (unabridged) (New York: Random House, 1966).
51. John L. Phillips, *The Origins of Intellect: Piaget's Theory* (San Francisco: H. W. Freeman & Co., 1969).
52. Jean Piaget, "The Stages of the Intellectual Development of the Child," *Bulletin of the Menninger Clinic*, 26:3 (1962), pp. 120-145.
53. Hans G. Furth, *Piaget for Teachers* (Englewood Cliffs, New Jersey: Prentice-Hall, 1970).
54. R. S. Moore, *op. cit.*
55. A. Morency and J. M. Wepman, "Early Perceptual Ability and Later School Achievement," *Elementary School Journal*, 73 (1973), pp. 323-327.
56. A. R. Jensen, *Understanding Readiness: An Occasional Paper*, 1969, ED 032 117; D. J. McCarthy, "Pre-Entrance Variables and School Success of Underage Children," *Harvard Educational Review*, 25 (1955), pp. 266-269; L. Kohlberg, "Early Education: A Cognitive-Developmental View," *Child Development*, 39 (1968), pp. 1013-1062; W. C. Olson, "Experiences for Growing," *NEA Journal*, 36 (1947), pp. 502-503; A. Brenner and L. H. Stott, *School Readiness Factor Analyzed* (Detroit, Michigan: Merrill-Palmer Institute, 1973).
57. J. W. Halliwell, "Review the Reviews on Entrance Age and School Success," *Journal of Educational Research*, 59 (1966), pp. 395-401; J. W. Halliwell and B. W. Stein, "Achievement of Early and Late School Starters," *Elementary English*, 41 (1964), pp. 631-639.
58. R. S. Moore, *op. cit.*
59. P. I. Yakovlev, letter to R. S. Moore (July 25, 1972); P. I. Yakovlev and A. R. Lecours, "The Myelogenetic Cycles of Regional Maturation of the Brain," in A. Minkowski (ed.), *Regional Development of the Brain in Early Life* (Oxford: Blackwell Scientific Publications, 1967), pp. 34-44; J. Scherer, "Electrophysiological Aspects of Cortical Development," *Progressive Brain Research*, 22 (1968), pp. 480-490; P. R.

Huttenlocher, "Development of Neuronal Activity in Neocortex of the Kitten," *Nature*, 211 (1966), pp. 91-92; R. J. Ellingson, and R. C. Wilcott, "Development of Evoked Responses in Visual and Auditory Cortices of Kittens," *Journal of Neurophysiology*, 23 (1960), pp. 363-375; T. Rabinowicz, "Some Aspects of the Maturation of the Human Cerebral Cortex," in S. R. Berenberg, M. Caniaris and N. P. Masse (eds.), *Pre- and Post-Natal Development of the Human Brain* (Basel: S. Karger, 1974). See also R. S. Moore, *op. cit.*, pp. 159-173.

60. R. S. Moore, *op. cit.*

61. T. Husen, letter to R. S. Moore (November 23, 1972); W. D. Rohwer, "Prime Time for Education: Early Childhood or Adolescence?", *Harvard Educational Review*, 41 (1971), pp. 316-341.

62. M. D. S. Ainsworth, "Object Relations, Dependency, and Attachment: A Theoretical Review of the Infant-Mother Relationship," *Child Development*, 40 (1969), pp. 969-1025; M. D. S. Ainsworth, "Attachment and Dependency: A Comparison," in J. L. Gewirtz (ed.), *Attachment and Dependency* (Washington, D.C.: V. H. Winston & Sons, Inc., 1972), pp. 97-137; S. M. Bell, "Early Cognitive Development and its Relationship to Infant-Mother Attachment: A Study of Disadvantaged Negro Infants," Final Report, Project No. 508, Johns Hopkins University (Washington, D.C.: OE, U.S. Department of Health, Education, and Welfare, 1971); S. M. Bell, letter to R. S. Moore (September 10, 1975); J. Bowlby, *Maternal Care and Mental Health* (Geneva: World Health Organization, 1952); J. Bowlby, *Attachment and Loss*, Vol. 1 (New York: Basic Books, 1969); J. Bowlby, *Attachment and Loss, II: Separation, Anxiety, and Anger* (New York: Basic Books, 1973); M. Gerber, "The Psycho-Motor Development of African Children in the First Year, and the Influence of Maternal Behavior," *Journal of Social Psychology*, 47 (1958), pp. 185-195; J. L. Gewirtz, *Attachment and Dependency* (Washington, D.C.: V. H. Winston & Sons, Inc., 1972); R. A. Spitz, "The Role of Ecological Factors in Emotional Development in Infancy," *Child Development*, 20 (1949), pp. 145-155; L. J. Yarrow and F. A. Pedersen, "Attachment: Its Origins and Course," in W. W. Hartup (ed.), *The Young Child: Reviews of Research* (Washington, D.C.: National Association for the Education of Young Children, 1972), pp. 54-66.

63. J. Bowlby, *Maternal Care and Mental Health*, *op. cit.*

64. J. L. Gewirtz, "Attachment, Dependence and a Distinction in Terms of Stimulus Control," in J. L. Gewirtz (ed.), *Attachment and Dependency* (Washington, D.C.: V. H. Winston & Sons, Inc., 1972), pp. 139-177.

65. B. E. Ruebush, "Child Psychology," *Yearbook of the National Society for the Study of Education*, 62:part 1 (1963), pp. 460-515.

66. M. Engel, "Rapunzel, Rapunzel, Let Down Your Golden Hair: Some Thoughts on Early Childhood Education," unpublished manuscript, National Demonstration Center in Early Childhood Education, U.S. Office of Education, Washington, D.C.

67. *Fortune* (February 15, 1988).
68. Parents' prior rights to determine the education of their children derive primarily from a series of U.S. Supreme Court decisions, *e.g.*, *Meyer v. Nebraska*, 262 U.S. 390 (1923); *Pierce v. Society of Sisters*, 268 U.S. 510 (1925); *Farrington v. Tokushige*, 273 U.S. 284 (1927); *Cantwell v. Connecticut*, 310 U.S. 296 (1940); *Martin v. Struthers*, 319 U.S. 141 (1943); *Wisconsin v. Yoder*, 406 U.S. 205 (1972); and many others.
69. J. I. Goodlad, "A Study of Schooling: Some Findings and Hypotheses," *Phi Delta Kappan*, 64:7 (1983), p. 465.
70. Betty W. Long, assistant to the Tennessee State Commissioner of Education, letter to attorney Mike Farris, 731 Walker Road, Great Falls, Virginia 22066 (February 10, 1987).
71. Wilford M. Aikin, *The Story of the Eight-Year Study*, 4 vols. (New York: Harper, 1942).
72. E. Mermelstein and L. S. Shulman, "Lack of Formal Schooling and the Acquisition of Conservation," *Child Development*, 38 (1967), pp. 39-52.
73. P.O. Box 9, Washougal, Washington 98671.
74. John Wesley Taylor V, "Self-Concept in Home Schooling Children," doctoral dissertation, Andrews University, Berrien Springs, Michigan (May 1986).
75. Other studies relating to the significance of parental educational level and homeschool excellence include: John Wartes, "Homeschooler Outcomes," a presentation made at a symposium on homeschooling during the American Educational Research Association's National Conference, New Orleans (April 5, 1988); and Jennie Rakestraw, "An Analysis of Home Schooling for Elementary School-Age Children in Alabama," a dissertation presented to the Graduate School of the University of Alabama, Tuscaloosa, Alabama (1987).
76. James Bryant Conant, *The Education of American Teachers* (New York: McGraw-Hill, 1963); Donald Erickson, UCLA, letter to Raymond Moore (April 27, 1988); Harold Orlans, *Private Education and Public Eligibility* (Lexington, Massachusetts: Lexington Books, 1975), pp. 207-229; Donald M. Medley and Homer Coker, "How Valid Are Principals' Judgments of Teacher Effectiveness?", *Phi Delta Kappan* (October 1987), pp. 138-140.
77. Zimmerman, *op.cit.*
78. A. Suviranta, "Home Economics Answer to the Problems Raised in Industrialized Countries," *XIIth Congress of the International Federation for Home Economics, Final Report* (Boulogne, France: Federation internationale pour l'economie familiale, 1973), pp. 92-99.
79. Irving L. Janis, "Groupthink," *Psychology Today* (November 1971).
80. If scholars, legislators or others are interested in research data or homeschool methodology or ways of helping school systems, write to the Moore Foundation, P.O. Box 1, Camas, Washington, 98607.

Chapter 8

HEALTH RISKS FROM
DAYCARE DISEASES

by Reed Bell, M.D.

A pediatrician describes the diseases to which infants and small children are especially vulnerable in the daycare environment, because they are naturally immuno-deficient and because group care produces an increased rate of exposure to infection.

Dr. Reed Bell is a pediatrician in private practice in Pensacola, Florida. He received his medical degree from Duke University, and received postgraduate pediatric training at Cincinnati General Hospital and at Baylor. In the private practice of pediatrics since 1957, Dr. Bell is on the staff of Sacred Heart Hospital in Pensacola.

Dr. Bell's resume contains many pages of academic and professional credentials, mostly in pediatrics and endocrinology and as a teacher of those subjects. He holds memberships in a dozen pediatric and medical associations. He is active in the American Academy of Pediatrics, presently serving on the executive committee of the Section on Bioethics.

Dr. Bell has been elected president of most of the professional organizations to which he belongs, including the Florida chapter of the American Academy of Pediatrics, the Florida Pediatric Society, the West Florida Pediatric Society, and the Escambia County Medical Society. He has received numerous awards for outstanding community service. Dr. Bell served in the United States Navy in World War II. He is married and has six children and 12 grandchildren. As a practicing pediatrician, Dr. Bell lives and works in the world of children as they really are.

The mass movement of children into daycare (an estimated one-third of children under six years of age, or approximately seven million young children) over the past decade has created significant and serious child health problems.

Karl Zinsmeister[1] observes this profound change in human history as a giant experiment, and he has noted the damage reports coming in. He notes that many pediatricians, child psychologists and educational theorists have warned of the potentially serious consequences of non-parental care. This includes harm not only to the child but to society. He and others raise the seminal issue, *i.e.*, what will the ultimate outcome be? Zinsmeister frames the issue in terms of intellectual, emotional and cultural effects. The debate is progressing in earnest regarding the long-term risk to the child's development. What kind of person will the child become?

My task as a pediatrician is to focus on the impact on physical health — on the medical aspects of child health, of daycare-related illnesses (DCRI). These may be viewed as short-term effects, but all too often there are long-term consequences as well.

A substantive body of clinical reports and research studies shows that children in daycare are at greater risk for a wide range of childhood illness and disease. With the marked increase in the number of infants and children in daycare, crowding increases the concern about this problem. The development of daycare standards[2] for the prevention, control and management of infections, and the need for safety requirements, point to the risk of physical harm from infectious disease and injury.

Historically, prior to vaccines and antibiotics, children were cared for in relatively protective isolation — the home — for the first few years of life, due to infectious disease risks. Significant and serious health risks persist today, and they are all too often ignored.

Children in daycare, especially infants and toddlers, are at increased risk for acquiring and spreading infectious diseases, compared to children not in daycare. They have more respiratory, gastro-intestinal, skin and epidemic childhood infections, and are at a higher risk for serious secondary infections, *e.g.*, meningitis, than are children in home care.[3] Infectious diseases are more common and more severe, and more complications occur in the younger ages. Important also is the fact that daycare-related illnesses, *e.g.*, hepatitis A, may be spread to members of the household and to the community at large.

Why are infants and children in daycare at such high risk for becoming infected? Because of their young age, their immune systems are naturally immuno-deficient and have had no prior exposure to the infectious agents abounding in the daycare setting. In group care, particularly involving the very young infant and toddler, there is an increased rate of exposure to infection—*i.e.*, the infectious agents are more prevalent—compared to home care.

Additionally, because of the nature and size of anatomic structure in the young, they are at greater risk for secondary bacterial complications such as otitis media (ear infections), pharyngitis (sore throats), tonsillitis, laryngitis (croup), bronchitis, bronchiolitis, and pneumonia. Because of the children's lack of immunity, they are at greater risk for the development of complicating invasive blood-borne infections, such as septicemia (blood poisoning), meningitis, septic arthritis (infected joints), osteomyelitis (infected bones), and abscess formation.

The Public Health infectious disease model is an excellent depiction of the relationships involved in the spread of infectious disease. If you visualize three circles which overlap a bit, you can see the three factors or elements in the spread of infectious disease.

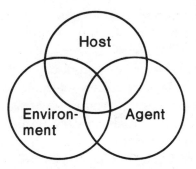

In the instance of young children: (1) the *host* is at high risk due to relative immuno-deficiency and small anatomic structures; (2) the daycare *environment*: hygiene, crowding (grouped), personnel; (3) the *agent*: the prevalence of infectious disease agents in young children.

Children become ill at totally unpredictable times. The parents often are not available, the facility commonly does not have sufficient space or qualified personnel to care for sick children properly, and the identification of diseases which require exclusion is complex. Striking a balance between the needs of the child, the other children in the group at risk, and the parents' quest for substitute child care is not just difficult, it is many times impossible.

The Categories of Illnesses

What are the infectious diseases in daycare which place infants and young children at risk? They may be classified into four categories according to the mode of transmission, as follows:

Category 1. Infections spread by the fecal-oral route include viral gastroenteritis, hepatitis A (liver inflammation), salmonellosis, shigellosis, campylobacter, giardiasis, and pinworms. These enteric (bowel) infections are greater risks for infants and toddlers who are not yet toilet-trained, since they mouth objects, handle their diapers and excretions, and place their hands in their own and other children's mouths.

Salmonellosis and shigellosis characteristically occur under five years of age, with the highest attack rates among infants younger than one year. Infectious diarrhea represents an approximately eleven-fold increased risk in centers with children younger than two years. Giardiasis has an estimated six-fold increased risk. One-third of hepatitis A outbreaks originate in a daycare setting, and over 70 percent of clinical cases can be traced to daycare, such as through household contacts with siblings and parents.[4] Daycare children are often silent carriers because hepatitis A is relatively asymptomatic in the young child; but in an adult it is potentially a very serious disease.

Category 2. Infections spread by the respiratory route represent 60 to 70 percent of DCRIs. Upper and lower respiratory tract infections are caused by viral agents which cause non-specific febrile illnesses with or without respiratory symptoms, *i.e.*, influenza, para-influenza, respiratory syncytial virus, adenovirus, enterovirus and rhinovirus; by micro-organisms such as Chlamydia and Mycoplasma; and by pathogenic bacteria such as Streptococcus, Staphylococcus, Pneumococcus, Hemophilus Influenza B, and Meningococcus.

It is notable that even the isolation of children with active respiratory infections has not been shown to be helpful in reducing the spread of airborne diseases in daycare centers. This is because the agent has already been transmitted before symptoms are noted in the youngster. It's almost impossible for a daycare center to adequately screen for an infected child, since before he becomes symptomatic, he may be infectious or contagious.

The major dreaded epidemic bacterial pathogens, such as the Hemophilus Influenza B and the Meningococcus organisms, produce acute overwhelming invasive disease, especially in the young, including septicemia, meningitis, septic arthritis, and osteomyelitis.

Studies indicate an approximately 12 times greater risk for Hemophilus Influenza B infection in children in daycare centers, and the risk of developing serious secondary disease is two to three percent of contacts.[5] Meningococcal disease occurs most commonly in children below one year of age with a high infectivity and mortality. Streptococcal infections with their sequelae of scarlet fever, nephritis (kidney inflammation), and rheumatic fever (carditis or heart inflammation), also cause, along with the staphylococci, severe local invasive infections of common concern, *i.e.*, furunculosis (boils), cellulitis (soft tissue infection), and lymphadenitis (swollen lymph nodes).

Category 3. Infections spread by direct contact include conjunctivitis due to viruses or bacteria, and skin and hair infections such as impetigo, scabies, lice, and ringworm.

Infections also may be spread via contact with urine, blood, saliva and other body fluids including herpes simplex, cytomegalic virus disease (CMV), hepatitis B, and AIDS. Normal asymptomatic children, as well as children with congenital CMV infections, excrete virus, and pregnant women may acquire CMV, potentially damaging their unborn child. Skin and oral lesions such as herpes require covering the lesions to prevent their spread. Hepatitis B and AIDS have not yet been shown to be spread in daycare centers.

Category 4. Potential epidemic childhood infectious diseases which are preventable by vaccination include: diphtheria, pertussis (whooping cough), poliomyelitis, measles, rubella, and mumps.

The younger the infant and child, the less likely they are to be completely immunized. Therefore, the child under one year of age is at particular risk for epidemic infections. This represents a catalog of infectious diseases of infancy and childhood, many of them serious as to morbidity and mortality.

The Daycaritis Syndrome

Loda[6] found that parents of children in daycare can expect the infant to be sick nine to ten times per year, and a preschool child to be sick six to seven times per year, with respiratory infections. In addition to such "colds," other bouts with diarrhea, pharyngitis, otitis media, conjunctivitis, skin infections, and epidemic illness such as chickenpox, constitute a frequency of illness that Jordan entitles "The Unresolved Child Care Dilemma: Care for the Acutely Ill Child."[7] Professional staff in primary care offices refer to this syndrome as "Daycaritis."

A University of California School of Public Health study[8] showed that, in the previous one year of daycare, 53.8 percent of preschool children were ill zero to nine days; 21.2 percent for ten to 15 days; and 25 percent for 20-35 days. A subsequent study[9] found that the parent-employee stayed home from work a median of 5.2 days (ranging from two to 14 days) for each episode of illness. Add to this a seasonal pattern of illness with peaks in March, and the problem of sick-child daycare grows in complexity.

Jordan[10] concludes, "The frequency of childhood illness, the exclusion practices of most licensed child care programs and the limited sick leave policies of many employers, all combine to create a particularly difficult dilemma for the working parent." Jordan's solution to the dilemma is: (1) "sick child" daycare programs, *e.g.*, in-home by parent or trained caregiver, on-site in integrated or "get-well" rooms, or, infirmary models in daycare facility or hospital; (2) changed employment policies and practices with expanded sick leave benefits as a supplement to the employee benefit of family sick leave; and (3) decreased exclusionary practices which screen-out children with indications of illness. Since 61 percent of employee absenteeism is due to unmet child care needs, these efforts would arguably "decrease absenteeism and increase productivity in addition to improving employee morale and corporate benefits."[11]

Additional preventive health measures, such as careful hand-washing by the child and the caretaker, as well as other hygienic measures, may help reduce the rate of spread of infectious disease. Objects, toys, and materials are easily contaminated and require cleansing and sanitizing. Adequate ventilation, separate food-preparation and diapering areas, as well as adequate space and staff, are factors that may ameliorate some risks of infection, but they are only marginally effective in the daycare setting.

In sum of fact, there are legitimate concerns regarding infectious diseases and significantly increased health risks to infants and toddlers in group care. These physical risks, along with the risks to the child's development and personality formation, warrant serious concern about the health of children placed in daycare.

In sum of opinion, there are obviously instances where it is necessary to provide paid, substitute, non-parental daycare because the parent has no option. However, what about the child, in particular the infant or toddler, where there is the choice or option for the mother to care for her child at home, especially when sick?

When are the child's best interests to be the primary objective? Do we deny the infant or the toddler's best interest, and perhaps his rights, by providing risky alternatives to the ideal of parental care, protection and nurture? If the *children* had a choice, what do you think it would be?

Notes

1. Karl Zinsmeister, "Brave New World: How Day Care Harms Children," *Policy Review*, Heritage Foundation, 44 (Spring 1988), p. 40.
2. "Health in Day Care: A Manual for Health Professionals," American Academy of Pediatrics (1987).
3. J. O. Klein, "Infectious Diseases and Day Care," *Reviews of Infectious Diseases*, 8:4 (July-August 1986).
4. Charles Marwick, "Changing Childhood Disease Pattern Linked with Day Care Boom," *Journal of American Medical Association*, 251:10 (March 9, 1984), p. 1245.
5. Cynthia Trump, M.D. and R. Karasic, M.D., "Management of Communicable Diseases in Day Care Centers," *Pediatric Annals*, 12:3 (March 1983), p. 219.

6. F. A. Loda, W. P. Glenzen and W. A. Clyde, Jr. "Respiratory Disease in Group Day Care," *Pediatrics*, 49 (1972), pp. 428-437.

7. A. E. Jordan, "The Unresolved Child Care Dilemma: Care for the Acutely Ill Child," *Review of Infectious Diseases*, 8:4 (July-August 1986).

8. A. Chang, P. Armstrong and G. Kelso, "Management of Day Care Children During Episodes of Illness," Berkeley, California, School of Public Health, University of California (1978).

9. A. Chang, G. Kelso, M. Harris and A. Jordan, "Care of Mildly Ill Children Enrolled in Day Care Centers," *Western Journal Medicine*, 134 (1981), pp. 181-185.

10. "Sick Child Care," Greater Minneapolis Day Care Association, Minneapolis, Minnesota (1983).

11. D. A. Wilson and C. R. Bess, "Establishing A Community-Based Sick Child Center," *Pediatric Nursing*, 12:6 (November-December 1986), pp. 439-441.

Chapter 9

DAYCARE: A
CHILD'S VIEW
by Wendy Dreskin

A daycare provider explains how, after running a high-quality center, she discovered that the stress on children who are placed in full-day daycare is so oppressive that she closed her center in order to spend time urging that we develop other options for families who need help with the cost and care of children.

Wendy Dreskin and her husband William founded and directed a nonprofit preschool in the San Francisco area. As more and more parents became employed, they opened up the school for full-time daycare.

The Dreskins believed they could provide quality daycare that would enhance children's development. The school was staffed by credentialed teachers (which in California means a B.A. and an additional year of graduate work), had low ratios of children to teachers, and had a wide range of educational equipment. Despite this, the Dreskins noticed that the children were under stress. They observed changes in children who had attended the program half a day as preschoolers and then attended full-time. Some children became aggressive. Others became withdrawn or lost previously acquired skills.

The Dreskins became so concerned about these stressful effects that they closed their center permanently. They began to observe other centers, talked to other daycare professionals, and read all the studies they could find. The result was their book, The Day Care Decision: What's Best for You and Your Child. *Wendy Dreskin and her husband are frequent guests on radio and television talk and news shows in the United States and Canada. They have two daughters, ages eight and five.*

I was on a national Canadian news show shortly after our book was published, and I heard a comment that to me summarized the plight of children in the 1980s. The producer chose to tape a segment showing "daycare graduates" talking about their experiences. It was supposed to show what nice, normal kids they were, and how daycare hadn't harmed them a bit. A boy who looked like he was about nine years old was talking. The interviewer didn't seem to notice what he said, but to me, the child's words were tragic. This little boy, this child, said, "I think daycare is a good thing because it frees parents from the burden of children." Here is a *child* saying that children are a burden and an encumbrance to our society.

The phenomenon of children feeling unwanted is the great crisis of daycare in our time. Only the family unit can give children a sense of belonging and of being valued. Substitute care cannot give young children a sense of identity. Yet the development of this sense of identity is vital if these children are to become caring adults and productive members of society.

In a *Cathy* cartoon that headed the Viewpoint article my husband and I wrote for *Glamour* magazine, a mother with a baby in her lap asks, "How do you like daycare all day, Cindy?" Bubbles show the child's thought: "It's just miserable. Do you have any idea how long eight hours is to a one-year-old? Where's my emotional bonding? Where's my continuity? I'm spending the most important time of my life surrounded by little maniacs!" The Dad walks in and says: "We think daycare will really help Cindy develop her verbal skills." The baby thinks, "By the time I can talk, it will be too late."

It's a joke, and yet it is urgent that parents do heed warning signs and act before it is "too late." A hundred years ago there was very little understanding that the experiences of babies and young children have a lasting effect on them even if these experiences were at an age they were too young to remember. The fields of psychology and child development have expanded dramatically since then, and we know now that the first years of life are critical, and that what happens in the early years will affect a human being for his whole life.

When my husband and I decided to open up our preschool program to full-time daycare we thought, like everyone else at the time, that there was such a thing as "quality care," and that quality care would be good for the children. As directors, we were in complete control of the situation and we planned to do everything right. We sincerely believed we could meet the children's needs.

We planned to have a maximum of 24 children. We would not have one of those big, impersonal warehouses where children get lost in the shuffle! We ourselves both had teaching credentials, which in California means a year of graduate training beyond a B.A., and my husband had a Master's degree. The state requirement for daycare workers was a mere 12 units of early childhood education courses, but we hired credentialed teachers. We had low ratios to ensure that each child would get enough attention.

Our facility was a large, bright room in a public school which had been closed due to dropping enrollment. We had the best educational equipment. Our preschool program had been very successful in meeting our educational goals for the children, and we assumed we would continue to meet these goals in our expanded daycare program.

Our math center had attribute blocks, Cuisenaire rods, play money, trundle wheels for measuring, and balances for weighing. Our science area had shells, birds' nests, magnets, and magnifying glasses. The library had hundreds of books. And of course we had all the time-tested toys including Lincoln logs, tinker toys, blocks, trucks, and trains.

Our program included art projects from fingerpainting and gluing to candle making and paper weaving. We had nature walks and frequent field trips.

The Stress From the Long Day

Yet despite all these educational activities, despite all the attention we gave them, we saw that the children still missed their parents. The day was too long for them.

Many of the children who were in the daycare program had started with us as preschoolers when we ran a half-day program. We knew them well. We could see the stress which the change to a long day placed on them. They responded in different ways. Some became withdrawn and stopped participating in activities. Others became aggressive. We had children who had never once hit another child in a full year in the half-day program. But in daycare, these same children were suddenly hitting, scratching and kicking other children.

The books and articles on helping your child adjust to day-care say that, if a child isn't happy, there's a problem with the center or it isn't right for that particular child. Nowhere do they say that daycare itself is the problem. And yet, after two years of doing daycare, that is exactly what we concluded. The stress that children in daycare are experiencing is not attributable solely to poor quality care. Lengthy separation from their parents is stressful regardless of the quality of care. Once we realized this, we could not in good conscience continue to operate a daycare center. Since the demand was for full-time care, we could not go back to a half-day program. Although it meant putting ourselves out of a job, we decided we had to close the center. It was not an easy decision.

My husband and I went on to write our book, *The Day Care Decision: What's Best for You and Your Child*. Since we wrote the book, long-term studies have proved that full-time daycare, even in model university centers, has an adverse affect on children who enter daycare in the first year or two of life. Our observations of withdrawal or aggressive behavior and other problems are so similar for children who enter daycare at age three or four that I cannot believe it is a coincidence. I will not be surprised if, in the next five years, research shows that the stress of full-time daycare is measurable even if a child begins daycare at three or four.

There are special circumstances which exacerbate the already stressful situation of a young child in daycare. One of these is divorce. Moving to a new home and starting a new school are both trying for a young child. Divorce often means enduring both these changes at once. When divorce also means that Mom must get a job outside the home and the child must face the additional stress of lengthy separation, the results can be devastating. Just at a time when the child needs to feel loved, and to feel there is some stability in this world of changes, he is separated for most of his waking hours from the only two people in the world who could give him this sense of security.

Jason was a little boy at our school. He started in the half-day preschool program. He was a very bright little boy. At two years and nine months, he knew all his colors and shapes. He knew the alphabet and could count to one hundred. He enjoyed a wide range of activities from painting delicate water colors to roaring around on a tricycle playing Batman. He started to read at four.

Then his parents got a divorce and he began coming for a longer day. He became withdrawn and lost all desire to read. He no longer sang at music time or participated in circle time. He even began slipping on his toilet training. Eventually, his parents sought professional help. But with two homes to maintain instead of one, they could not afford to eliminate a major source of stress in Jason's life by greatly reducing the number of hours per day and days per week he spent in daycare.

Unfortunately, finances are not the only factor in parents' decisions to use full-time daycare. Allison was a pretty child with brown curls that always smelled of shampoo. She came to our school three hours a day, three days a week. She was a gentle child who loved flowers and babies. After her parents' divorce she began to attend 50 hours a week.

One day when another little girl was sitting in a teacher's lap I heard Allison cry, "I want teacher's lap." When the other child did not move, Allison attacked her, raking her nails across the girl's face. She reminded me of a starving urchin fighting for a scrap of bread.

I knew that her need had to be very great for this gentle child to deliberately hurt another child. I called a conference with her parents. Her father admitted he had the money to support his ex-wife until Allison and her sister were older, but he did not want to. He wanted to punish his wife. He said, "If she's not cooking and cleaning for me, why should I support her?" I pointed out it was Allison who was being punished. She badly needed her mother's care. Although he cared about his child, this father's animosity towards his wife was stronger. "I'm not letting my wife off easy," he insisted, "so Allison will just have to make the best of it."

Children Want Their Parents

Children cannot fight their own battles. When their needs are put on the back burner, they cannot sue their parents. They cannot accomplish change through the electoral process. They have no vote. The littlest ones cannot even speak to voice their outrage. They need caring adults to speak up for them. Unfortunately, daycare advocates claim they are working in the interests of children when, in fact, many are simply feathering their own nests.

In a debate on public television, the director of child development with the California State Department of Education made the statement, "Children want daycare." I responded, "Working parents want daycare. What *children* want is their parents." I talked about the children at our center, and how they had missed their parents. He replied that he'd visited many daycare centers and that every child he'd talked to loved daycare.

Children's behavior can be manipulated. By threats or actual punishments, it is relatively easy to get them to "not tell" even in the extreme of a physically or sexually abusive situation. It is not so easy to change their real feelings. To feel comfortable expressing their real feelings, children, like adults, need to feel they can trust the person they are opening up to and to feel that person genuinely cares about them.

At our school we kept a journal for each child. The children would dictate into these journals, and we wrote down whatever they said. They told us their dreams, their thoughts, and their feelings. A single sentence in the simple words of a child says so much. Allison wrote, "I love my Mommy so much I wish she didn't have to work." And a little boy told how he started each day. "In the morning I cry and want my Mommy. Then I go to school."

There are many ways parents are misled. Pop psychology and feminist pseudo-research have come up with many theories and studies to reassure employed mothers who feel a natural concern about leaving their child's rearing to strangers. I'm sure you've read these theories in articles in women's magazines and heard them on radio and television. One of the most popular ones is, "If I'm happy in my work, my child will be happy in daycare."

Propagating such lies is not only unethical, it is downright dangerous. I received a letter from a mother who read our book. She had decided to leave her toddler with a woman who was also caring for her own granddaughter. Her child cried and tried to pull away from her every morning when she was dropped off at the sitter's house.

"I read all the books and articles," she wrote. "They told me my daughter was manipulating me. They told me to ignore her tears and enjoy my work. If I was happy, she'd be happy." When her daughter finally grew old enough to talk, this mother learned that the tears were not mere manipulation. The sitter locked the toddler out of the house all day in the backyard with a large dog which frightened her. The sitter deliberately sat at the kitchen table where the lonely, frightened little girl could look through the sliding glass door and see her giving her own granddaughter cookies and soda. That mother left her job and decided to stay home with her daughter, but she will always feel guilty when she thinks of the terrible months her daughter spent in the sitter's home.

This mother was a caring mother, and yet she was misled by what she had read. Her daughter survived, but such mistakes can be fatal. One mother placed her four-month old infant in a daycare home with a woman who cared for five other children. The baby turned blue, but pinked up again. The daycare mother was busy with the other children and didn't bother to call a doctor or the mother. She put the infant down for her nap. The little girl never woke up.

Psychological abuse, physical abuse and neglect, and sexual abuse are all realities of daycare in this country. My husband and I were on a radio show with Senator Paula Hawkins. She told of a daycare home in Florida where abuse was discovered only after dozens of children were found to have gonorrhea of the mouth. We know of abuse in daycare homes, with sitters, and in centers. In many cases the parents had made a real effort to determine if the situation was suitable and had been deceived.

A lot of the children feel really sad when they are dropped off in the morning. It is not unusual for them to arrive crying, their parents pulling them by the hand. The teachers try to distract them, to show them what interesting projects they have in order to get them involved. The parents feel a real pull—feel very sad about leaving the child.

One of the major daycare corporations has the slogan, "He stopped crying the minute you left." Well, sometimes that is true, and it's often what directors instruct the daycare worker to say because it makes the parents feel better. Daycare workers will be told, "Tell the mother he stopped crying the minute she left." Unfortunately, this is not always the case. Children's unhappiness can last for much longer than a few minutes.

At pickup time the children are waiting, and they are so anxious. Our daycare center was on a hill, and every child in the group knew the sound of the engine of his mother's car trying to come up that hill. The children would listen and say, "Cathy, I hear your mother coming," or "Eric, I hear your mother coming." They were so anxious to be reunited with their mothers that they were tuned in to the motors in their parents' cars.

At pickup time, the parents are often hurried and hassled, and they don't really have time to look at what their children did during the day. Often the child is trying to say, "Look, here's a painting I did," and the mother says, "Come on, come on, we've got to go now; I'm double-parked." I remember one mother who said to her little boy, "Bring your truck that you brought this morning." The little child sighed and said, "What's the use of bringing it home, Mommy? I'm here more than I'm home anyway."

Many daycare advocates have tried to create a smokescreen of rationalizations, distortions, and outright lies. They have a seemingly limitless supply of rationalizations to confuse parents who are considering daycare for their child and to reassure parents who are already using it.

Rationalizations for Daycare

"We're professionals," they claim. "We can teach your children better than you can." Dr. Burton White, the country's foremost authority on educational development in the first three years of life, has determined that without question parents are the best teachers in a child's early years. He has found that young children learn best from the person to whom they have a strong emotional attachment.

Recently new evidence has come in. A study of third graders by researchers at the University of Texas found that full-time daycare children had poorer grades and poorer study skills than children who were home-reared or whose mothers were employed part-time.

Another rationalization is the need for peer contact. Infants simply have no need for peer contact. Toddlers may enjoy each others' company, and preschoolers certainly do, but they do not need to attend a full-time program to get this contact. Parents who have made the decision to use substitute care often try to persuade their children to say they want to go to daycare by making the situation black or white. "You'd be bored staying home with me all day."

The children at our center were not fooled by such false choices. A four-year-old boy dictated this letter to his mother: "I wish you didn't have to work, Mommy. I wish you could just stay home and take care of me. I wish I could just come to school in the morning and then come home and have lunch with you. I like school, but I don't like it all day because I want to play with you sometimes."

You have probably heard the claim that daycare makes children more independent and more mature. What responsible mother could deny her children the opportunity to develop these valuable traits? How can your children succeed in a competitive world if you keep them tied to your apron strings?

It is a great misunderstanding of child psychology to assume that the daycare baby who pushes his mother away is expressing independence. Rather, he is clearly showing signs of a disturbed attachment to his mother. We know now that true independence can only be achieved if children have formed secure attachment in the crucial early years. This process takes time and it cannot be hurried along by an impatient adult.

The word maturity can also be misleading. Studies have shown that young children who have been in full-time daycare from their earliest years are more defiant of adult authority and more likely to use bad language. Daycare advocates look on the bright side and report that studies show that daycare children are more mature. How does such behavior show maturity? Obviously, if a second grader is as defiant as a teenager and curses like an adult, he's "more mature" than his stay-at-home little friends who still show respect for their teachers and parents.

Studies of the long-term effect of daycare on children matter, but we must not lose sight of the fact that children's feelings *now* matter, too, even if there were no lasting effects. No one says to an adult, "Why complain about working for the next ten years at a job you hate. After all, it won't have any permanent effect on you and you'll be retiring at 65 anyway."

We had a third grade girl in the after-school-care part of our program. The center closed at 6:00 p.m., but her mother, a single parent, didn't get home until 6:30. Rather than hire a sitter for that half hour, she told Ellen to walk home. It was a mile walk. In the winter it was dark and cold. Ellen read in the newspaper about a rape in the park behind the school. She began to take her roller skates to school with the fantasy that on skates she'd be fast enough to escape any molester. But her mother was concerned she'd skate across streets without stopping to check for traffic and forbade her to take the skates.

The daycare worker who shut down the school in the evening began to walk the child home. She was not paid for this. She was just a kind, compassionate woman who cared about Ellen and knew that she was frightened and miserable. She knew Ellen's feelings mattered, whether or not this experience would cause lasting psychological trauma.

Daycare is not just a problem for children of employed mothers, but for all of us. We cannot avoid the problems of a daycare society simply by staying home with our own children. Our lives, and our children's lives, are affected in many ways.

Large centers for infants and toddlers provide a fertile environment for infections. Daycare diseases are not a problem only for children in these centers, but for the community as well. For example, a study in Phoenix, Arizona by Dr. Stephen Hadler, an epidemiologist with the Centers for Disease Control, found that 40 percent of the new adult cases of hepatitis A could be traced to contact with group care centers. The trend to put daycare centers on-site at the workplace is unfortunate because it puts all employees at risk. This risk is particularly great for pregnant women, who may bear a deaf or mentally retarded child if they contract cytomegalovirus, and for older employees and those with chronic medical conditions.

For those of us with preschool children, a major concern is the trend of turning preschools into daycare centers. Ten years ago, as a parent, I would have had a choice of dozens of preschools my daughter could attend. Now there are only two in the whole county. Some of these preschool/daycare center combinations no longer accept part-time children, denying our children the opportunity to have a nursery school experience.

Some centers do accept part-time children, but these combination preschool/daycare centers have many disadvantages over the traditional nursery school. Despite the problems of the daycare diseases, employed parents often do not have adequate arrangements when their child is sick. They dose the child with medication, which they hope will mask the symptoms, and then head for their job. The result is that children in half-day programs are exposed to the daycare diseases.

Daycare advocates would say such problems could be solved with more funding for sick child centers. In addition to being medically unsound, sick child centers are utterly inhumane. When young children are sick, their need for their mother's loving care is particularly great, and facing an unfamiliar center and strange daycare workers is stressful in the extreme.

Daycare Effects on Non-Daycare Families

The combining of preschools and daycare centers has other disadvantages for home-reared children. Children in our half-day program were enthusiastic about coming to school. I was happy to see that their first school experience was a positive one. I worried that seeing their daycare classmates balking at the door and crying would affect their attitude towards school. I heard one little girl who came three half-days a week tell her friend, "I love school." Her friend, a daycare child, replied seriously, "I can't wait for my days off."

Our elementary school children are affected by the daycare society as well. You have heard about studies showing that children who were in full-time daycare from infancy show increased aggressiveness in the elementary grades. But when your child comes home from school with a red swollen bite mark on her hand or a swollen lip as my daughter did, such aggression is no longer an abstraction. It is a reality our children live with daily in the schoolyard.

Our children's lives outside of school are affected as well. In a daycare society, the simple childhood pleasure of spending afternoons in the backyard playing with a friend becomes a luxury. My eight-year-old daughter Tanya goes to the local school where about two-thirds of the children come from single-parent families. Many go to the on-site after-school-care program. Tanya wrote an essay for a county writing competition last summer about her view of daycare. She discussed how daycare affects her, even though she is not in daycare herself.

> "Daycare . . . affects my friendships. When I ask a friend if she'd like to come over instead of going to after-school-care, my friend says, 'Sure.' Then my Mom calls her Mom, and her Mom says, 'No. It would waste money because I'm paying for the daycare.' Daycare makes it harder for a friend to come over.
> "When a parent says a friend *can* come over, even though she can come over I never get to go over to her house."

This year Tanya's friends are entering the latchkey stage. For the first time, when she invited a friend over to play, the little girl asked, "Will your mother be home?" Mothers of older children have told me about the problems they have in providing their children with a social life. They do not want their children to play unsupervised in a latchkey child's house, yet they do not want to become an unpaid daycare worker as their home fills up with their children's latchkey friends.

As our children grow up, there are new concerns. We hope to see our grown children happily married with families of their own. We have raised them with love and they have the capacity to trust, to love, to make a lifetime commitment to love and cherish another human being. But where will our children find loving husbands and wives among the swelling ranks of daycare graduates? The ability of these daycare graduates to form close attachments withered in those early years when substitute care did not provide adequate nurturing.

Dr. Byrna Siegel, child psychologist at Stanford University Medical School, studied the child care decision-making process of professional couples expecting a baby. She found that these parents-to-be were making decisions about the care of an infant before the child was born and so, of course, before they could know anything about the infant's individual needs. It was striking that half the women and three quarters of the men had never in their lives so much as held an infant under the age of one month. They not only did not know their own child, they had minimal experience to give them a baseline. And yet they were making decisions about the type of care the baby should receive, and in some cases choosing the person who would do that care.

Legislators are often in the position of those mothers, choosing what kind of care the children of this country will receive without a first-hand understanding of what caring for young children means. Before being qualified to vote on any daycare legislation, I would like to see members of the House or Senate have five babies under the age of one in their sole care for nine hours. I would be very surprised if they emerged from that room at the end of the day saying that group care makes any kind of sense!

Families Must Have Options

Mothers who care for their own children are doing an important job. They are not old-fashioned, following some outmoded tradition. They are giving their children the upbringing which the most up-to-date research has determined is best.

There are those who say we cannot afford to have mothers remain at home. They must enter the workforce and be productive, we are told. What could be more productive than raising children to be caring, compassionate, ethical adults? What we truly cannot afford is a society of daycare children, a society where the problems of violence, drugs, and divorce increase.

Our government must find ways to give families choices. We must educate parents about the effects their choices will have on their children and on society as a whole. Currently, government policy is not neutral. There are no incentives to choose mother care that would counterbalance the incentives to choose daycare. Taxpayers' money is now used to help only those employed parents who choose to use daycare. We badly need a system which offers parents a choice by including incentives for families who want to raise their own children.

We can gain from looking at what other countries offer in the way of options. Part-time work is one way in which parents can balance work and family life. In Austria, the government is the largest employer. If an Austrian government employee chooses to go back to work while her child is still young, she can request that her job be converted to part-time until the child reaches four years of age. Studies show that the risks daycare poses to infants and toddlers are related to the number of hours they spend in daycare. If this option of part-time work was available to federal employees in the United States, it would be tremendously valuable in helping parents who want to protect their children's development. The Federal Government could set an example for state governments and for the private sector.

Another area where I see a lack of balance is in the financial incentives to employers to set up on-site daycare centers. If there are going to be government subsidies for corporate day-care, there should at least be equal financial incentives for corporations to set up job sharing programs and telecommuting programs, and to give the first choice of these jobs to parents of young children.

I would like to see the government explore the option of a family integrity loan. Such a loan would help families where a mother wants to stay home while her children are young but cannot afford to do so without an unacceptable drop in the family standard of living. This would not be welfare, but simply a deferred-interest loan which the family could use to help offset the loss of a second paycheck during the child's early years. It could be made available to families of all income levels. Perhaps special low-interest loans could be given to low-income families. Since the money would be loaned, and not given away, actual expenses would be only the expenses of administering the program. The government offers loans for students so they can go to college. Why not offer loans to the families of this country so they can give their children the best start in life?

These solutions of part-time work, work at home, and tax breaks for families who do their own child care, can all combine to create realistic, affordable solutions for the families of this country.

The Myth of Quality Affordable Daycare

The daycare solution is not affordable. You've all been hearing a lot about "quality, affordable care." Quality care and affordable care are contradiction in terms. There is not, and could never be, such a thing as quality, affordable substitute group care.

Most child development experts, whether they favor daycare or not, believe that consistency of care, a well-trained staff, and low ratios of children to each adult are the prerequisites of quality care. Proponents of the Act for Better Child Care say that more funding will provide quality care.

Let's take a careful look at what quality care would cost. Currently, many daycare workers are paid the minimum wage. The median income is about $9,500 per year, and only the top ten percent make as much as $16,000 per year. Because of low salaries and the lack of benefits, daycare workers have the highest job turnover of any job in the social service field. It is reasonable to suppose that a higher salary and more benefits would attract a better trained staff and reduce job turnover. Let us suppose we raised the salaries to the level of preschool and kindergarten teachers, which is $8.11 per hour. And let's suppose we gave them a standard benefit package which, according to the Department of Labor, would add 30 percent to the employers' costs. The cost of one hour of a daycare worker's time would now be $10.54. In a typical budget, salaries are half the cost of the program, with rent, insurance and equipment being the other largest items. Now let us assume that we follow the guidelines of the Department of Health and Human Services, which are very close to the recommendations of most child development experts, and have a ratio of 3:1 for ages zero to two, and 4:1 for two-year-olds. This would be a cost of $7.02 per hour or $17,550 per year per child for a typical 50-hour week for children under two, and $13,175 per year for each two-year-old. Assuming a very conservative ratio of 8:1 for children from three to five, the cost per child would be $6,587 per year. Using these very reasonable standards for salaries and ratios, the total cost for quality center-based care for all children whose mothers are currently employed would cost from $60 to $90 billion each year. That is equivalent to roughly half the current annual federal budget deficit.

Obviously, this is not affordable whether parents, the government, employers or some combination of the three pick up the tab. And what would we achieve if we did spend this money? This gargantuan sum would buy our children a form of care which has been shown to be second best, a substitute which puts them at risk emotionally, socially, physically, and educationally.

Once the people of this country see through the myth of "quality, affordable care," I believe they will conclude that it is imperative to seek other solutions. These solutions must include giving parents choices, and supporting, instead of penalizing, those families which choose to give their children true quality child care — care at home.

Children's needs are the same whether they are rich or poor, black, Hispanic, Asian or white. They miss their parents just as much, whether those parents are Republicans or Democrats, married, divorced, or even unwed. This is not a time to think about differences. This is a time for the childrearers of every religion, every race, every ethnic background and every political persuasion to join together. All mothers who feel love and respect for their children have a common bond. Let's work together to create a society where childrearers are respected and where children's feelings are respected, a society which offers childrearers real choices and gives them the flexibility and options they need to meet their children's needs *and* their family's economic needs.

Recently, the mother of a five-year-old told me of a conversation she overheard. Her son told his friend, "My Mom really thinks I'm special. She could have a job and make lots of money, but she'd rather take care of me."

We have a choice. We can choose a future where children feel unwanted, where they feel they are a burden to their parents and to society. Or we can choose a future where children feel they are special to their parents, where they feel loved and valued. We cannot offer our youngest citizens substitutes and compromises. That is why we must reject daycare and support the family.

Chapter 10

HOW DO WE MEASURE
QUALITY CHILD CARE

by Gene Armento

A professional daycare provider with 22 years' experience explains why "quality" daycare is an elusive goal. He tells why full-day daycare is a heartrending experience for both mother and child.

Gene Armento is the largest daycare provider in one of the most densely populated areas in America, Bergen County, a residential section in northern New Jersey just 20 minutes from midtown Manhattan. He and his wife, Judy, who has her degree in early childhood education, are in their 22nd year in the daycare business.

Mr. and Mrs. Armento have four centers licensed by the state of New Jersey. One is licensed for 45 children, one for 60, one for 100, and the fourth for 105. Though all the centers are secular in their operations, two are housed in church-based facilities. The children in their centers come from widely varied economic groups, ranging from high-income, two-earner, upwardly-mobile families to poor children in single-parent, foster or adoptive families whose fees are paid by the state.

Mr. and Mrs. Armento have five grown children of their own and two grandchildren.

Daycare: What is it? Do we need it? If so, why? Is there such a thing as "quality" daycare? In these next few minutes, I shall attempt to cover the most salient points which address these questions.

Daycare in America had its inception during World War II when women became "Rosie the riveters" while America's men were defending her freedoms on foreign fields. There was a real need for the care of young children by other than their mothers in their own home environments. When that need for daycare ceased at the close of the war as our servicemen came home and America settled down to enjoy affluence and peace, for most, the need for daycare dropped dramatically, but not altogether. The seeds of the breakup of the American family were being spawned even then.

Nursery schools, with their half-day programs for socialization and enrichment to enhance children's growth and development, gradually came into vogue for those who could afford them. These programs were almost always only a half-day and, most often, children attended only two or three days a week. Many were in cooperative settings with parental participation, fathers included.

The divorce dilemma had not yet hit. Then, most parents were not faced with the multiplicity of pressures which today have resulted in ever increasing numbers of women going into the workforce outside the home. Children did not have to face the emotional pressures of being forced to go to nursery school. If Johnny needed or wanted to stay home on a given day, Johnny stayed home. The option was available.

The nursery school day was usually 9:00-11:30 A.M. or 1:00-3:30 P.M., or thereabouts. Ten to 15 years later, daycare centers usually open between 6:00-7:00 A.M. and close at 6:00-7:00 P.M., or even later. There are even centers affiliated with large hospital or university facilities which are open 24 hours a day to accommodate shift work. We have children in other-than-parental care for a 3:00-11:00 P.M. shift, and others who are lifted from their own beds in the dark of night to sleep on a cot or mat in a daycare facility.

We call what we do "quality daycare." For years as daycare center owners and operators we worked to reassure mothers entering the job market that it was not the *quantity* of time they spent with their child, but the *quality* of time that truly counted. We stated, "If a woman is fulfilled in the workplace, she will bring a greater quality of care to her offspring." This statement implies the gross misassumption which our society has ever so subtly moved to embrace, namely, that motherhood is not fulfilling or work of optimal "quality." This simply is *not* true.

Random House Dictionary defines quality as, among other meanings, "a degree or a grade of excellence." Interestingly enough, lower on the same page appears the word quantity, which is defined as "the measurable, countable, or comparable property or aspect of a thing."

This brings us to the first and most salient fact about quality daycare. There is no center, there is no program, there is no caregiver whose attributes could *ever* be compared with the "properties" which a mother, who has given life to her child and who has the greatest and deepest commitment to that child, can give her own child.

When we discuss "quality," what standard are we using to measure what that quality is? Whose value system, whose way of life, is being lived out before each child on a day-in-day-out basis? It is certainly not the parents'.

Confusion reigns supreme in the full-day daycare center of today. It is not the fault of the parents. In order to attain the all too elusive American dream of the two-car garage and house on a cul-de-sac in the woods of suburbia of any U.S. megalopolis, we are told that both mommy and daddy *must* go to work.

It is not the fault of the caregivers. Most are highly dedicated, highly motivated, caring, hard-working, nurturing women who are doing what they do best and love most, caring for and nurturing children.

There is only one problem — these children are not their own. There has been no bonding with that child to that caregiver, as there was with that child to his own mother and father. *This* is the reason why confusion reigns. The child truly does not know or understand what is going on and to whom he should turn for security and trust. Simultaneously, the child may continually receive mixed messages — one set of values, rules and functions at home and, probably, another set in the daycare facility.

Mother has had a maternity leave of six weeks, eight weeks, three months, maybe has been able to stretch it to six months, and then the "tearing" comes — the rending of that bond, the trust which a child develops in his parents.

I have witnessed daily in my own centers, three of which have infant care, the daily rending of these bonds. I've seen the mothers leave their precious bundles of joy, lovingly, caringly, tenderly placing them in the hands and arms of another woman. They walk reluctantly out the door, lean against the wall of the building, and weep with body-racking sobs because of this rending.

Inside the building, a concerned caregiver cuddles and coos to a screaming baby who struggles and wrestles to try to escape the unfamiliar arms and scents, and frantically reaches towards the door which has closed on that last visage of Mommy. This happens no matter how carefully we try to ease the baby into the unfamiliar setting. The rending always comes: as day follows night. This is "quality"?

In these daily rendings, children lose that most basic bonding trust. Many do, eventually, bond with the caregiver. Some do not. Many toddlers form a closer relationship in the daycare center than with their parents. And why not? Virtually all their physical and emotional needs are being met by this caregiver with whom they spend nearly all of their waking hours. But this caregiver is simply a daycare center employee whose life is subject to change. Caregivers frequently leave their jobs, and the baby goes through another rending, another tearing.

As the baby grows and develops and moves on through the various age groups of the center, he experiences a series of tearings and bondings before age six and the first grade. Many daycare facilities today offer a full-day kindergarten because the half-day program of most public schools does not meet the demands of the employed parents. In this process of repeated rending, tearing, and hurting hearts, a basic, deep-seated mistrust and resentment frequently develops in these children because of that early, continuous confusion.

As daycare children struggle for their control and autonomy, for their own sense of self and a base of trust, various phenomena will manifest themselves. Professionals in the field often say that the children write the psychology textbooks which we read in training. Children become total experts at pushing parents' (and, yes, caregivers', too) "buttons," sending their authority figures into orbit.

Here is one example, and I could give you many. One mother is a professional, a trained teacher for emotionally disturbed children, each day working with and facing the many challenges of a job in that field, including the drain on one's own inner resources. Her own child, who is in our daycare center, habitually, repeatedly throughout the day, week in and week out, month in and month out, soils his pants at the slightest provocation, often for no apparent reason. The caregivers and the director schedule and hold conferences with the parent. Social welfare is involved to "evaluate" possible/probable causes. A neighbor has registered a suspicion of child neglect or abuse. Social welfare, after a full investigation agrees to pay the tuition of $180 weekly for the child and his sibling in our daycare center. The mother continues, daily expending her energies and abilities in her job assisting emotionally disturbed children. Her career is rewarding and fulfilling to her.

Now for some questions. Where does this mother's value system lie? Would these two young children not be better served by giving this mother the $180 a week to enable her to stay at home with her own children, utilizing her abilities and expertise with them? She previously admitted that, if her husband had a $180 per week raise in pay, she could well afford to stay at home.

Daycare Dropouts and Disease

We hear the hue and cry about the need for quality daycare centers, for funding, and on and on regarding this issue. Today we are seeing the amber light of caution demonstrated by some parents. One in every three infants who are enrolled in daycare centers today, in hands-on, day-to-day care, drop out within three weeks to a month of starting in a daycare center. Where do they go? Usually to a grandmother, an aunt, a sister or sister-in-law, or close friend of one of the parents. Sometimes it is to a nanny who is hired to come into the couple's home. Frequently, it is to a trusted neighbor or hired sitter who herself has a young child at home and is supplementing her income (usually unreported).

If one peruses the classified advertisements on any given day, or skims the community bulletin boards in local supermarkets, the ads are there for daycare alternatives from both caregiver and receiver. This is all too frequently misinterpreted to mean that there is an insufficient supply of adequate "professional" daycare available. That is simply not true.

Why do these families with their babies and young children leave daycare facilities? The answer is often illness coupled very directly with economics. Any pediatrician worth his salt today will tell the young parent who will heed words of wisdom, that young children do *not* have the body's natural immune systems sufficiently matured to withstand the onslaught of the multiplicity of infectious exposures which come into play in any assembly of numbers of young children.

One of the biggest battles the daycare center fights is illness and the spread of bacteria and viruses. No matter how careful the center may be, disease is unavoidable.

Any professional daycare setting must exclude, usually by state standards if for no other reason, the unwell child. Few centers can provide the type of facility necessary to isolate unwell children, as costs to center operators for this "quality" of care would be beyond the reach of all but the most affluent of young parents.

What are the parental alternatives? Parents, where two are present, take turns at taking their sick days. When these are exhausted, time is taken off the job without pay. Mothers have been known to lose their jobs because of taking too much time off, usually spent nursing unwell children.

Single parents frequently resort to a phenomenon which we have come to call "masking." With fewer backup helpers, the single parent, usually the mother, will give her offspring aspirin or Tylenol to mask a fever and other symptoms so that the unsuspecting caregivers at the center will be unable to detect that Johnny isn't well until several hours after the mother has left him behind at the center and put in some time at her job. In this way, she is usually able to be paid for the full day, preserves her job credibility, and then collects her child who has, by mid-day, again spiked a temperature. The unwell child has, once again, had to pay the price. But so has a frazzled, worried, guilt-ridden Mommy, trying to keep body and soul together for her family.

The private setting, therefore, presents an increasingly inviting alternative because of the minimal exposure to illness and the maximizing of on-the-job time. However, this does not help anyone deal with the lack of monitoring of the "in home" daycare situations which exist all across our nation.

What price does an employed professional mother pay? What price are the offspring made to pay? What price is society paying with its most valuable resource, our children? Is the quality that we speak about, and say we prize so highly, really there — or are we just giving lip service to our nation's children? As yet, we do not know what a generation of children totally raised in daycare will bring to our society.

Giving It Up

The real reason why both Mommy and Daddy "must" work is a multi-pronged dilemma. It is partly a desire to live the American dream and partly that our society today has taught us to focus on "I," "my," "me," self-gratification and "I've got to have it *now.*" The development of a push-button, instant-results mentality has occurred. Working, saving, and planning toward future goals are, for many, particularly lower-income and single-parent families, difficult, if not impossible attributes to inculcate.

The largest portion of this pie lies with the fact that the tax base for deductions for dependents has not kept pace with the inflationary spiral. If it had, two-thirds of the women of child-bearing and child-rearing age in the workforce today would be able to make the quality decision which so many are coming to realize they really want — that is, to stay at home to raise their children, and not have to work outside the home while at the same time juggling all the demands placed upon the woman who takes that course.

I have witnessed more and more young couples who have come to the New York City area for the fulfillment of their dreams say, "The price this is exacting on us and on our children is simply too high. We are packing it up, going back to Middle America, and settling for a more modest home and a simpler lifestyle with fewer gadgets. With a less fancy car, taking a camping vacation with the kids instead of a ten-day cruise on the bright blue sea, our children can be at home with Mom instead of with strangers."

These couples are defining their "quality" of child care. Personally, my wife and I have come to that point of agreement with them, and so we are presently moving to divest ourselves of our daycare involvements and channeling our lives into other areas where we can work to preserve the American family as a unit.

I thank you all for giving me your ear, as you are the people who have the ear of those who can truly impact on the quality of life for the children of America. No matter how hard we may strive, quality will never be found in a daycare center.

Chapter 11

CHILD CARE IN A
GENDER-NEUTRAL SOCIETY
by George Gilder

An economist explains why a civilized and productive society depends on the nurturing of children by a mother in the home and a father as provider. He says that public facilities, no matter how costly, can never substitute for the commitment and the care that mothers voluntarily provide. He also explains that the victims of the changing roles of men and women are not only children, but also women, men, and our competitiveness in the world's economy.

George Gilder is known worldwide for his views on economics, especially in relation to family institutions. His best-selling book Wealth and Poverty *provided the theoretical foundation for supply-side economics and gave conservatives new confidence in American capitalism. In studying what causes wealth, prosperity, and economic growth, George Gilder discovered that human motivation is based largely on family and faith. Therefore, the family structure is essential to prosperity because it motivates husbands and fathers to work to provide for their families, now and in the future. He is the first modern American economist to write with sensitivity to moral values, family integrity, gender identity, and cultural differences.*

In another recent book, The Spirit of Enterprise, *Mr. Gilder writes with enthusiasm and admiration for the entrepreneurs who are the prime movers of economic growth. His next book will be on the semiconductor industry and how computers have changed our lives. Mr. Gilder also writes frequently for* The Wall Street Journal, National Review, *and* The American Spectator.

George Gilder's 1986 book, Men and Marriage, *is an update of his 1973 book called* Sexual Suicide. *It shows how the sexual revolution and the breakdown of defined sex roles have undermined the*

147

Irving Kristol has written that "the unintended effects of social policy are usually both more important and less agreeable
than the intended effects." The advocates of massive new federal
child care programs imagine that they are providing options for
beleaguered mothers. They claim to offer necessary preschool
training for disadvantaged children. They purport to be saving
"latchkey" children from a dangerous and depraved life on the
streets. Their intentions seem good. Even some conservatives
have succumbed to the siren appeal of helping children. But
perhaps never in the catalog of government programs has a proposal entailed a greater gulf between its intentions and its likely
consequences than the current government daycare initiatives.

This is a strong statement. The marmoreal buildings of
Washington provide a veritable street map of the hell that can
be paved by federal good intentions. Health and Human Services (HHS), Housing and Urban Development (HUD), Education, Justice all ring with high purpose and compassion. But
HHS is the source of welfare policies that have given America
at once the richest and most wretched poor people on the face of
the earth. The Justice Department heads a system of criminal
justice that is a holy terror toward small Christian colleges and
deadly toward police departments with single-sex squad cars,
but that fosters a rate of violent crime 62 times higher than
Japan's patriarchal society.

HUD is the source of public housing so afflicted with crime
and drugs that a resident or visitor would be safer in Beirut or
Belfast, Soweto or Sinai. HUD is also the focal point of the single greatest propaganda triumph for socialism since the Great
Depression: the homeless in America who—from the beaches of
Los Angeles to the center of Manhattan—occupy some of the
most valuable real estate on the face of the earth. Like the Great
Depression, which was caused by massive tax and tariff hikes,
the homeless problem is a harvest of government good intentions: deinstitutionalizing the mentally ill, overthrowing

vagrancy laws, stifling cheap housing with regulations, codes and controls. But the answer, in the morbid feedback loops of liberalism, is yet more government subsidies and benefits for homelessness and thus yet more homeless — and yet more propaganda for the enemies of America.

The Department of Education symbolizes a U.S. school system in which the top one percent of 18-year-olds perform less well in mathematics achievement tests than the average Japanese, while spending far more money than Japan per student. In some cities, moreover, this public school system boasts some 400 times as many administrators per capita as Catholic schools that perform far better.

The good-intentioned array of governmental programs against racism and poverty, covering a gamut from affirmative action and black studies to workfare and AFDC (Aid to Families with Dependent Children), have inflicted more damage on America's blacks than centuries of slavery. But the dire achievements of government in the ghetto probably pale before its achievements on Indian reservations. For the catastrophic results of liberal good intentions, it is hard to imagine beating the record of the Bureau of Indian Affairs.

Now, in a new climax of liberal presumption, the same people who paved the road to hell in America's inner cities want to take care of your small children. It is an utter outrage. And yet, it is perhaps the most seductive of all the liberal offers. Conservative Senators and Congressmen, tough-minded with terrorists and only rarely intimidated by the *Washington Post*, go weak at the knees and wet in the eyes when confronted with feminist staffers proposing a new program of daycare centers.

You've got to admit it sounds appealing. Small children are one of the enduring problems of life. They constantly make demands, disrupt projects, spill food on your word processor or new copy of *National Review* or Phyllis Schlafly's newsletter. They bawl and shriek. They distract you from important work. They run into the kitchen and knock over the coffeemaker during your most romantic moments. They are an impossible nuisance at the country club or the local prayer breakfast for Oliver North. They are miserably embarrassing on airplanes. They fail to listen politely while Daddy explains supply-side economics to Dan Rather. They interfere with human fulfillment courses and aerobics classes. They undermine and subvert your career. No way around it, small children are a major problem. All of us from time to time may be tempted to let the government solve it for us.

It is, in fact, the ultimate liberal temptation. Karl Marx and Friedrich Engels described it in broader terms in *The German Ideology*: "In Communist society, where nobody has one exclusive sphere of activity but each can become accomplished in any branch he wishes, *society* regulates the general production and thus makes it possible for me to do one thing today and another tomorrow, to hunt in the morning, fish in the afternoon, rear cattle in the evening, criticize after dinner, just as I have a mind, without ever becoming hunter, fisherman, shepherd or critic."

The contemporary liberal wishes to banish male bias from the dream. This is where government daycare comes in. In order to have a gender-neutral society, we must assign to society the duties not only of "general production" but also of reproduction. Thus the liberals could extend to women, as well as to men, the life of a British country squire.

It was Marx's dream and it is the liberal dream today. Liberating both sexes from restrictive roles and moral codes, the dream would bring a new spirit of sharing—of jobs, bodies, vocations, and pleasures. People would be full "human beings" rather than oppressed men and women.

There are two serious problems with this arrangement. Both are fatal. In the first place, there is no such thing as "society." There really isn't. Therefore both production and reproduction will be left to particular human beings.

The second problem is that there is no such thing as a "human being." There are just men and women. The profound differences between the sexes dictate that men will do most of the production and women all the reproduction. Thus we are back where we started.

The gender-neutral communal dream always fed on the vast ignorance of intellectuals like Marx about the production of wealth. To Marx and Engels, the role of men seemed so simple that it could in due course be passed on to a few bureaucrats managing the machines of mass production. The most striking fact about Communist writing is its contempt for labor. Marx really believed that the means of production were machines.

The Challenge of the Mother's Role

Liberals show a similar contempt for the lives of ordinary men and women. To the average sexual liberal, the role of women seems so routine that it can be assumed by a few bureaucrats managing child development centers. To the current advocates of a gender-neutral society, both the work of the world and the duties of the home are so undemanding that they can be accomplished with part-time effort.

The truth is that, even beyond fulltime duties nurturing infants, the mother's role imposes continual and unremitting challenges. Raising several children is a project that exacts a constant alertness and attention that none of the sexual liberals remotely understands when they urge that "society" do it.

With fewer children, kept longer within the household, the focus on each child is even more intense than it was in the past. The decline of extended families, though crucial to the Industrial Revolution, also increased the burdens of the mother alone.

New technologies relieve the mother of some household burdens. But the lesson of Japan is that, from birth through high school, children can learn far more than previously believed. For example, the best time to learn a foreign language is between the ages of two and six. Mathematics, through calculus, can be learned early in high school. Compared to the Japanese, Americans do a dreadful job in raising children.

Two things are clear about Japanese families. From the point of view of Americans, they are entirely patriarchal. But women are in charge of young children and the women stay in the home in the early years.

I believe that new technologies will soon bring a wide array of educational possibilities to the home, making homeschooling a much more attractive option. High definition television transmitted over fiber optic cables will offer a wide range of vivid and beguiling educational programs, with interactive graphics. Churches may focus their educational efforts in this medium. Parents will be able to control still better the educations of their children. It is nonsense to say that children can benefit more from going to lousy secular public schools than from watching and responding to brilliant television at home. Children will both learn more from good educational programs and enjoy them more. But someone will have to be in the home to make it happen.

As many sociologists have discovered to their surprise and dismay, housewives usually pursue more varied and challenging lives, with more options and intellectual opportunities, than do either employed men or employed women. Women's activities are far richer in intellectual and social challenge than most academic writers understand. As Helen Lopata wrote: "The role of the housewife provides her a base for building a many-faceted life, an opportunity few other vocational roles allow, because they are tied down to single organizational structures and goals."

It is foolish to imagine that the complex domestic and social roles of women can be assumed by outside agencies. The woman's role is nothing less than the hub of the human community. All the other work—the business and politics and entertainment and service performed in the society—finds its ultimate test in the quality of the home.

The central position of the woman in the home parallels her central position in all civilized society. Both derive from her necessary role in procreation and from the most primary and inviolable of human ties, the one between mother and child. In those extraordinary circumstances when this tie is broken—as with some disintegrating tribes—the group tends to sink to a totally bestial and amoral chaos.

Most of the characteristics we define as humane and individual originate in the mother's love for her children. Men have no ties to the long-term human community—no ties to the future—as deep or tenacious as the mother's link to her child. People who foresee men taking over the roles of child care forget that men need be nowhere around when a child is born. For raising healthy children, all societies must depend on the mother's love.

Springing from this mother's love are the other civilizing concerns of maternity: the desire for male protection and support, the hope for a stable community life, and the aspiration toward a better long-term future. The success or failure of civilized society depends on how well the women can transmit these values to the men.

What is true for individual moral issues is also true for the practical needs of a nation: the maternal role remains paramount. There is no way to shunt off child care to "society" or to substantially reduce its burdens. If children lack the close attention of mothers and the disciplines and guidance of fathers, they tend to become barbarians or wastrels who burden or threaten society rather than do its work. Raising children to be productive and responsible citizens takes persistent and unrelenting effort.

The prisons, reformatories, foster homes, mental institutions, and welfare rolls of America already groan under the burdens of children relinquished to "society" to raise and support. In the sense of becoming self-sufficient, all too many of these children never grow up at all. To reproduce the real means of production—men and women who can uphold civilization rather than subvert it—the diligent love of mothers is indispensable. In fact, the only remedy for the "overpopulation" in female-headed families is the creation of a larger population of children brought up by two active and attentive parents.

Zero population growth is crucial to the liberal dream. Because each individual no longer depends on his children to support him in old age, many observers seem to imagine that children are less important then they were in the past. But with so many children blighted by childhoods spent in female-headed families, we will need more productive workers than ever. No less than in the past, the new generations will have to support the old. The only difference is that now the medium is coercive taxation and Social Security rather than filial duty.

The Challenge of the Father's Role

Just as the female role cannot be shared or relinquished, the male role also remains vital to social survival. For centuries to come, men will have to make heroic efforts. On 40-hour weeks, most men cannot even support a family of four. They must train at night and on weekends; they must save as they can for future ventures of entrepreneurship; they must often perform more than one job. They must make time as best they can to see and guide their children. They must shun the consolations of alcohol and leisure, sexual indulgence and flight. They must live for the perennial demands of the provider role.

On 40-hour weeks the world dissolves into chaos and decay, famine and war. All the major accomplishments of civilization spring from the obsessions of men whom the sociologists would now disdain as "workaholics." To overcome the Malthusian trap of rising populations, or to escape the closing circle of ecological decline, or to control the threat of terrorism and nuclear holocaust, or to halt the plagues and famines that still afflict the globe, men must give their lives to unremitting effort, day in and day out, focused on goals in the distant future.

They must create new technologies faster than the world creates new challenges. They must struggle against scarcity, entropy, and natural disaster. They must overcome the sabotage of socialists who would steal and redistribute their product. They must resist disease and temptation. All too often they must die without achieving their ends. But their sacrifices bring others closer to the goal.

Nothing that has been written in the annals of feminism gives the slightest indication that this is a role which women want or are prepared to perform. The feminists demand universal daycare in the name of liberation. But the male role means bondage to the demands of the workplace and the needs of the family. Most of the research of sociologists complains that men's work is already too hard, too dangerous, too destructive of mental health and wholeness. It all too often leads to sickness and "worlds of pain," demoralization and relatively early death. The men's role that feminists seek is not the real role of men but the male role of the Marxist dream in which "society" does the work.

These are the facts of life. A single-parent family is almost always a broken family and a burden on society. Both the man's role and the woman's role remain indispensable to a civilized and prosperous nation. The advocates of government administering daycare in a gender-neutral society live in a dream world. No government program in the world, however expensive, can make up for the economic and emotional disaster of broken homes. No daycare scheme can enable most single women to both raise their children successfully and earn incomes above the poverty level. In most cases, female-headed families cannot even begin to discipline teenage boys or provide role models for them; in many families that I have interviewed, the mothers are actually afraid of their teenage sons.

Governments grow by the pretense of solving problems. By solving the immediate problem of where to park the kids, government daycare creates an illusion that families may break down without major damage — and an illusion that women can bear children without marrying the fathers. By solving the immediate problems of female-headed families, government thus creates the deadly long-term problem of a society full of them.

Don't solve problems, pursue opportunities, is Peter Drucker's rule for the successful executive. The broken families of America already constitute an insoluble problem that can absorb unlimited funds and efforts and provide a pretext for unlimited expansion of government. The current welfare programs already do all that the state can do to provide minimal care; an enrichment of these programs with job training and daycare will further accelerate family breakdown. With every new initiative of the state, the problem will grow inevitably worse and demand ever more extreme government action.

As Jack Kemp says, "If you want more of something, subsidize it; if you want less, tax it." The new government daycare proposals will tax families that care for their own children in order to subsidize families that place their children in another's care. The more the state subsidizes the breakdown of family responsibilities, the more families will break down. But there is no way on earth for government to supply the love and attention and self-sacrifice that mothers spontaneously offer their children. There are not enough resources on this entire planet to raise a new generation of civilized children if mothers defect. Every government daycare center entails an irretrievable net loss for children.

The Current Child Care Opportunity

The current daycare mania, however, does provide a major political opportunity. For decades the tax burden has been shifting from single people and families without children onto families with children. The child deduction in the federal income tax code would be worth some $6,000 today if it had risen apace with inflation and incomes, not to mention educational costs, since 1950. Whenever the liberals demand support for children outside the home, we must demand support for children in the home as well. Conservatives do not like the idea of child allowances: payments to every mother of some income for each child. But it is the only alternative to a steady erosion of the economic viability of families.

In the January 1989 issue of the Rockford Institute's superb newsletter, *The Family in America*, economist Richard K. Vedder demonstrates that the market continues to increase the real wages of male providers in the workforce. Adjusted for inflation, the wages of married men have risen slightly since 1970. But the government continues to focus the brunt of taxation on intact families with the woman at home, and continues to focus government benefits on female-headed families. Thus the opportunity cost of divorce and separation has steadily declined for the last two decades.

The government has been paying for divorces and broken families. It has been paying lavishly for illegitimacy. It thus should not be surprising that it has been getting more broken families and illegitimate children. The government has been paying women to leave their families or refrain from marriage, and to enter the workforce. It is not surprising that women follow the dictates of these powerful government incentives. Government statistics may even identify this process of familial deterioration as an expansion of our Gross National Product.

The average social scientist spends his life ignoring what is important in order to aggregate data. He sees concepts such as "poverty lines," "comparable worth," "productivity," and "daycare facilities" as more significant than morality, family loyalty, religious faith, male solidarity, motivation, knowledge, and maternal love. He believes, as a professional hypothesis, that what is easily measurable and aggregatable is more important than what is not. This hypothesis can yield interesting observations about the economy and society. But unless the social scientist understands the limitations of his data, he can blithely propose absolutely monstrous errors of policy.

He will imagine that women can be combat Marines or police officers without disrupting morale, or that girls can participate in male sports without demoralizing the underdeveloped boys, or that differences between girls and boys in mathematical apti-tude are the result of discrimination, or that welfare benefits can rise to near the poverty line without expanding poverty and de-stroying families, or that the spread of promiscuity, divorce, pornography, and homosexuality are irrelevant to the health of an economy or society. He will suggest that government day-care facilities can replace loving mothers and fathers. These so-cial scientists thus have no sense of the social prerequisites of civilization and prosperity.

The stable families of America both sustain the American economy and raise virtually all the nation's productive new citi-zens (most of the rest are immigrants from stable families over-seas). The child-free families of today are the freeloaders on Social Security tomorrow, for they have failed to produce the next generation of workers to support them in their old age. The female-headed families of today create an unending chain of burdens for tomorrow as their children disrupt classrooms, fill the jails, or throng the welfare rolls. Then they gather as bit-ter petitioners and leftist agitators seeking to capture for them-selves the bounty produced by stable families.

There is no doubt that American competitiveness suffers more from the declining quality of American family life and resulting deterioration of school performance than from any other factor. But we have no trouble competing with European welfare states, which have gained virtually all their growth for a decade from increased government consumption and exports to America.

The competitors who give trouble to American firms mostly come from the patriarchal family structures of Asia where women take care of their children and where schools teach physics and calculus rather than sex education and Indian rights.

Liberalism today is chiefly a movement of the voluntarily dependent *against* the society's productive citizens and intact families. It is a movement of amoral secularism against the reli-gious codes and disciplines that uphold civilized life. There is no way to compromise with this force of self-destruction at the heart of Western culture. We must fight it. The issue of child care presents the challenge in its most stark and menacing form.

The family is the place where we are formed as individuals, the place where we partake of the great religious traditions that

inform civilized life, the place where the sanctity of human life
is cultivated and thrives. The family gives us our links both to
the past and to the future. Although sought as liberation, government daycare threatens all these links that make us free men
and women.

The Powerful Piety of Gender Neutrality

Twenty years ago, as a liberal Republican, I was editor of a
magazine called the *Ripon Forum*, the journal of the Ripon
Society. I had been doing some research in the ghetto, interviewing unemployed ghetto youth. I was chiefly interested in
poverty at the time. That was before I was married; since then I
have acquired a new interest in wealth.

While I was running the *Ripon Forum*, the Mondale-Brademas
Child Development bill passed Congress. Although it seemed
like a fairly innocent proposition to most people, President
Richard Nixon vetoed it. Since we were a Republican magazine
and President Nixon was a Republican, I wrote a short editorial
supporting his veto of the daycare bill. My editorial ignited a
complete uproar. Nothing I'd ever written in my life had ever
approached the emotional eruption that was provoked by my
innocent little declaration in support of President Nixon's valid
and good decision.

Within a day, the leading ladies of the Ripon Society were
on the NBC *Today* show denouncing me. I'd never even imagined
that television was so easily accessible to Republicans, but the
Ripon ladies were promptly invited on the *Today* show to de-
nounce my editorial written in a publication with a circulation
of about 2,000.

After that I was invited to appear on a television program
called *The Advocates*—a debate show that was being run at the
time by Michael Dukakis. On that program, I made the innocent
argument that maybe it wasn't the best thing to do to spend what
would have been about $22 billion in today's money to finance
the somewhat reluctant entry of more people into the workforce
at a time of substantial unemployment. It was already absolutely clear to me that the key problem of the ghetto was the
abandonment of families by their fathers. It seemed to me that
this Mondale bill, which was often linked with workfare and

public support, would take away the mothers as well; so it seemed to be a proposal to "help" ghetto youth by making them orphans, which I thought was an unpromising approach.

I said some of these things on *The Advocates*, where I appeared along with a group of eminent people, and a throng of women rushed forward to argue with me at the end of the program. For years I'd been exploring various ways of arousing the intense interest of women, and it was obvious that I'd hit paydirt with the child care issue.

I resigned from my job as *Ripon Forum* editor minutes before I was to be fired, as I learned later. I was told by the head of the Ripon Society and all the other people in charge at the time that they had resolved to fire me because of my violation of what, even then, was the supreme liberal piety of the day, which is that men and women are essentially the same. This notion had never occurred to me before, but at major universities it's still the essential piety. Most of the speeches that are being delivered at this conference on child care could not be delivered on most university campuses. I can't speak on this subject on most campuses. On several occasions, colleges have invited me to speak, but there was a protest and my speech was cancelled.

It is also true that one can't publish these kinds of ideas because of the power of this piety among the leading New York publishing firms. In Gretna, Louisiana, I found a bold publisher named Pelican Books willing to release *Men and Marriage*. Before I had to resort to Gretna and Pelican, following the big sale of my *Wealth and Poverty*, I was being besieged for a manuscript by publishers all over New York. I kept saying, "Yes, I do have another book idea that you might want to consider. I'd like to adapt *Sexual Suicide* for the new environment of the time." They'd all tell me yes, they could publish it. Then a few weeks later, there would be an embarrassed call: "Of course you'll be able to publish it somewhere else, but we have a special political problem at Harper and Row (Times Books, Crown, or wherever) that prevents such publication."

The Feminist Mistake

There is obviously something very emotional about this subject. I think the key to it is that lots of women in recent decades really did change their lives as the result of the women's movement. The essence of what they did was to spend their twenties and early thirties competing intensely with men for advancement in their jobs, making their first priority the achievement of career advantage. As they entered their thirties, they began to see that the gratifications of this kind of intense careerism are not as great as they anticipated, and they then sought to get married. At that point, they discovered that it is much harder for a woman to get married, or to marry the man she wants to marry, in her thirties or forties than it was in her twenties.

Thousands, perhaps even millions, of American women to some extent changed their behavior and made a terrible sacrifice of their very future as women. This was a dreadful, tragic mistake, but once they made it, they have a compelling need to defend it. They feel they need—and it's really a tragic need—to defend the mistaken choice which so many of them made. That is what accounts for the intensity of emotion surrounding this issue on campuses, in publishing houses, and in various other arenas.

The daycare issue is an extension of this mistake and of the illusion which so many women desperately want to justify and perpetuate. *That's* what this issue is all about. It's often declared to be about poverty or workfare or other conceptions, but it is essentially about ratifying the feminist mistake. It is an attempt to give massive public ratification to the appalling error which millions of American women made in the 1970s and 1980s, which only became fully manifest when they were confronted with that famous *Newsweek* cover article of June 2, 1986 about their diminished chances of ever getting married. That article really signified the end of American feminism when it showed the dimensions of the error which the leading feminists had induced American women to make. Then the real costs and significance of the women's liberation movement became clear.

The reason it's such a mistake, not only for society but also for the economy (and I write about economics), is that the family has two roles. It is often said that the key role of the family is socializing children, raising children, and this is obviously an absolutely central role of the family in every culture. It can't possibly be replaced to any significant degree by public facilities. Why we have to debate this subject is really peculiar, because it is not even vaguely conceivable that we could provide daycare centers all across the country which could replace the energies and commitment and attention and love and sacrifice which mothers are willing to make for their own children. You can't pay for that. There's no possible way to reproduce it.

It's not a matter of whether you could pay to have enough daycare centers built or to hire enough people (and they would be mostly women) for the daycare centers. That isn't the issue. If that could be done, it would be extraordinarily expensive. It would also probably be completely unsuccessful because mothers give far more than any routinized official bureaucracy could possibly offer. As we would pay and pay for more daycare, the conditions would become worse and worse; more and more families would break up because of the increasing financial burden incurred by supporting an ever larger apparatus of public services. The daycare costs would only be the beginning because, as families break down, then the prisons would have to be vastly expanded, the welfare programs would have to be vastly enlarged, and the social service programs would have to be extended, while the economy declined.

It just is not in any way possible to replace the complex of deeply intimate and powerful services which are transmitted in the home. The illusion that this can be done would be an even more terrible mistake to compound the initial mistake which was made when feminists declared that women during their twenties should focus chiefly on their careers and then later, if they decide that perhaps they want to "have it all," they might entertain the idea of marriage. That is exactly the wrong sequence for those decisions. The twenties are by far the best time to have a family and maintain it. Later on, women can have even longer careers, if they want, than men can, because women live longer and are generally healthier than men in their older years.

The idea that women somehow have to sacrifice their careers in order to have children is a fundamental misconception. The fact is that women today are probably less eager for employment, and actually work less than they did in previous generations. I was brought up in a farm family, so I have some sense of what life was like when most American families were farm families. It seems clear to me that women on farms made a larger contribution to the success of those operations than the average woman does in her career in America. Women in intact families still earn less than 20 percent of the family income—less than a fifth in intact families. In families that actually function and stay together, women make a relatively small contribution to the total family income.

The statistics which appear to show a massive entrance of women into the workforce, competing in increasing equality with men, are chiefly evidence of family breakdown rather than the activities of intact families. Yet intact families are the chief source of the next generation of real workers in the society. It is intact families that sustain the U.S. economy.

The statistics show that married men are the driving force of economic growth. Some single men, of course, make big contributions but, across the wide array of the economy, it is chiefly married men who make the kind of sacrificial lifetime commitments to work that produce the flow of income that sustains a growing capitalist economy. Single people just don't do it. They can't motivate themselves to make the kind of long-term commitments and sacrifices which are required for economic growth. Because women have the option of starting a family or withdrawing from the workforce more easily, they likewise do not make that sort of major long-term lifetime commitment which is necessary to sustain a prosperous economy.

The Family Socializes Children and Men

The family is not only a source of the socialization of children, it is also a key source of the socialization of men because it induces men—who have a more compulsive, short-term, erratic kind of sexuality and commitment to the society—to subordinate themselves to the long-term sexuality of women raising children and thus to become linked to the future of the race by their very bodies. It's this process whereby men commit themselves to the future through, in essence, the wombs of women which makes a civilized society work. This is why married men work some 60 percent more than single men do, why married men work far harder and exploit their earnings capacity so much more fully than married women or single women or single men or any other group in our society.

It is this kind of major lifetime commitment which makes possible economic growth. On 40-hour weeks, the world decays into stagnation and decline. To build a successful economy takes the kind of full-time commitment which men supporting children readily and reliably make. At the same time, it takes the kind of commitment which women routinely and readily make to their children to sustain both the man's effort and to create a new generation of men and women capable again of sustaining a prosperous and civilized society.

When this complex of roles and commitments is undermined, all the king's horses and all the king's men can't put the society together again. You can get an idea of what will happen just by looking at the areas where the government has played the largest role so far. All the social programs are most intensely focused in the inner cities, and we see that is the pattern which can easily spread throughout our society. As a matter of fact, it is already spreading through society as a result of the increasing propagation of the "we are the welfare-feminist-daycare government and we're here to help you" mentality.

One of the most important recent findings of Charles Murray is that this is not a racial problem at all. It is a complete misconception to think that the decay we find in the inner cities is somehow a reflection of the concentration of black people in the inner cities. White poor people are not concentrated in specific identifiable places, so their behavior is harder to identify in census materials. But if you make all the appropriate corrections, as Murray has done, you find that levels of illegitimacy, family breakdown, and crime among white poor people are almost identical to the pattern we see in the black ghetto. The idea that we are somehow exempt from this potential catastrophe which government policy has inflicted on black Americans is entirely an illusion, as much an illusion as that the declarations of feminism can exempt us from observing the facts of life.

This is a much broader issue than some of these debates may suggest. It is not an issue of the statistics of just how bad daycare is, or whether daycare can be made marginally positive if we spend some extraordinary amount of time and money on every child. There are probably ways to create experiments in which daycare may help some children; that might be possible if we devote the massive attention of lots of people to raising a few children. But it is a total illusion that any such "quality" daycare could be created across the whole nation of the United States. It's a completely quixotic, crazy idea that the kinds of commitments which women make for their own children can be reproduced in large numbers of public centers.

Child care is a competitiveness issue, it's a productivity issue, it's a moral issue, and it's a religious issue. Families everywhere require the support of religious institutions. You don't have monogamy without religious support. Even Margaret Mead understood this. She said that, in all societies where monogamy is sustained, you find both an expectation of permanence and a religious environment. Religion is fundamental to sustaining and perpetuating families. One of the most hopeful developments in this field, in relation to the economy and across society, is the revitalization of the conservative churches. They are essential to the task of creating a society that works and prospers and maintains its civilized values.

Child care is a critical issue of our time, but it is not just an issue of family; it's also an issue which affects the heart of the U.S. economy. It affects the motivation of all the workers in the U.S. economy. It affects the conditions in which our children will be raised and their likely contributions to society because, outside of the family structure, children don't grow up. They stay children all their lives. They may call themselves grown-ups but, outside of the family structure and its connections to future generations, children simply don't grow up. They remain dependents. It's the family which sustains the economy and, to the extent it breaks down, our economy will deteriorate.

Chapter 12

IDEOLOGIES ABOUT
CHILD CARE
by Midge Decter

A nationally-acclaimed writer on social, military, and economic trends examines the ideologies behind the current demand for daycare, and defines the central role that children play—or should play—in our lives and in our future.

Midge Decter has been since 1980 the Executive Director of the Committee for the Free World, a consortium of intellectuals who have a commitment to the survival of the United States against its enemies.

Prior to that, she had a distinguished career in the publishing field. She was managing editor of Commentary, *editor of the Hudson Institute publications, executive editor of* Harper's Magazine, *book review editor of* Saturday Review, *and editor for Basic Books.*

Midge Decter is the author of two significant books written in the early days of the women's liberation movement: The Liberated Woman and Other Americans *(1971) and* The New Chastity and Other Arguments Against Women's Liberation *(1972). She is also the author of* Liberal Parents, Radical Children *(1975).*

Midge Decter is a member of the board of directors of the Heritage Foundation and of Resistance International. She is the wife of Norman Podhoretz, the mother of four children, and the grandmother of eight.

In a way, the very notion of an ideology of child care defines the contemporary problem. It will not do to be sentimental about the lot of children in olden times. They have often been very badly treated, both by the poor and by the aristocracy. Brenda Hunter offered a chilling illustration of this in talking about 18th century France. When economic necessity dictated it, children were sent into the coal mines at age seven or eight, or sent out to beg even younger. There are places in the world today that we might visit, India being one, where babies are maimed by their parents in order to make them more effective beggars. As for the aristocracy, children lived in isolation in the nursery, and little boys were sent off around the age of seven to be ill-fed, ill-housed and ill-treated in some elegant boarding school—an experience described unforgettably by George Orwell.

As an exercise in remaining unsentimental about the lot of children in the past, try looking up in what year the state of Pennsylvania outlawed infanticide. You'll find that that year was in the 20th century. I don't mean to suggest that Pennsylvanians were widely practicing infanticide, but something must have induced someone to pass a law against it—some lapse, shall we say, in obedience to a higher law that necessitated this passage of an earthly one.

So children, precisely because they are small and helpless, have many times in the sad history of man's fallen estate had a pretty hard time of it. The one institution in which they have consistently found themselves protected and cherished, however, is the bourgeois family, that great and benign creation of the great and benign Industrial Revolution—that inventor of what is horribly called middle-class values. That family is our family, the American family, which, whether rich or poor, has granted children the right to ripen slowly, both in limb and in mind, so that they may achieve genuine autonomy and realize the full measure of their potential. Of course, middle-class parents, being sane people, wouldn't put it this way—they didn't have to. They took this for granted, which is what brings me to my point.

Today we *do* have ideologies of child care. Indeed, right now, the American middle class is engaging in what it is no exaggeration to call ideological warfare on this matter—because we no longer as a society take for granted what children are supposed to mean to us and we to them. Put it another way: over the past quarter century, there has been an influential group of privileged and articulate—hence influential—women who have refused to regard children as simply a natural given in their lives.

Some of these women—only a very small minority—refused to have children at all on the ground that women should no longer have to be slaves to the race. One of their chief philosophers, Simone de Beavoir, referred to the womb in her famous book as "that infirmity of the belly." However, this was really too radical a view for most of the women who were declaring their liberation. Sooner or later—mostly later, to be sure—they were bound to have children. But that far from ended the matter.

Having declared themselves oppressed, they still did not see why merely giving birth to a baby required one to be its mother in the traditional sense. Whole libraries of protest literature were produced on this particular point, literature in which, not surprisingly, babies and children were described exclusively as producers of soiled diapers, vomit, sleeplessness by night, and intolerable tedium by day. Betty Friedan, the original fountain of inspiration for this vision, once likened the condition of women looking after home and children to that of a certain group of war veterans who had returned from World War II with brain injuries. So, the having of children was not to be allowed by itself to answer to the question of how to shape and live one's life.

In general, what those privileged, educated, articulate women were seeking was an overarching structure of theories that would make it legitimate for them, first, to have husbands without being wives; and then to have children without being mothers. This dream might look like ordinary immature, infantile selfishness to you; to them it was the very ideal of social justice.

This, of course, is where the warfare comes in. If there was an ideological assault on children, then those of us who feared and fought that assault were forced to mount an ideological defense of them. Soon, what had been natural and instinctive and unthinking in our lives—motherhood and fatherhood—became something we, on the other side, had to argue about. The women's libbers' effort to violate what was natural to them came to violate what was natural to us as well.

We found, and still find, ourselves defending the family—which is a deeply absurd thing to have to do, if you think about it. It's rather like defending being alive. Of course, we're all pleased to be alive. Indeed, who could think of an alternative? But to go around talking about how wonderful it is all the time would make you sound like an insufferable prig. It's like telling people you'rc happily married; it's really bad manners!

But here we are, forced to construct a formal defense of the family, and talking about babies as if we were composing messages for the insides of greeting cards. Both ought to be — and in a better world would be — beyond speaking about. But since we are forced to speak, let us not lose our sense of humor. Children are after all one big pain in the neck, and we do have to get away from them once in a while.

Yesterday I listened to someone ask if she had perhaps damaged her child because she had been away for a weekend. That kind of problem and anxiety is what comes of our need to defend the family. Of course, no child is damaged by his mother having a few days off every five years.

Be all this as it may, wherever there is a radical movement, the contrivances of social science, of course, are not far behind. Thus, the child psychologists, particularly those involved in researching something called learning psychology — a field whose perhaps most eminent practitioner is a professor at Harvard named Jerome Kagan — very quickly, as if on demand, began to produce massive studies, replete with the most arcane statistical analysis, showing that infants and toddlers develop better both intellectually and socially in group settings. There was a great big fat book published by the publishing house I used to work for by Jerome Kagan which said that.

We heard yesterday that, now, he is not so sure. But the intellectual damage that he wrought has already been done. Thus these privileged, articulate women who wanted to have babies, for the purpose — as they would put it in their lingo — of "fulfilling" themselves were also given warrant for dumping these babies into daycare centers. "In order to be able to pursue their careers," they explained; in order to enhance the decor of their lives with children without having to be mothers was what they really meant.

In all the discussion about the economics of the two-career family, nobody mentions the Mercedes career. It is not to pay taxes, and it is often not even to improve one's standard of living; it is to buy the second Mercedes. Those of us who, in one way or another, have been granted the incomparable pleasure of such young women's company as these — and I worked in publishing, so I used to see lots of them — were even further enlightened by them on the subject of the daycare center. Placing ten or so infants under the supervision of one, rather harassed we should imagine, caregiver actually helps to socialize them, we are told. Relieving babies of this over-intense, neurosis-producing, smothering one-on-one relationship with a mother is actually healthier for babies — so said some theory invented to justify these women to themselves.

Thus by the 1970s, we witnessed the following fascinating phenomenon. Young people who had for years most actively been attempting to undermine the authority of all our public institutions — the police (those pigs), the presidency, the schools, the courts, you name it — these institution- and society-haters now commenced demanding that society provide a vast new network of institutions for bringing up their children.

Yet something curious has been happening at the same time. Try as you might, and as much damage as you succeed in doing — which, as far as women's lib is concerned, is a great deal of damage, indeed — in the end, as that old commercial used to have it, "you can't fool Mother Nature." The movement was causing too much personal misery. It was beginning to lose out with everybody but the blind, by which I mean, the politicians and the media.

The women's lib war on men and children was no longer selling. Young women were now growing quite desperate to find husbands and beat out the biological clock. Something had to be done. Enter what the redoubtable Mrs. Friedan, never at a loss for words, proclaimed to be the Second Stage. We love husbands and children, she declared, whoever said we didn't? It was just that we had to call attention to our little problem. Now that we have done so, the next step is to reorganize society — that's all — so that we can all have satisfying work and lovely families, taking a little time off, both men and women, or even a lot of time off, for the having of each baby, and then have one's employer fix it so the kiddies are looked after conveniently nearby. In the Second Stage, properly understood, one's ideal family would be a kind of trouble-less, gender-free, socialist heaven.

We are forever being told how many women are in the work-force, especially how many with children under six. Probably it is time for us to face the fact that an economy which makes so much use of women of childbearing age must have some kind of need of their services. It seems to me that somehow we will have to figure out what this means and what to do about it, and I'm not sure we yet know the answer.

By the way, we are now faced with another finding from so-cial science. Just the other day in the *New York Times* I read a story which said that latchkey children get along just fine—in-deed, by some measures of maturity and adjustment, they do better. The *New York Times* proclaimed this very proudly on the front page of its family section. The concern that these children might be lonely or frightened was unfounded, said the research-ers. So you see, even if you convince liberated mothers that daycare centers are bad, they now have a fall-back position. Very well—give the children no care at all—they'll do even bet-ter. So what in the end are we to make of all this?

It is important to bear in mind that we are not really talking simply about mothers in the workforce. There have always been mothers in the workforce, especially when it was an agricultural workforce. But also, the garment center of New York City, for instance, was full of employed mothers during the Depression. I had such a mother myself, in the Midwest. Nor are we talking about the sufferings of individual children. As we have learned from history, and from the books of Charles Dickens, some chil-dren can overcome an awful lot of childhood misery.

We are talking about us as a society and the ideas that threaten to—in fact are even intended to—tangle our minds and poison our souls.

Children stand at the heart of these ideas because they stand at the heart of human existence. It is through them, through what we feel about them and what we say about them, that we give flesh to what we think and feel about life itself. Having chil-dren, and caring for them, is, among other things, one's way of expressing gratitude for the life that one has been given. A life for a life, so to speak.

When the women's liberation movement came along, those of us who turned our faces against it did so not because it was politically unsound, but because it was unholy. There is no more radical thing to say—certainly V. I. Lenin himself was not so radical as to say it—than that there are no differences between the sexes. Lenin only wanted to overturn history—the whole history of man's social and political arrangements. The women's liberation movement set out to overturn nature itself, that is, to tinker with God's very design for our existence. Of course, the ladies of the National Organization for Women and all their various partners in the sisterhood could not have set out to do such a fundamental thing on their own. It does not relieve them of their own noxious responsibility to say that they could not by themselves have released such a tide of nihilism without massive underlying support in the culture.

In the 20th century, people who are not grateful to the United States of America, just to give one example, are not grateful to life. And people who are not grateful to life do not open their hearts to children. Of course, they feel a primitive attachment to their own children. That, to some people's surprise, cannot be avoided. But to children, our children, our collective hostages to the future, our anchor, the base of our common commitment to be a decent people living in a decent society, to children in this sense, they can only respond with some theoretical formulation about adult rights.

There is, of course, a lot of individual hope. The career women of whom Brenda Hunter spoke so interestingly are evidently beginning to discover that there is more to this motherhood business than anyone told them—not only more guilt and responsibility, but more pleasure. Will wonders never cease! Their mentors forgot to tell them about the miracle of growth and development—a miracle just as fresh and new to contemplate with each and every additional child as it was with the first. You never believe it is going to happen again, and then it does. Someone neglected to tell them what infant flesh feels like and smells like.

It's a pity those young women had to be so tiresome to themselves and others, and had to put their husbands through so much anxiety, before they could make this great discovery: that babies give you easily as much as they take. But these women are beginning, *beginning*, in any case, to understand this. My

prediction is that those educated young mothers, if they still have
husbands (a big if, to be sure) and can afford it, will soon be
seen departing the executive suite and the law firms in droves.

My friends, we are more than half way down a very, very
slippery slope. We must fight the legislators and the bureaucrats. All of us in our separate and individual capacities, as
women, as wives, as citizens, simply as human beings, and
above all as mothers, have got to carry society with us on a long,
slogging, dirty, painful climb back up that slope. Fighting off
the daycare centers will not be enough—something else will
take their place. We must fight off the hatred of life, the love of
sterility, the narcissism, which lie behind them. How do we do
this? I don't know. Let's start by making a pact: I will hold your
children and grandchildren, and you will hold mine, to be precious—sight unseen, pain in the neck, and all.

Chapter 13

THE RETREAT
FROM MARRIAGE

by Bryce J. Christensen

A philosopher identifies the trends that have caused the fall in the marriage rate and the declining American commitment to marriage. He discusses the social costs of allowing these trends to accelerate through public policies on divorce, daycare, a reduction in the family wage, and the changing of gender roles.

Bryce Christensen is the editor of The Family in America *and director of the Rockford Institute Center on the Family in America, a research organization devoted to investigation of the cultural, economic, ethical and political issues affecting family life in the United States. In addition to writing and editing this Rockford Institute journal, he coordinates the Center's conferences on family issues and writes on family topics for other publications.*

Dr. Christensen's articles have appeared in The Wall Street Journal, Baltimore Sun, Chicago Sun-Times, Cincinnati Post, St. Louis Post-Dispatch, Indianapolis Star, Houston Post, *and numerous other newspapers. He has also written scholarly and literary articles for* Philosophy and Literature, Modern Age, The Public Interest, Forum, New Oxford Review, Christianity and Literature, *and* Chronicles. *Much of his journalism has focused on the family, on parental rights, and on demographic trends. His scholarly writing has analyzed the philosophical foundations of modern science and the religious implications of literature.*

Dr. Christensen's previous experience includes four years in various editorial positions for Chronicles, *a publication of the Rockford Institute devoted to literature, history, and the arts. He received his Ph.D. in English literature from Marquette University in 1984. He*

*received his M.A. (1980) and B.A. (1978) in English from Brigham
Young University, where he won numerous academic honors. He is
married and has three children.*

Permit me to begin with a story. A businessman decided to
visit a farmer friend in the country. As he arrived at the farm-
house, he noticed that one of the pigs in the pigpen had two
wooden legs. This struck the businessman as odd, so he asked
the farmer: "Why does one of your pigs have two wooden legs?"
"I'm glad you asked," the farmer replied. "Let me tell you about
that pig. Why just last month, our house caught fire in the middle of the night. That pig saw the smoke, leaped over the pigpen
fence, ran into the house and woke everyone up. He probably
saved all of our lives." "Amazing!" the businessman responded.
"But why does the pig have two wooden legs?" "Let me tell you
some more about that pig," the farmer continued. "Just last week,
I was working on my truck when the jack slipped, pinning me
under the rear axle. I thought I was done for. But once again,
that pig saw the trouble, leaped out of the pigpen and ran for
help." "Astounding," said the businessman. "But why does the
pig have two wooden legs." "Don't you see?" the farmer asked.
"When you've got a pig like that, you don't eat it all at once."

Today, we find a number of Americans whose attitude toward
the family resembles that of the farmer in this story: they're not
going to consume it all at once. Indeed, some people now cham-
pion daycare and similar programs with misleading pro-family
rhetoric. Senator Christopher Dodd (D-CT), for instance, has
offered a pro-family rationalization for his support for such
measures as federally-mandated parental leave and federally-
subsidized daycare. "The basic unit of society is the family,"
Dodd told *The New York Times*. "And when that begins to deteriorate, it falls apart, and we don't do things to encourage that."
Apparently, the editors accepted this line. Not long after the
Dodd interview, the *Times* published an editorial proclaiming
that, even if "publicly funded daycare" was once an "anti-
family" idea, "it isn't any more."[1]

A closer look, however, raises troubling questions. A number of recent studies have shown that daycare weakens a child's
bonding to both mother and father, often causing later emo-

tional and social problems.[3] Far from providing a support for healthy family life, daycare may best be interpreted as one more symptom of our national repudiation of family life. In particular, I wish here to explore the relationship between the widely publicized daycare issue and the much-less recognized social trend: the declining American commitment to marriage.

Since 1950, the marriage rate has fallen a remarkable 35 percent. The fall has been particularly steep in the last 20 years, dropping more than 20 percent since 1970. The average age for first marriage has climbed to 26.8 years for men and to 24.5 years for women. One American in eight now remains unmarried for life.

Surveying the statistics, the prominent demographer Robert Schoen discerns a "continuing retreat from marriage" over the past two decades. Schoen even wonders if we are not witnessing "a fundamental change in the nature of marriage." Thomas Espenshade of the Urban Institute has similarly concluded that "marriage is weakening as a social institution in the United States." Stanford scholar Kingsley Davis concurs: "A weakening of marriage is certainly occurring, at least in the sense that matrimony is rapidly becoming less prevalent." Officials at the National Center for Health Statistics report that since 1970 "the status of marriage in America" has been in "steady decline," since "a rising share of eligible people are choosing not to marry."[3]

What, though, is causing this decline in wedlock? A number of profound cultural developments, stretching back over at least two centuries, have rendered marriage both less attractive and more difficult to maintain. Patterns of American life, long defined by religion, agriculture, and community tradition, have slowly been displaced by secular, urban, commercial, and individualistic variants.

Since the Industrial Revolution of the 18th and 19th centuries, the family has surrendered ever more of its educational and economic functions to the state or to the marketplace. The normative status of marriage has naturally suffered in this realignment, especially as traditional religious belief and morality have faded among the cultural elite.

Despite these long-term trends, however, Davis is right to insist that, "compared to most other aspects of human society, marriage has changed surprisingly little" since the late 1700s. Indeed, Davis supposes that "the weakening of marriage as an institution" did not become particularly pronounced in the United States until the end of World War II.

Even the sudden eruption of divorce that occurred during the late 1940s can be partially explained as an aberration, an after-effect of the war that was quickly erased by the fervid domesticity of the 1950s. Contemporary sociologists need look no further back than the early 1960s to find "relatively early and widespread marriage, relatively low divorce rates, and relatively high fertility" in the United States.[4]

In retrospect, though, the remarkable blooming of marriage and family during the 1950s was largely a cut-flower illusion. After a decade and a half of depression and war, Americans were eager to spend their newly won prosperity in a family way, but were not willing to reverse the deep-seated historical forces that were eroding the family's place in society. As unbelief, modernity, and consumerism continued to rise during the 1950s, any reasonable observer could have predicted a slow, steady fading of marriage and family life in America.

The Rapid Unraveling of Marriage

But America has witnessed a far faster unraveling of marriage and family than can be explained simply by extrapolating pre-1960 trends. By the late 1960s and early 1970s, identifiable new forces were grievously exacerbating the long-term trends. Particularly deserving attention are five new influences, all of them either engendered or emboldened by imprudent government actions.

Beginning with the founding of *Playboy* in 1953, the publishers of "girly" magazines and of hard-core pornography began a surprisingly strong and effective attack upon marriage. In his very first issue of *Playboy*, editor Hugh Hefner emphasized that "we aren't a 'family magazine.'" Subsequent issues repeatedly ridiculed marriage as a "bondage of breadwinning" and an impediment to sexual fulfillment. In *The Rape of the A*P*E* (*American *Puritan *Ethic)*, published in 1973 by Playboy Press, Allan Sherman chronicled the "obscening of America" and the passing of the "incredibly clean-cut and impossibly wholesome"

American culture of the 1950s. After the sex revolution which *Playboy* helped to foment, "nothing was reduced to less recognizable rubble than the revered . . . institution of Marriage." In fact, Sherman boasted, by 1973 "it was getting increasingly difficult to explain why marriage was necessary at all." In the view of Judith Reisman, pornography has helped foster attitudes of "mutual distrust" and "heterophobia" between the sexes, so weakening the emotional foundations for marriage.[5]

The Supreme Court did its part to encourage pornography and undermine marriage in 1966 when it imposed an impossibly vague three-point test for obscenity. Prosecutors soon learned that it was almost impossible to prove the absence of "socially redeeming value" in smutty publications. In 1973 the Supreme Court finally abandoned its "redeeming social value" test for obscenity and replaced it with a more reasonable test of "contemporary community standards." Unfortunately, once the evil genie of pornography had been released from his bottle, it has not been easy to force him back in. Although in some cities — Atlanta and Cincinnati, for instance — vigorous law enforcement is rolling back the tide of smut, pornography is vastly more prevalent in America now than it was in 1965.

Even as court-induced paralysis prevented officials from stopping the flood of pornographic pollution, radical environmentalists persuaded government leaders of the need to protect the country's forests and wildlife against the unrestrained fertility of traditional families.

Partly because of groundless fears about "the population bomb," policymakers deliberately turned against the family by shifting the nation's tax burden. Between 1960 and 1984, the tax rate remained essentially flat for singles and childless two-earner couples. But one-earner couples with two children saw their federal taxes rise by 43 percent, while one-earner couples with four children witnessed a phenomenal 223 percent hike.[6] This unprecedented shift in tax responsibility occurred at the very time that the traditional family was also paying markedly higher payroll taxes for Social Security. Since Social Security actually favors the deliberately childless at the expense of parents, the system further discourages marriage, childbearing, and family life.

Government policy during the 1960s and 1970s not only weakened marriage by taking in money but also by giving it out. The dramatic growth of the welfare system since the early 1960s has made marriage appear unnecessary to many single women. Charles Murray has shown that current welfare benefits actually seem both to inhibit new marriages and to weaken existing ones.

Family sociologists Randal Day and Wade Mackey believe that current welfare policies encourage the formation of "the mother-state-child family," while weakening the traditional family. In the welfare state, they point out, married fathers must "pay directly for their own children and, in addition, must pay a heavy tax burden to underwrite the state, as the state takes over the role of the supportive 'traditional father' " for the children of unwed and divorced mothers. Day and Mackey warn that such a system discourages men from marrying or from staying in marriages with children.[7]

The Feminist Assault on Marriage

Growing welfare benefits only partially account for America's "divorce revolution" of the last 20 years. Although American divorce rates had been inching up steadily since the turn of the century, they shot up remarkably after the enactment in the early 1970s of innovative "no fault" statutes permitting couples to divorce for no cause other than "irreconcilable differences." In many states, the new laws permitted one spouse unilaterally to terminate the marriage without grounds. The author of a major new study on the unintended side-effects of no-fault divorce, Lenore Weitzman, observes that "a radical change in the rules for ending marriage inevitably affects the rules for marriage itself and the intentions and expectations of those who enter it." No-fault divorce, she reasons, is now "redefining marriage as a time-limited, contingent arrangement rather than a lifelong commitment."[8]

No-fault divorce counts as only one of the anti-marital initiatives promoted by the feminist movement during the late 1960s and early 1970s. Because they viewed the family as "patriarchy's chief institution," feminists launched many attacks on marriage. What began in 1963 with Betty Friedan's fairly restrained complaint that early marriage was "regressive" and an obstacle to "women's growth to autonomy," soon amplified into hysterical rant. In 1971 Germaine Greer indicted marriage for laying the foundation for "the prison of domesticity." "Rape is the first model of marriage," shrieked Andrea Dworkin in 1975. Dworkin decried the awful pattern of "male domination in Amerika [sic]," where "every married man, no matter how poor, owned one slave—his wife." The same year, Susan Brownmiller struck a similar chord when she alleged that marriage and rape were "philosophically entwined" and that it was "largely impossible to separate them out."9

While Greer, Dworkin, Brownmiller, and others helped provide the polemical artillery, feminist foot soldiers carried out a war of attrition in the legislative and bureaucratic trenches. Through a series of federal measures and their enforcement—the Equal Pay Act of 1963, Title VII of the Civil Rights Act of 1964, the Equal Opportunity Act of 1972, Title IX of the Education Amendments of 1972, the Equal Credit Opportunity Act of 1974, and the Civil Rights Restoration Act of 1988—feminists steered the government away from its traditional posture of nonintervention and toward sex-role engineering. School texts had to be rewritten, affirmative action "goals" enforced, girls' sports programs expanded, wage scales rewritten. Every available government program was enlisted in the effort to root out every vestige of "sexism," to erase the last public acknowledgment that fundamental differences separate men and women.

Despite the defeat of the Equal Rights Amendment, the feminist movement has largely succeeded in abolishing the traditional gender prescriptions that once existed in the nation's schools and workplaces. During the 1970s feminism helped to coax, encourage, and push record numbers of women into paid employment, while ensuring that they receive "equal pay for equal work" in their wage competition with men.

The new cultural and economic relationships between the sexes have profoundly undermined marriage. Kingsley Davis points out that marriage in the past has rested on the principle of "complementarity," requiring "a differential commitment to childbearing and child care" and "a division of economic labor, with husband and wife pursuing different activities in the production of goods."

The distinguished economist Gary Becker corroborates Davis' views in a probing analysis proving that marriage makes the greatest financial sense when men and women offer one another different kinds of services. In the past, wives have "traded" homemaking and child-rearing for a share of their husband's income. In modern America, Becker observes, "the gain from marriage is reduced by a rise in the earnings and labor force participation of women and by a fall in fertility because a sexual division of labor becomes less advantageous."[10]

At the same time that feminism has weakened the economic logic of marriage by putting more women into paid employment, the new competitive pressures in the wage market have seriously eroded the average man's ability to earn a "family wage" sufficient to support a wife and family. Even Robert S. McElvaine, former speechwriter for Walter Mondale, believes that the massive movement of American women into the workforce between 1965 and 1980 was "detrimental to the economy" with "a depressing effect on real income levels." In 1973, almost 60 percent of young men aged 20-24 could earn enough to keep a family of three out of poverty, but by 1984 only 42 percent could.[11]

The effects of female employment upon marriage are especially visible in countries such as Sweden and Denmark, where feminist policies have been in effect longer. Danish demographer Paul C. Matthiessen offers this assessment of why marriage rates have plummeted in Sweden and Denmark, while divorce rates have climbed: "The improved economic position of women — a result of their increased participation in the labour force — has probably contributed to the decline in the number of legal unions (marriages). The woman's earning ability has made marriage less important as a means of support. . . . It is also probable that the woman's improved economic position has contributed to an increase in dissolution of marriages which have failed to meet the expectations of the couples concerned."[12]

Daycare's Effect on Marriage

Clearly, daycare fits within this overall pattern. Contrary to the rhetoric of daycare advocates, daycare does not support family life. Rather, daycare serves chiefly to facilitate female employment. Among feminists, an ideological commitment to female employment makes daycare sacrosanct, beyond criticism.

Consequently, feminists have attacked researchers who have recently documented the risks of daycare. Professor Jay Belsky of Pennsylvania State University is a case in point. Once a cautious defender of daycare, Professor Belsky has recently incurred feminist wrath by publishing new studies exposing psychological risks of daycare, especially for infants. Feminist psychologist Sandra Scarr of the University of Virginia dismisses Belsky's work as part of the "backlash against the women's movement." "The advice to women has always been to get out of the workforce," complains Scarr. "This is just another way of saying the same thing." In the same spirit, feminist psychologist Tiffany Field has labeled Belsky's recent work "bunkum," accusing Belsky of relying on poor research.[13]

Herself a former employed mother who has written compellingly about her decision to stay home with her children after a personal investigation of daycare, Deborah Fallows understands why critics of daycare have become objects of abuse. "In feminist eyes," she explains, "day care is indispensable to the formula for women's equality. For feminists, it is but a short step from criticizing day care to suggesting that there are fundamental conflicts between parenthood and career."[14]

By easing women out of parenthood, daycare further erodes the complementarity of the sexes and so weakens marriage. Professor Steven L. Nock of the University of Virginia observes that, among career women, "being a good mother may imply much the same thing . . . as being a 'good' father has to men for years—the provision of adequate material and financial resources to permit the child a rewarding and successful life."

But why, then, would two "fathers" be married to each other? In fact, recent studies show that among two-career marriages—marriages of the sort that require daycare if they have children—the divorce rate runs high. Professors Bijou Yang and David Lester find a clear pattern: "The higher the percentage of wives working full-time [in the United States], the higher the divorce rates." Yang and Lester suggest that "a working wife encounters a wider variety of men than a housewife and may increase her chances of finding an alternate mate. Entering the labor market also gives a wife another source of gratification, making her less dependent upon her marriage for happiness."[15]

The availability of daycare does not remove these pressures breaking up two-wage-earner marriages. In its recent cover story on daycare, *Time* magazine hailed Denmark as a country with one of the most highly developed daycare systems in the world. "Nearly 44 percent of Danish children younger than three and 69 percent of those between ages three and five are enrolled in a public facility," *Time* reported. Yet Professor Matthiessen notes that between 1971 and 1984 Danish divorces outnumbered new first-time marriages by fully ten percent. Over 40 percent of Danish births now occur out of wedlock, compared to less than ten percent in 1965. Matthiessen attributes these trends largely to the "changing role of women in society."[16]

Some advocates have alleged that easier access to daycare would strengthen family life by encouraging more women to bear children. Paul Demeny questions this argument, countering that because daycare helps women into the workforce it might effectively decrease the birth of a second or third child. Demeny points out that government provision of daycare has not bolstered the depressed fertility of West European women. And to the degree that daycare suppresses fertility, it further weakens marriage, since research shows that parenthood defines a "basis for marital stability" and that children reduce the likelihood of divorce.[17]

Clearly, then, the rise of daycare and the decline of marriage are related developments, both symptoms of a social retreat from family life. Byrna Siegel believes that the aggressive individualism fostered by daycare will translate into fewer and less stable marriages in the decades ahead.[18] Some, however, may view both the rise of daycare and the retreat from marriage as appropriate adjustments to modern life and not as issues for public concern. A closer look, however, reveals problems. I will leave to others the task of detailing the many psychological and health risks of daycare. But permit me to outline some of the negative consequences of our national retreat from marriage.

The Decline of the Birth Rate

Demographers who are worried about America's low birth rate in recent decades invariably cite the decline of marriage as one of the principal causes. In the view of Ben Wattenberg, the nation's "birth dearth" reflects the trend toward fewer, later, and less permanent marriages. "A sharp increase in never-married women," he reasons, "has the effect of reducing the likely universe of potential mothers." Because "fertility delayed is fertility denied," the postponement of marriage likewise depresses the birthrate. Leading sociologists fret about the growing tension between the generations as a declining number of youthful voters must pay for the Social Security and medical benefits for a growing number of retired elderly. Health authorities at Vanderbilt University predict that "intergenerational conflict will intensify" as the costs of caring for the elderly climb and as "mother-to-daughter ratios" grow out of balance.[19]

America's retreat from marriage not only reduces the number of youthful taxpayers carrying the nation's public-health burdens, it also increases the size of those burdens. Numerous studies prove that married people of all ages and ethnic groups enjoy better physical and mental health than the unmarried. Writing recently in *Social Science and Medicine*, Catherine K. Reisman and Naomi Gerstel observe that "one of the most consistent observations in health research is that married [people] enjoy better health than those of other marital statuses."

In a study presented just two months ago to the American Public Health Association, researchers found that, "in spite of the recent changes in American marital patterns, there was still a clear association between being well and being married in 1987." This new study further suggests that the "surge in divorces" in recent decades has imposed "hidden health costs on the population" that should be recognized. Indeed, a 1988 study at Ohio State University found that divorced men are less healthy and exhibit weaker immune systems than married men even if their personal health habits are identical. According to Peggy Thoits of Indiana University, "married persons have significantly lower anxiety and depression scores than unmarried persons, regardless of gender."[20]

Costs of the Retreat from Marriage

Adults are not the only ones hurt by the retreat from marriage. Children growing up in single-parent—usually female-headed—households, suffer in a number of ways. More than one third of all children living in female-headed households live below the government's official poverty line, with many more living perilously close. In contrast, only one in 19 two-parent households lives in poverty. Over 40 percent of all single-parent households receive welfare, compared to only 12 percent of two-parent homes.

Naturally, children who grow up in impoverished one-parent homes are handicapped in their access to medical, academic, and recreational services. Their mental outlook is consequently constricted and their emotional life is often insecure. Studies show that, compared to children raised by two parents, children in one-parent homes are more likely to develop mental illness, to cause trouble and to fail in school, to use drugs, to engage in premarital sex, to have an illegitimate child, to commit crimes, and to attempt suicide.[21]

Nor is poverty to blame for many of the problems found among the children of unmarried parents. Professor Nock stresses that many of the problems encountered by these children cannot be traced to household income, to race, to sex, or to region of residence. Rather, Nock reasons that children in one-parent homes fare so poorly because they fail to learn how to recognize and defer to authority, how to accept order and discipline. Lessons in order and authority are rudimentary in the intact family. Perhaps that is why a University of Maryland study recently concluded that crime rates can be better predicted by the percentage of single-parent homes in an area than by the socio-economic class of the residents. In fact, the children of single-parent households — regardless of social class — are not only more likely to commit crimes than peers in two-parent homes, they are also more likely to have crimes committed against them.[22]

Unfortunately, children raised in one-parent households are far less likely to make successful marriages as adults than peers raised in two-parent households, meaning that the dismal pattern of broken homes repeats itself across the generations. A pattern of economic dependence likewise repeats itself: living with an unmarried mother raises the likelihood that a daughter will receive welfare benefits by 125 percent for whites, 65 percent for blacks, compared to peers raised by two parents.[23]

Inevitably, the retreat from marriage imposes public costs. Higher costs for police protection, for court proceedings, for prison construction, for Medicaid and Medicare, for remedial education — these and other social burdens will mount because of the retreat from marriage. On the other hand, the community's non-economic resources dwindle when fewer adults marry or remain married. Surveys show that it is the married and not the unmarried who usually support civic and voluntary organizations.[24]

The public costs of the retreat from marriage ought to be borne in mind at a time when many now call for additional government subsidies for daycare despite the likelihood that such subsidy will further weaken marriage. It seems patently unjust to impose heavy tax burdens on traditional families for family-surrogate services that they neither want nor need. When I speak of family-surrogate services, I speak not only of daycare but of the whole range of law-enforcement, medical care, therapeutics, and social services made necessary by the repudiation of family life. Why is it that the very idea of "imposing values" offends many public officials who are quite willing to impose the costs of repudiating those values? The imposition of these costs on traditional families appears especially dubious at a time of depressed birthrates, since fulltime homemakers bear a disproportionate number of the nation's children, the nation's future taxpayers. I am glad that proposals are now being discussed that would alleviate the unfair tax burdens now borne by traditional families.

Yet, I wish to conclude by stressing that both the retreat from marriage and the rise of daycare signal problems deeper than economics or tax policy. In 1957, Harvard sociologist Pitirim Sorokin argued that both the erosion of the "sacred union of husband and wife" and the trend toward "earlier and earlier" separation of parents from children were symptoms of a crisis in moral and spiritual purpose. These two trends could be reversed, he argued, only if society could be "purified and brought back to reason, and to eternal, lasting, universal, and absolute values."[25]

I agree with Sorokin's assessment. It is no accident that countries with well-developed daycare systems are also countries in which religion is weak and fading.[26] Nor is it surprising that couples who are religiously devout are less likely to use nonmaternal child care than couples without strong religious convictions.[27] For that reason I believe that, as Americans consider the current push for daycare and the present retreat from marriage, we must do more than debate public policy. It is a time for soul-searching, for prayer, and for bearing witness.

Notes

1. See Peggy McCarthy, "The Basic Unit Is the Family," *New York Times*, sec. 23 (September 20, 1987), p. 3; "Stumbling Toward Day Care," *New York Times*, sec. 1 (March 26, 1988), p. 30.
2. See Jay Belsky, "Infant Day Care and Socioemotional Development: The United States," *Journal of Child Psychology*, 29 (1988), pp. 398-401.
3. See Robert Schoen, "The Continuing Retreat From Marriage: Figures from 1983 U.S. Marital Status Life Tables," *Sociology and Social Research*, 71 (January 1987), pp. 108-109; Thomas J. Espenshade, "The Recent Decline of American Marriage: Blacks and Whites in Comparative Perspective," in Kingsley Davis (ed.), *Contemporary Marriage: Comparative Perspectives on a Changing Institution* (New York: Russell Sage Foundation, 1985), p. 53; Kingsley Davis, "The Future of Marriage," in *Contemporary Marriage, op. cit.*, p. 32; Barbara F. Wilson and Kathryn A. London, "Going to the Chapel," *American Demographics* (December 1987), p. 29.
4. Kingsley Davis, "The Meaning and Significance of Marriage in Contemporary Society," in *Contemporary Marriage, op. cit.*, p. 19; Susan Cotts Watkins et al., "Demographic Foundations of Family Change," *American Sociological Review*, 52 (1987), pp. 346, 354.
5. See Allan Sherman, *The Rape of the A*P*E* (*American *Puritan *Ethic): The Official History of the Sex Revolution* (Chicago: Playboy Press, 1973), pp. 11, 338-339; Allan Carlson, "Family Breakdown and Other Cancers of the 'Post-Capitalist' Era," *Persuasion At Work*, 6 (October 1983), pp. 2-3; Telephone interview with Judith Reisman, November 30, 1987.
6. See Eugene Steuerle, "The Tax Treatment of Households of Different Size," in Rudolph G. Penner (ed.), *Taxing the Family* (Washington: American Enterprise Institute, 1983), p. 75; Allan Carlson, "Children in Poverty and Other Legacies of the Redistributive State," *Persuasion At Work*, 10 (January 1987), p. 2.
7. Charles Murray, *Losing Ground: American Social Policy, 1950-1980* (New York: Basic Books, 1984), pp. 154-162; Randal D. Day and Wade C. Mackey, "Children as Resources: A Cultural Analysis," *Family Perspective*, 20 (1986), pp. 258-262.

8. Lenore Weitzman, "The Divorce Law Revolution and the Transformation of Legal Marriage," in *Contemporary Marriage, op. cit.*, pp. 305, 335.
9. See Kate Millett, *Sexual Politics* (New York: Doubleday, 1970), pp. 33, 126-127; Betty Friedan, *The Feminine Mystique* (New York: W.W. Norton & Company, 1963), p. 176; Germaine Greer, *The Female Eunuch* (New York: McGraw-Hill, 1971), pp. 216-220; Andrea Dworkin, *Our Blood: Prophecies and Discourses on Sexual Politics* (New York: Harper & Row, 1976), pp. 32, 82; Susan Brownmiller, *Against Our Will: Men, Women and Rape* (New York: Simon and Schuster, 1975), p. 376.
10. Davis, "The Future of Marriage," *op. cit.*, p. 47; Gary Becker, *A Treatise on the Family* (Cambridge: Harvard University Press, 1981), p. 248.
11. Associated Press, "Young men's earnings fall by nearly one-third," *Rockford Register-Star* (June 12, 1987); Robert S. McElvaine, *The End of the Conservative Era: Liberalism After Reagan* (New York: Arbor House, 1987), p. 100.
12. Paul C. Matthiessen, "Changing Fertility and Family Formation in Denmark," *World Health Statistics Quarterly*, 40 (1987), p. 64.
13. See Thomas E. Ricks, "Day Care for Infants is Challenged by Research on Psychological Risks," *Wall Street Journal* (March 3, 1987), p. 37.
14. Deborah Fallows, "A Closer Look at Day Care," *The UTNE Reader* (May-June 1987), pp. 88-89.
15. Steven L. Nock, "The Symbolic Meaning of Childbearing," *Journal of Family Issues*, 8 (1987), pp. 373-393; Bijou Yang and David Lester, "Wives Who Work Full-Time and Part-Time: Some Correlates Over the States of the USA," *Psychological Reports*, 62 (1988), pp. 545-546.
16. Claudia Wallis, "Children of the World," *Time* (June 22, 1987), pp. 54-60; Matthiessen, "Changing Fertility and Family Formation in Denmark," pp. 63-73.
17. Demeny cited by Michael Klitsch, "Scholars Disagree on Economic, Social Impact of Continued Low Fertility in Developed World," *Family Planning Perspectives*, 19 (May-June 1987), p. 131; S. Philip Morgan et al., "Sons, Daughters, and the Risk of Marital Disruption," *American Journal of Sociology*, 94 (1988), pp. 110-129.
18. Siegel cited by Brenda Hunter, "Breaking the Tie that Binds," *Christianity Today* (February 21, 1986), p. 33.
19. Ben J. Wattenberg, *The Birth Dearth* (New York: Pharos Books, 1987), pp. 99, 126; see Wayne A. Ray et al., "Impact of Growing Numbers of the Very Old on Medicaid Expenditures for Nursing Homes: A Multi-State, Population-Based Analysis," *American Journal of Public Health*, 77 (1987), pp. 699-703.
20. Catherine K. Reisman and Naomi Gerstel, "Marital Dissolution and Health: Do Males or Females Have Greater Risk?", *Social Science and Medicine*, 20 (1985), p. 627; Charlotte A. Schoenborn and Barbara F. Wilson, "Are Married People Healthier? Health Characteristics of Married and Unmarried U.S. Men and Women," paper presented at the American Public Health Association (November 15, 1988), pp. 9, 15; Susan Kennedy et al., "Immunological Consequences of Acute and

Chronic Stressors: Mediating Role of Interpersonal Relationships,"
British Journal Of Medical Psychology, 61 (1988), pp. 77-85; Peggy Thoits,
"Gender and Marital Status Differences in Control and Distress:
Common Stress versus Unique Stress Explanations," *Journal of Health
and Social Behavior,* 28 (1987), pp. 7-22.

21. See Terry Arendell, "Women and the Economics of Divorce in the
Contemporary United States," *Signs,* 13 (Autumn 1987), pp. 121-122;
William P. O'Hare, "America's Welfare Population: Who Gets What?",
Population Trends and Public Policy, 13 (September 1987), pp. 9-14; Heather
M. Blum *et al.,* "Single Parent Families: Academic and Psychiatric
Risk," *Journal of the American Academy of Child and Adolescent Psychiatry,* 27
(1988), pp. 214-219; Sheila F. Krein and Andrea H. Beller, "Educational Attainment of Children from Single-Parent Families: Differences by Exposure, Gender, and Race," *Demography,* 25 (1988), pp.
221-234; Murray M. Kappelman, "The Impact of Divorce on Adolescents," *American Family Physician,* 35 (June 1987), pp. 200-206; Susan
Newcomer and J. Richard Udry, "Parental Marital Status Effects on
Adolescent Sexual Behavior," *Journal of Marriage and the Family,* 49
(1987), pp. 235-240; Sara S. McLanahan, "Family Structure and Dependency: Early Transitions to Female Household Headship," *Demography,* 25 (1988), pp. 1-16; Bruce Chapman, "Fairness for Families: An
Organizing Theme for the Administration's Social Policies," *The Journal of Family and Culture,* 2 (1986), p. 23; John S. Wodarski and Pamela
Harris, "Adolescent Suicide: A Review of Influences and the Means
for Prevention," *Social Work,* 32 (1987), pp. 477-484.

22. Steven L. Nock, "The Family and Hierarchy," *Journal of Marriage and
the Family,* 50 (1988), pp. 957-965; "Children From Single-Parent
Families: Differences by Exposure, Gender, and Race," *Demography,*
25 (1988), pp. 221-234; Douglas A. Smith and G. Roger Jarjoura,
"Social Structure and Criminal Victimization," *Journal of Research in
Crime and Delinquency,* 25 (1988), pp. 27-52.

23. McLanahan, "Family Structure and Dependency," *op. cit.,* pp. 1-16.

24. See Robert J. Sampson, "Crime in Cities: The Effects of Formal and
Informal Social Control," in Albert J. Reiss, Jr. and Michael Tonry
(eds.), *Communities and Crime,* Vol. 8, in Michael Tonry and Norvel
Morris (eds.), *Crime and Justice* (Chicago: University of Chicago
Press, 1987), pp. 271-307.

25. Pitirim Sorokin, *Social and Cultural Dynamics: Ethics, Law, and Social Relationships* (1957; rpt. New Brunswick: Transaction, 1985), pp. 700-702.

26. See, for instance, Ole Rijs, "Trends in Danish Religion," *Social Com-
pass,* 35 (1988), pp. 45-53.

27. See T.R. Balakrishnan *et al.,* "A Hazard Model of the Covariates of
Marriage Dissolution in Canada," *Demography,* 24 (August 1987), pp.
398-400; Mary Y. Morgan and John Scanzoni, "Religious Orienta-
tions and Women's Expected Continuity in the Labor Force," *Journal
of Marriage and the Family,* 49 (1987), pp. 367-379.

Chapter 14

CHILDREN—OUR GREATEST RESOURCE

by Harold M. Voth, M.D.

A psychiatrist with long experience in dealing with real problems in the real world explains the importance of giving children good mothering and good fathering in order to develop healthy citizens who can meet the challenges of today's world problems.

Harold M. Voth, M.D., is Chief of Staff at the Veterans Administration Medical Center in Topeka, Kansas. He is also a professor at the University of Kansas Medical School and at the Karl Menninger School of Psychiatry, where he was a senior psychiatrist and psychoanalyst for many years.

Dr. Voth received his medical degrees from the University of Kansas School of Medicine, the Menninger School of Psychiatry, and Topeka Institute for Psychoanalysis. He is a charter fellow of the American College of Psychoanalysts, and a fellow of the American Psychiatric Association. He speaks nationally on social issues and has testified before many Congressional committees.

Dr. Voth is the author of the anti-drug program that cleaned up drugs as a problem in the United States Navy, for which he received the Legion of Merit. He is a retired Rear Admiral in the United States Navy. He served on the White House Conference for a Drug Free America. He is the author of more than a hundred articles in professional and popular journals, including all the major journals of psychiatry. He is also the author of several books on the family endorsed by such diverse persons as the late Senator Sam Ervin and Ann Landers. Dr. Voth and his wife have three sons.

Our meeting is focusing on child care, on what constitutes good care and what constitutes bad care and the consequences of each. How we care for infants and children is a central, crucial and, I believe, the most important element in the future of America and of the earth itself. I have placed our topic in this context in order to emphasize the profound importance of childhood development, not just education but personality development. Society must awaken to the depth of the child care crisis.

The survival of any organization depends foremost on its members putting as much, or more, into the organization as is taken out of it. As much money has to be taken in as is disbursed or an organization will soon be bankrupt. If all the talent is recruited away, no organization will be able to keep abreast of its competitors. When material resources dry up, products cannot be manufactured. This principle is self-evident. We humans must see to it that we put into civilization, and into our very existence, as much as or more than we take out.

Enlightened and thoughtful people the world over—and, fortunately, this number is growing rapidly—have awakened to the fact that man is using up the resources of the earth, and also seriously damaging the ozone, the air, the earth, and the water, thereby imperiling all forms of life, including man. Recycling programs have increased, cleanup efforts are underway, and we are more conscious of our gluttonous use—and misuse—of energy. By nature, and because of the cultural values he has created, man seeks territory; he strives to possess material objects. These natural and cultural imperatives may exhaust the earth's material resources and destroy our environment unless we begin using our intelligence, our knowledge, and our wisdom to reverse this trend. Some progress is being made, but woefully little.

How we care for infants, the children and the youth of this earth will, in my judgment, determine whether or not we avoid an irreversible race toward disaster. Our planet must be inhabited by a sufficient number of people who have the ability and the inner psychological resources to strive for and achieve excellence, as well as to find joy through ways of living which do not require endless gratification of narcissism, selfishness, and egocentricity. These are the people who are able to give of themselves and find joy in doing so, rather than take for themselves, and who are perceptive and responsible enough to tackle the horrendous problems facing man. These are the people who make any organization flourish, be it a family, a small business, a corporation, or a society. The reason is very simple. They put more in than they take out.

The creation of people like this depends in great measure on the quality and quantity of care the child receives from birth forward into youth. No period in life is more crucial to the future of the individual and to mankind's future than the first few years of life, for what you become determines to a substantial degree what you believe and what you do, including the values you create and live by.

Mothering is the central factor of this period. How the child is mothered — good mothering — leads to a variety of human qualities and personality development. Courage, the ability to trust, trustworthiness, reliability, to be able to love and to be loveable, the capacity to form intimate relationships, the ability to mate physically and psychologically, competence, mastery, the ability to experience beauty, the capacity to be a parent (over time, not briefly or part-time), and above all to find more pleasure and personal fulfillment in giving rather than receiving — all these qualities derive either directly or indirectly from the mother-child relationship. There is no adequate substitute for a mature, psychologically healthy mother who is bonded to and loves her child.

For the mother to function best, she should have a good man by her side whom she loves, to whom she is committed and who loves her, provides for her, is committed to her, and so on. Men have a direct impact on child development during the first three to five years of the child's life, but not to the extent of the mother. Men can carry out maternal functions to be sure, but their effect on the child is by no means comparable to the mother's. Men should be good fathers, not try to emulate mothers, as seems to be the vogue these days.

It is, then, the solid, healthy, intact family which will ensure the future of mankind. This basic human unit can produce the kind of people who do *not* have a gluttonous desire to devour everything in sight, oblivious to the consequences of such behavior. From such people, the creative process will produce the

knowledge and the techniques for halting and reversing the dis-
astrous course we are now on. Women who can provide such
maternalism need good men to provide for the family, so that
these vital processes can take place within the children.

It is hard for me to believe that a civilized society such as
ours treats millions of children the way we do. Child care in the
United States is shocking. Our own society is paying a high
price, not only in terms of the personal suffering these children
are experiencing and will experience throughout their lifetimes,
but also in terms of the damage they do society and what they
do *not* do for society. They will crave input of all kinds into their
psyches. They hunger for material possessions, drugs, alcohol,
freewheeling sex, instant pleasure, in short, narcissistic gratification of any kind. Others lead slothful, unproductive lives and
become a serious drain upon society. All of them lack altruism,
the capacity to be giving, to tolerate solitude, to be able to draw
upon inner resources instead of constantly seeking fulfillment
through external sources, to make permanent commitments, to
be able to recognize and master the challenges which ensure
man's existence and progress.

Much of man's behavior today is out of harmony with
nature's laws; and when these laws are defied, disaster is the inevitable result. Nature's laws are immutable, but man's behavior is not. We must adjust our childrearing practices so that
what we do for and with our children is responsive to the natural imperatives governing child development. Children reared
in this way will discover how to be in harmony with the other
laws of nature that govern both life processes and inorganic
events. Children whose development conforms to natural imperatives can love, they recognize beauty, they seek to build not
to destroy, they care for living things, both human and animal.
Millions of the world's children, and most shockingly even here
in the United States, are not receiving the kind of care which
will create these human qualities.

All known forms of aberrant behavior in this country are on
the increase: homosexuality, pornography, child abuse, spouse
abuse, grandparent abuse, neglect of the elderly and the unfortunate, crime, drug abuse, transient relationships, obesity in
the young, violent and delinquent behavior. Our educational

standards are below those of other industrialized nations. The history of Western civilization is even being rewritten because of these very destructive current forces. Excellence in all aspects of society is waning.

Most ominous of all is that the one weak link in the entire chain of earthly events is the fragility of the heterosexual bond — the ability of a man and a woman to remain bonded to each other and to create new life within the context of that bond. The latest figures indicate that fewer than 20 percent of America's children will grow up within a classical family. I just heard that by the year 2000 three-fourths of all children under age 12 are predicted to be in some kind of care situation other than a home where the mother makes the home and the father provides for it, wherein family life proceeds in the best possible fashion. Divorce is rampant; about one-half of all marriages fail. Illegitimate births amount to about one-fourth of all babies born. One-half of the workforce are women, and one-half of this workforce has preschool children (about 9.5 million — 7 million are a little bit older).

The trauma being inflicted on our children is sin of the worst kind, for millions are doomed to a life of suffering and will never become what they might have been. Have you ever been in a daycare center and watched those babies lie there and cry, seeing nothing but empty emotionless faces? It is terrible. I can't stand it — I don't go there very often. It upsets me too much. The assault on them is a composite of repetitive premature separations, as the mother goes to her job each day, leaving her child with so many empty hours filled with largely mechanical events. Instead of the rich experiences of family life, especially maternal care during the first few years, these children suffer confusion as to who are the solid anchors to emulate and from whom to find security. Too many children face empty or absent family life, instability, transience, and broken bonds.

We are a weakened and progressively weakening people. Vigorous people are invading us economically. They are buying up our material wealth. Japan, which has virtually no natural resources, is buying up the United States at an alarming rate. The profits from the enterprises they purchase go to their homeland. Why is that possible? The answer is simple. They work hard. Why can they work hard? Because they have it in them to do so. Their greatest resource is the energy and strength of their people. The family is still intact in Japan, and I believe this is the key element in their robust culture. Their people put more into a society than they take out of it.

More and more women are entering the workplace in order to pay the bills for goods and services which steadily increase in price. As the cost of living increases, people have to work more to pay their debts. The feminist movement thrives on this trend and seeks to legitimize the woman's exodus from the home, such as through enactment of the Equal Rights Amendment. As written, it would mandate that the law treat men and women as interchangeable in all walks of life. That's utter nonsense. No surer route exists for further lowering the efficiency of our productivity than to place women where men should be, or men where women should be. Efficiency depends not only on hard work, but also on placing people where they function best.

The very quality of people has changed and continues to change toward greater narcissism, less capacity for commitment, competence and mastery, as this cycle proceeds from generation to generation. The constructive values which were created by psychologically strong and healthy people, which have stood the test of time, are being cast aside. Inevitably, sick values replace the good ones. Vast numbers of people cannot see what is happening to our country and to the earth. This is so because what you are determines in large measure what you can experience, believe and think, and all of that determines what you do.

The French have a saying, "If you trample on nature, nature will come roaring back." I believe this simply means that man can defy the laws of nature for just so long, and then nature's inexorable laws will prevail.

If I have ever seen a self-destructive life course—and I have seen many in my 40 years of professional work—I am now seeing such a course taken by our country. The politicians speak beautiful words about our country and its people and, while some of what they say is true, they don't see the trend, or if they do, they don't talk about it. Of course, they have to tell people how wonderful they are, and of course there are many fine people in America.

A few religious leaders are warning us of the peril facing the family, but missing in this voice are the professional organizations that should be expending every possible effort and resource for the purpose of preserving the family and thereby ensuring the proper development of infants, children, and young people.

Healthy, intact families produce strong-willed generous people who can perpetuate the human race along a healthy and productive road. Such people are capable of living by the highest and most constructive social values and, as time passes, they create new and better ones. Brilliant scientists and other professionals spring from such people, and they possess the courage, the intelligence, and the creativity to guide mankind.

Signs exist that constructive trends are underway. Man's instinct for survival is one of nature's laws. Man is awakening to the earth's destruction and to the flaws in his social orders. We have the resources, a marvelous tradition, great freedom, and a way of life that permits creativity to flourish. The turnaround should come. We have all the ingredients for it to happen, but one element is uncertain. And that is the key one: What currently is the relative balance between strong, healthy, unselfish people versus their opposite kind? Are we producing the quality of people who possess the inner resources of sufficient abundance, and in sufficient numbers, to *give* more than they *take* and thereby continue to breathe life into our values, improve upon them and on our social structure, and lead all nations, and ultimately the earth, to survival?

We may be in a situation analogous to an airplane flying in a box canyon. We may all be dead and just don't know it yet, or we may be turning the plane around and moving man to new heights of existence. I can tell you with absolute confidence that we in the United States must soon restore the family, and thereby ensure better rearing of our children, or our country will fall into an ever decreasing status among nations.

Chapter 15

PUBLIC POLICY
ABOUT CHILD CARE

by William J. Bennett

The Reagan Administration's leading spokesman on family issues enunciates five principles that should govern federal policies about child care, and describes the role that the Federal Government should play in order to help families care for their children.

William J. Bennett was U.S. Secretary of Education during the second term of the Reagan Administration, from 1985 through 1988. As Education Secretary, he stimulated a vigorous national debate about excellence in education. He urged that our public school emphasize the "Three C's"—content, character, and parental choice. Dr. Bennett was also a leading advocate of traditional family values. His principal speeches during his tenure were published in 1988 by Simon and Schuster under the title, Our Children & Our Country: Improving America's Schools & Affirming the Common Culture.

From 1981 to 1984, Dr. Bennett was Chairman of the National Endowment for the Humanities, and before that he was President of the National Humanities Center. He has a law degree from Harvard Law School and a doctorate in political philosophy from the University of Texas. He has taught at the University of Texas, the University of Southern Mississippi, Harvard University, Boston University, and the University of Wisconsin.

In 1989 President Bush appointed William Bennett to serve as Director of the Office of National Drug Control Policy. He and his wife have one child.

The First Book of Kings tells us that, when Solomon was king of Israel, two women came before him, each claiming to be the mother of the same infant. They asked for a judgment. Solomon ordered that the child be cut in two, and that half of the body be given to each woman. When, at this command, one of the women immediately gave up her claim, Solomon decreed that the child be given to her, because he knew then that she was the child's mother. That was the wisdom of Solomon.

I offer as my thesis today the same truth that Solomon relied upon when he made his judgment. That truth is this: No one is more important to the care, the nurture, and the protection of a child than that child's parent. As Solomon knew, sensible government policy recognizes and takes advantage of this truth. There really is no choice where this truth is concerned. No government policy or action can match or replace the care that a parent can offer a child.

I believe that the issue of "child care" policy is really part of the broader issue of how we can best care for and raise our children. During my term as Secretary of Education, I was reminded time and time again of the importance of parents in the education of their children. It is parents who impart to their children moral standards, life ambitions, and the security and confidence that comes from a deep sense of permanent love. As the Reverend Martin Luther King Jr. once said, "The group consisting of mother, father and child is the main educational agency of mankind."

With that in mind, let me state the fundamental principles that I believe should guide our efforts in the development of public policies bearing on child care.

The first principle is that any government policy or program in the area of child care worthy of our support must meet one standard above all others. It must strengthen, over the long term, the vital social institutions—especially the family—that bear primary responsibility for the nurture and the protection of our children. As President Reagan said, "Sound public policy must support the family in its mission of child care."

In our society, families have the basic responsibility for the care of children. It has been said that the family is the original and the best Department of Health, Education, and Welfare. If our public policies—however inadvertently—undermine and weaken families; if our public policies do not pay sufficient attention to supporting and strengthening families; then no amount of additional money and no new government programs will be able to undo the damage.

The primacy of the family in this area does not, of course, mean that government has no role to play. Government can and government must support and supplement the efforts of families in a variety of ways. But the best policies on behalf of children will be those that strengthen the families.

Now, this may seem unobjectionable. Everyone says he is *for* families. But not all public policies are equally good for families. Some public policies may—sometimes inadvertently, sometimes indirectly—damage our nation's families. If thcy do, we should resist them.

Some of the daycare proposals now pending before Congress seem to put families to one side. They seem to accept as inevitable the declining importance and role of the family. They seem more concerned with creating new structures than with supporting the very best structures possible for our children and our families.

It has been said that child care has important implications for the workforce. Of course, it does. But finally and fundamentally, child care is and must be seen as a family issue.

A second principle is this: We should resist policies that discriminate against families that choose to have a parent stay at home to care for their children. The choice as to whether a parent, particularly a parent with young children, should or should not seek employment out of the home must be made by each family. The government should not bias that choice through its policies.

It is troubling that we should even have to defend the traditional family against discriminatory public policies. But in our time, in our age, the family is too often an institution that is being undercut. We therefore need to remind lawmakers about first principles and fundamental social truths. The policy analyst Karl Zinsmeister has written about the responsibility of being both parent and citizen. It means deciding, he says, "that we are going to live not only for ourselves, for our short-run prosperity and material advancement; . . . that we can, and yes, we want to, participate spiritually in the future of our culture; . . . and that raising a child by our own code and ethics is both a worthy goal and a profoundly rewarding undertaking."

Many of the child care proposals being debated before Congress address themselves only to the situation of two employed parents or a single employed parent. These proposals would take tax dollars from *all* families — including families in which the mother or father, often at considerable financial sacrifice, stays at home to care for the children. These proposals would then take taxpayers' money and spend it in most cases on families where both parents are employed. Many of these families are financially better off than families who would receive no benefits at all.

A third principle: For those parents who do choose non-parental care for their children, we should insist on fair and equal treatment for the various types of child care available to them. Government programs should not favor or promote secular daycare over religious daycare; nor should government favor institutional care over informal care. It's worth noting that many disadvantaged families use informal or religiously-affiliated daycare, and church-run centers in the inner city are among the types of child care which some current legislative proposals wouldn't help at all. In short, parents should be able to make decisions about the kind of child care they want — and the government should respect their choice. Government should not bias that choice.

A fourth principle: When we do spend public money, we should target funds on those most in need — on lower-income families. As social policy analyst Douglas Besharov has written, "The criterion for evaluating any federal child care program . . . is whether its benefits are directed to those in greatest need."

A fifth principle is this: In seeking to improve the care of our children, we should not set up government programs that will result in overlapping responsibilities and ever-growing bureaucracies. We shouldn't create a child care "blob" to model the education "blob" we've used in many discussions of our educational problems. We don't need a child care "blob." In particular, we must avoid the all-too-familiar pattern of establishing a federal program that manages to spend large amounts of taxpayer money without actually benefiting those who most deserve the help, and ends up finally just funding bureaucracies rather than benefiting the intended recipients. We don't need more money for bureaucracies. It is families that need the help.

We need not be satisfied with the status quo—and we need not accept bad daycare legislation as an alternative to the status quo. There is pending legislation that contains proposed changes in current tax laws, and there are other public policy reforms we should consider. These might include a crackdown on absent fathers for the child support they owe. We might ensure that regulations do not hamper the availability and affordability of daycare. We should also explore ways to encourage employers to institute practices such as flex-time and part-time work. We should consider changing laws and regulations that hamper parents from employment at home. We should continue our efforts to improve the delivery of existing federal services that help disadvantaged children prepare for school, to ensure that such programs are doing all they can and should.

We have heard much in the child care debate about the needs of employed parents. We are told, for example, that "employed parents require child care." But in the end—when the arguments have been made, when the debate has been waged, when a decision must finally be made—we should remember this: It is *children* who require child care. We must be sure that our policies recognize that *first* purpose and recognize that the child's best protection is, in almost all cases, his family.

Chapter 16

MYTHS AND FACTS ABOUT
FAMILIES AND DAYCARE

by Robert Rector

A policy analyst exposes the stereotypes and myths that underlie much of the current debate about family patterns and daycare affordability. He shows the essential justice of formulating government policies that allow parental choice to accommodate different family priorities.

Robert Rector is a Policy Analyst on Social Welfare and the Family at the Heritage Foundation. As Coordinator of the Foundation's Federalism Project, he works on poverty issues, specifically on welfare reform and the family. Mr. Rector is also Director of the Executive Development Program at the Heritage Foundation, a training program for presidential appointees. Nearly 800 political appointees attended this program during the Reagan presidency.

Mr. Rector has a B.A. from the College of William and Mary and a Master's degree from Johns Hopkins University. Before joining Heritage, he worked as a legislative assistant in the Virginia House of Delegates and as a management analyst in the U.S. Office of Personnel Management.

Since joining the Heritage Foundation, Mr. Rector has written on the policy process, government management, defense spending, trade policy, family issues, and welfare. He is co-editor of Steering the Elephant: How Washington Works, *a book on the internal management of the presidency which* The Wall Street Journal *said "illuminates the Reagan Presidency better than any other book to date."*

The United States Government is presently embroiled in a debate over the fundamental principles of a family/child care policy. At the heart of this debate are five questions:

First, should a national policy to help families with children assist only families with employed mothers? Should it exclude those families that make an economic sacrifice so that the mother can remain at home to raise her own children?

Second, in aiding families with employed mothers, should the Federal Government support those families that use daycare provided by relatives, neighbors, and churches—recognizing that a majority of daycare for preschool children takes these forms? Or, should the Federal Government assist only those families that use institutionalized daycare in professional centers?

Third, who gets the money? Should funds go directly to parents through tax relief to be spent according to the parents' priorities? Or should funds go to bureaucrats and institutions to meet priorities that may be selected by a slim majority of members of a few Congressional committees?

Fourth, which family income levels should be assisted?

Fifth, should the Federal Government deliberately adopt a policy which diminishes the role of religion in American society against the wishes of parents, especially when other options are available?

In answering these questions, we must recognize that whatever the government chooses to subsidize, we will get more of. If the government subsidizes a limited set of child care options, we will certainly see the use of those options expand even though parents might have preferred other choices in the absence of federal intervention.

On the other hand, if the Federal Government follows a broad-based policy of tax relief and financial assistance to families with young children, parents will be enabled to raise their own children in a manner of their own choosing. At the foundation of the current debate, we find the financial interests and eccentric ideological designs of certain segments of the daycare/child development industry pitted against the freedom and integrity of American families and parents, and the well-being of American children.

I am struck by the "trendiness" of this debate. It seems that our society can accept only one stereotype of women at a time. In the 1950s, all mothers were supposed to be at home baking cookies. In the 1980s, all mothers are supposed to have degrees in bio-chemistry; they are supposed to be employed full-time from their early twenties until they retire. When they have a child, they are supposed to stay with it for a few weeks and then plunk it in a daycare center for 40 or more hours a week, while they get back to things that are really important. But most mothers today don't fit this stereotype — nor do they want to.

There is an underlying premise to much of this debate: that it is both inevitable and desirable that, within a few years, some 80 to 90 percent of two-year-olds will be raised in daycare centers. I don't believe this is either inevitable or desirable, and most Americans would agree. We need a more humane model for helping families with young children meet their needs and for helping women to integrate their careers and motherhood. That model would be rooted in parental choice, not in a one-dimensional policy of subsidizing the use of daycare centers.

How To Help Families: An Analogy

The following analogy contrasts conservative and liberal approaches to policies for families with young children. Suppose the government wanted to help parents feed their children. On the one hand, it could offer families greater income through tax cuts and — to very low income families — cash payments through an expanded Earned Income Tax Credit.[1] On the other hand, the government could set up a government restaurant or heavily subsidize a non-profit restaurant in selected communities.

The government restaurant could provide "HUDburgers" to the public. If the HUDburgers were free or their price were heavily subsidized — bringing it below market rates — families would use the restaurant and there would even be waiting lines. In this situation, we would expect the advocates from the HUD-burger industry to show up in Washington claiming that the waiting lines at the government restaurant showed a pent-up public demand for HUDburgers which was not being satisfied. I suppose one could even whip up a media campaign on the HUDburger "crisis."

The HUDburger advocates would tell us that the only way to help parents feed their children is to get more money and build more government restaurants. None of this, of course, would show that parents actually preferred government cuisine or that this rather stupid policy was an efficient or fair approach to helping families feed themselves.

The same is true for daycare. The best way to help parents meet the problems of child care is to stop taking so much of their hard-earned money away in taxes. Parents would then be free to use their own money to care for their children in ways which they—not the lobbying interests in Washington—actually prefer. They could use the money to help themselves stay afloat financially while the mother remained at home with her young children. Or, if they wished to use the money to pay for day-care, they would be able to choose from a wide range of options excluded by the Big Brother/HUDburger approach of the Act for Better Child Care (ABC) bill. Parents—not bureaucrats—should determine how their children should be raised.

Much of the irrationality in proposed federal policies concerning daycare is a result of basic misconceptions about American families and child-rearing. In order to make the real elements of these issues more clear, I would like to address twelve myths about families and child care.

Myth 1: The Traditional Family Is Obsolete

Daycare advocates contend that the "traditional family," in which the mother remains at home to care for children while the father is employed, is a thing of the past, and that nearly all mothers with young children are in the workforce or soon will be. Thus, the argument goes, a massive increase in daycare services is needed and only the Federal Government is capable of financing it. Since nearly all mothers with young children allegedly are or want to be in the workforce, the interests of families and the interests of the daycare industry are treated as if they were synonymous.

But the traditional family is far from dead. According to data in *Who's Minding the Kids?*, a 1987 Census Bureau report, only 45 percent of children under age five have employed mothers.[2] Fewer than one preschool child in three has a mother employed full-time, and fewer than one in five has a mother employed full-time throughout the year.

It is clear that traditional parental care is overwhelmingly regarded by American families as the most preferred mode of child care. More than 80 percent of mothers state that they would prefer to remain at home with their children if they could afford to do so. Young mothers overwhelmingly feel that the increase in the number of children in daycare centers in recent years has not been a good thing.[3]

Myth 2: Traditional Families Are Affluent

A second myth is that families with young children using daycare do so out of economic necessity, while other families have the economic luxury of having the mother stay at home to raise her infant children. This also is untrue. Certainly, single employed mothers with young children do use daycare out of economic necessity — but 80 percent of preschool children with employed mothers come from two-parent/two-earner families. The median income of two-parent/two-earner families is around $38,000, which is about 50 percent more than the median income of families where only the father is employed.

If we compare the Smith family — the average family where both husband and wife are employed — with the Jones family — representing the average traditional family where the husband is employed and the wife is not — we get surprising results. We find that Mr. Jones' and Mr. Smith's salaries are roughly the same.[4]

It is simply untrue to claim that families where the mother is employed are driven by overwhelming economic necessity while other families have the luxury of choice. The reality is that different families have different priorities: some families choose to increase family income through the mother's employment; others choose to make economic sacrifices so that they can provide what they believe is the best possible care for their children, care by the mother.

Traditional families, where the father is employed and the mother remains out of the labor force, are among America's least affluent families. Looking at families with children under six, there are actually more traditional families with incomes less than $15,000 per year than there are families headed by employed single mothers. These low income traditional families are "America's forgotten families"; few politicians and commentators recognize that they even exist.

If making an economic sacrifice so that a mother can remain at home to care for her own children were in some sense anti-social or reprehensible, then we could understand a federal policy, such as the Act for Better Child Care, which ignores these families. But the only real sin of these families is that they have not conformed to the prevailing cultural stereotype of this decade, and so can be conveniently ignored.

Myth 3: It Takes Two Salaries to Live Like Ozzie and Harriet

Organized daycare advocates maintain that it now takes two salaries to provide the same standard of living that a husband's salary alone could bring in the 1950s. This is again untrue, as is illustrated by Chart A. The median income of husbands today is 40 percent higher, after adjustment for inflation, than the median income of traditional families in 1955. Families where the husband and wife both are employed full-time actually have a median income which equals 250 percent of the median income of traditional "Ozzie and Harriet" families in the 1950s.

As noted, 80 percent of preschool children with employed mothers come from two-parent/two-earner families. On the average, these families have chosen to have both parents in the workforce in order to obtain a standard of living far higher than that of previous generations. The government should respect these parents in their choice; however, it should not ignore or discriminate against other families which choose to make a financial sacrifice so that one parent can remain at home to care for the children.

Myth 4: The Shortage of Daycare

Advocates of the ABC bill claim that the legislation is needed to solve the "shortage of daycare" in the U.S. They argue that the current daycare system of private sector, non-profit, and government daycare centers has failed to expand rapidly enough to meet parental demand. There is a chronic economic bottleneck in the daycare industry which prevents expansion, daycare advocates argue; consequently, direct federal subsidization is needed to create a new daycare "infrastructure."

But the daycare industry is expanding rapidly. Between 1960 and 1986, the number of children in formal group care centers increased by 1,500 percent, from 141,000 to 2.1 million. The number of centers grew from 4,400 to 39,929. In addition, there are at least another 1.65 million unlicensed neighborhood daycare providers.[5]

If the demand for daycare did greatly exceed the supply, then the price of daycare would increase rapidly. But the costs of both formal daycare centers and smaller neighborhood daycare providers have remained the same or increased only slightly in real terms over the last ten years.[6]

Some daycare centers have waiting lists, but this does not necessarily prove a supply shortage. Other daycare centers in the same communities will have vacancies. Centers with waiting lists are generally those providing subsidized care at below market rates—a practice which makes waiting lists inevitable regardless of supply elsewhere in the industry. The national daycare chains, such as Gerber and Kinder-Care, have an average vacancy rate of 30 percent. A preliminary survey by the National Child Care Association, which represents private sector daycare providers, has found average vacancy rates of between 15 and 30 percent in various states across the country. In some states, it would be fair to say there is a daycare "glut" rather than a daycare shortage. A recent report of the Labor Department reached the same conclusion: "Considerable concern has been raised that a 'shortage' of child care exists. This report finds no evidence in support of the contention that there is a general, national shortage of available care."[7]

However, there is a "shortage" of daycare in the sense that many parents would like to have more or better-quality daycare for their children than their family budget will currently permit. The way to assist these families is not to construct a new government daycare "infrastructure," but simply to cut their taxes, giving them greater disposable income to purchase the daycare they want.

Myth 5: The Prevalent Use of Daycare Centers
Popular wisdom maintains that a significant portion of American children are now being raised in formal daycare centers. In fact, the use of daycare centers is still quite rare, as is illustrated

by Chart B. As noted previously, more than half of preschoolers are still cared for by parents at home. But even among families where the mother is employed, few families actually use professional daycare. The most common type of daycare for preschool children with employed mothers is by the father, grandmother, or other adult relative. Twenty-two percent of children under age five are cared for in this manner. Note that this means that three out of four preschool children are in parental or relative care during the average day.

Only one child in four is in some form of daycare provided by a non-relative, and even among these children a majority are in small unlicensed neighborhood daycare homes rather than formal daycare centers. Overall only about one preschool child in ten attends the formal licensed daycare institutions which would be subsidized under the Act for Better Child Care.

Myth 6: The Latchkey Crisis

In recent years, there has been a rise in concern about "latchkey" children: young school-age children who are left without parental supervision for long periods before and after school. However, a Census Bureau survey of child care arrangements in 1984 shows that both the extent and the character of the latchkey phenomenon have been grossly misreported. Census data show that there are approximately 2.1 million latchkey children between the ages of five and 13 who are left without adult supervision for at least brief periods before and after school. The overwhelming majority of these children are over age ten; only two percent of school-age children under age ten care for themselves either before or after school. Among younger children, aged five to seven, the figure is even lower; less than one percent or 70,000 are in self-care before or after school. Another 218,000 children aged five to seven are cared for by another child under age 14, generally an older brother or sister.

Contrary to popular accounts, latchkey children remain alone for only short periods. Among children under ten who care for themselves or are cared for by a sibling under 14, a third are without adult supervision for less than one hour each day; 89 percent are alone for less than two hours.[8]

While polemicists have argued that latchkey children come mainly from low-income families — particularly families headed by single employed mothers who are forced by economic necessity to leave their children unattended, the facts again show otherwise. Latchkey children disproportionately come from intact two-parent families and from higher-income families. Latchkey children disproportionately tend to be white, to live in the suburbs, and to have better educated parents.

In a detailed examination of latchkey children, Drs. Virginia Cain and Sandra Hofferth of the National Institutes of Health found that parents are selective in determining whether or not to have a child take care of himself or herself. The relative maturity of the child and the security of the neighborhood, rather than economic necessity, appear to be the key factors in the decision. Drs. Cain and Hofferth conclude: "There are substantially fewer latchkey children than popularly believed, and latchkey children are such for only a short period of time. . . . The characteristics of latchkey children are substantially different than popularly believed. They are not comprised of children of low income single parents whose parents cannot afford to provide stable child care arrangements for them. . . . The latchkey phenomenon is a white middle-class phenomenon."[9]

This does not mean that latchkey children represent no potential problems. The 307,000 children under age ten who are in self-care are a cause for some concern; but the scope of the problem (roughly four children for each elementary school nationwide) is clearly limited and can be dealt with at the local level. There is no national "crisis" requiring a new federal program and the allocation of yet another layer of federal funding. The appropriate response by local governments would be modest programs offering before and after school supervision within the elementary school. Such programs should be financed by fees paid by the relatively small number of parents who would use the service; exceptions to the user fee principle could be made for very low-income families.

Myth 7: The Government Spends Little on Daycare

Another common misconception is that the Federal Government spends little on daycare. Total nationwide spending on daycare, both public and private, is about $15 billion per annum. Through tax credits and direct outlays, the Federal Government provides between $5 and $6 billion in financial subsidies for daycare use. Thus, more than 35 percent of the cost of daycare nationwide is financed by the Federal Government. It is likely that at least part of the recent increase of mothers with young children in the labor force is due to the high degree of federal subsidization of daycare use.

The Federal Government already provides roughly twice as much financial assistance, through tax exemptions and credits, for each young child in a two-parent family using institutional daycare, as it does for a young child in a traditional family where one parent remains at home. If the ABC bill is passed, this ratio would rise to three to one.

Myth 8: The "Magic Dollar" Argument

An underlying premise of most of the current daycare debate is that one dollar provided to parents who spend it on daycare will *not* cause an increase in daycare supply, but that the same dollar given as a direct federal subsidy to a daycare center *will* cause an increase in daycare supply. This argument is, of course, completely without economic validity. However, it has been used to rationalize the fact that little or no money from the ABC bill would go directly to parents. ABC proposes a "trickle-down" daycare strategy, filtering funds through multiple layers of expensive federal and state bureaucracies in order to ultimately subsidize government-selected daycare centers at the local level. Even when the funds actually reach local daycare centers, there is nothing to prevent them from being swallowed up by increased salaries and supervisory costs.

Practical experience demonstrates that, contrary to the "magic dollar" argument, direct bureaucratic subsidization of services is the least efficient means of expanding supply and meeting public needs. For example, public housing units cost 40 percent more to construct than comparable private sector units and often begin to fall apart within months after completion. Providing funds directly to parents, on the other hand, inserts an automatic quality control mechanism into the process: parental choice and competition will ensure that monies are spent usefully and efficiently.

Myth 9: Daycare and the Impending Labor Shortage

Daycare advocates contend that the U.S. economy will face a labor shortage in the mid-1990s. They argue that we need to build a daycare infrastructure to encourage even more mothers with very young children to enter the labor market to fill this shortage. But the elementary principles of economics tell us that "shortages" of any commodity are only temporary; they are quickly eradicated as prices or wages rise until supply and demand reach a new equilibrium.

The argument concerning the impending labor shortage could be rephrased as follows. During the 1990s, the demand for labor will grow more rapidly than supply; wages will rise quickly unless the government artificially stimulates an expansion of the labor supply of young mothers through daycare subsidies. The labor shortage/daycare argument is in reality little more than camouflage for policies that seek to artificially restrain increases in the wages of American workers.

Myth 10: Unregulated Family Daycare Is Harmful

In the United States there are two basic types of daycare provider: "group daycare centers" caring for more than six children, and "family daycare providers" which care for six or fewer children. All would agree that group care centers should be licensed, and all states do license and regulate such centers. But some states do not attempt to license the smaller family daycare providers, and even in states which do impose licensing and regulatory requirements, a majority of family daycare providers remain unlicensed and unregulated. Nationwide, approximately 90 percent of the estimated 1.75 million family daycare providers operate without a license.

Proponents of institutional daycare have for many years argued that unregulated neighborhood family daycare providers are less safe and less healthy than large regulated daycare centers. But all available scientific evidence flatly contradicts this claim, and much evidence actually suggests the opposite. For example, the nationally publicized cases of sexual abuse in daycare, such as the West Point Daycare Center and the McMartin School in California occurred, not in small, unregulated neighborhood facilities but in large, fully regulated day-care centers.

The *National Day Care Home Study* by the Department of Health and Human Services found no evidence that unregulated family daycare was harmful or dangerous. It concluded that family daycare was: "stable, warm, and stimulating . . . [it] caters successfully to the developmentally appropriate needs of the children in care; parents who use family daycare report it satisfactorily meets their child care needs . . . [The study's] observers were consistently impressed by the care they saw regardless of regulatory status."[10]

The average non-licensed family daycare provider is a woman caring for one related child as well as one or two other children in her own home. A majority of parents using unregulated family daycare knew the provider before the daycare arrangement began; a majority regard the provider as a "personal friend." Most providers live within a few blocks of the child's home. Ninety percent of parents stated that their children's needs were met by the unlicensed daycare arrangement—and 75 percent of parents stated that their child had a "loving relationship" with the daycare provider. Only 17 percent of the parents using unregulated family daycare stated that they would prefer to place their child in a formal daycare center. In contrast, a quarter of the parents with children in regulated family daycare stated that they would prefer less formal daycare arrangements.

The *National Day Care Home Study* rebutted the notion that unregulated family daycare was largely "custodial." The study found few significant differences in the quality of care or in children's activities between licensed and unlicensed family daycare. There was no evidence of neglect in either case. Unlicensed daycare providers were actually found to be more likely to be in compliance with state regulations concerning staff/child ratios for different age levels than were licensed facilities.

Moreover, unregulated family daycare poses far less threat to children's health than do licensed daycare centers. Researchers from the Centers for Disease Control have determined that "large, licensed daycare centers . . . are major transmission centers for hepatitis, severe diarrhea and other diseases."[11] Daycare centers cause over 3,000 cases of meningitis among children each year.[12] One study found that nearly one percent of children under age one in daycare centers contracted meningitis over the course of a year, more than 12 times the rate for children who were not in daycare centers.[13] Ten percent of children with meningitis will die and a third will suffer long-term neurological damage.

Diseases picked up in large daycare centers are also passed on to parents and siblings. Dr. Stephen Hadler of the Centers for Disease Control has estimated that 14 percent of all infectious hepatitis cases in the U.S. are acquired through daycare facilities. Other daycare diseases include cytomegalovirus infection, which does not harm the daycare infants but can be transmitted to a pregnant mother, resulting in birth defects to the unborn fetus.

Smaller, generally unlicensed, neighborhood daycare facilities pose far less threat of infectious disease than do large regulated facilities, because larger centers place more children in direct contact with each other thereby dramatically raising the risk of contagion. "The larger the center or the longer the hours, the greater the chance [of infectious disease occurring]," says Dr. Hadler.[14]

But the ABC bill would deny assistance to parents who place children in the small unregulated family daycare homes which are best for the child's health. The bill would also force states to tighten regulations, thereby driving many small-scale providers out of business. Such policies would restrict parental choice, decrease the quality of daycare, and undermine the health of American children.

Myth 11: Daycare Regulation Has No Impact on Cost or Supply

There is a consensus in this nation that the states, not the Federal Government, should set standards for the operation of primary and secondary schools. State or local authorities, for example, determine appropriate classroom size, staff-pupil ratios, and teacher qualifications. While states can apparently be entrusted with the regulation of schools, when it comes to the regulation of daycare, ABC advocates insist that the Federal Government must take charge.

The ABC bill would impose federal daycare regulations on the states, including federal standards for daycare workers. The two most important regulatory requirements would be: (1) mandating that no state may ever make its current daycare regulations less stringent, even if its regulations exceed federal standards; and (2) requiring that all states establish staff-child ratios at least equal to the current median staff-child ratios nationwide.

The ABC bill is supposed to expand the availability of daycare. But the inescapable fact is that more stringent daycare regulations will raise costs and restrict supply. Chart C shows the relationship between the strictness of daycare regulation and the availability of daycare in different states. Those states which have more severe regulations regarding staff-child ratios clearly have far fewer daycare slots relative to their populations than do states with less strict standards.

The proposed regulatory standards of the ABC bill would actually increase daycare costs for many parents while forcing many daycare centers to close. A 1988 study in *Child Care Review* found that the proposed ABC regulations would increase the cost of providing daycare nationwide by $1.2 billion per year.[15] The study concluded that 12,600 daycare centers, or roughly 20 percent of all the daycare centers in the United States, would be forced to close as a result of the cost increases imposed by the ABC regulations.

Southern states would be particularly hard hit by the ABC regulations. For example, in Texas daycare costs would be increased by more than $300 million and 3,100 daycare centers would be forced to close. In most southern states, the increases in daycare costs as a result of federal regulation would exceed the value of ABC subsidies entering the state. These states would experience an increase in average daycare prices and a net reduction in daycare supply. Ironically, the states that would be hardest hit nationwide are the states with the largest supply of licensed daycare relative to their population.

The ABC bill itself provides excellent evidence of why the Federal Government should not regulate daycare. There is a delicate tradeoff between increasing daycare standards and decreasing supply by making daycare operations unaffordable. The ABC proponents have addressed this tradeoff with great simplicity: they have ignored it. In the year or so that this bill has been debated, they have not produced one study of how ABC's proposed regulations would affect supply. This cavalier and irresponsible attitude is the clearest evidence possible as to why we should continue to let state legislatures take the lead in wrestling with this difficult issue.

Myth 12: Daycare and Welfare Dependence

Another argument by daycare proponents is that a shortage of daycare facilities blocks mothers on AFDC (Aid to Families with Dependent Children) from employment. AFDC mothers are currently guaranteed payments (termed "earnings disregards") of $175 per month per child, or the average cost of daycare in their locality, to pay for daycare while the mother is employed or in training. In many states, the average AFDC mother can work full-time at a minimum wage job, receive a full daycare subsidy for each child, and still be eligible for Medicaid, food stamps, and partial AFDC benefits. Even after the daycare subsidies are discounted, such a mother would have a combined family income from earnings and welfare which exceeds the poverty level.

Nevertheless, few mothers on AFDC are employed. The reasons for prolonged welfare dependence are complex.[16] But the evidence indicates that a shortage of daycare facilities or a lack of funds to pay for daycare has little effect on a welfare mother's decision to take a job or not to take a job.

The data from rigorous controlled experiments on this question are clear. The income-maintenance experiment in Gary, Indiana provided free, high-quality daycare to welfare mothers who were employed or in school. It also provided subsidized care to other low-income parents. But only 15 percent of eligible children were actually enrolled at the height of the program. In the Seattle-Denver income-maintenance experiments, only three percent of low-income mothers who were not employed stated that lack of daycare was a reason. While the experiments in both Seattle and Denver provided substantial daycare subsidies, use of licensed daycare centers and daycare homes among the experimental group increased by only six percent in Seattle and did not increase at all in Denver.[17]

The evidence also demonstrates that, when existing daycare arrangements are disrupted, low-income mothers are quickly able to locate alternatives. One study of low-income mothers in South Carolina showed that when their daycare center was shut down, nearly all the mothers continued to work in the same job and found alternative care arrangements for their children within a few days.[18]

Additional experimental evidence is available from the recent Manpower Demonstration Research Corporation (MDRC) study of workfare programs in Arkansas.[19] Unlike most job search, work, and training programs, more than half the welfare mothers who were required to participate in the Arkansas program had children between three and six years old. The MDRC research did not find that a lack of daycare barred mothers with young children from participating in the program.

According to the Arkansas officials in charge of the program, AFDC mothers who were required to participate were encouraged to arrange for their own daycare. Formal daycare centers were not available in many cases, but this was not an impediment to participation. Most mothers used informal care and this seems to have been preferred. Clarence V. Boyd, Manager of Work Programs for the state of Arkansas, stated: "We did not find that a lack of child care inhibited large numbers of AFDC recipients from participating in the program. . . . We tried to encourage mothers to make their own arrangements. The mother is best able to determine what care is most appropriate for her needs and the needs of her child."[20]

The available evidence also indicates that, when welfare mothers are employed, they prefer informal child care, generally by relatives.[21] This preference is shared by the population in general. The national debate on daycare has generally been distorted by the fact that the professionals who dominate public discourse are inappropriately projecting their own personal experience onto the rest of society. The child of a professional mother working in Washington, D.C. is likely to have a grandmother in Buffalo and an aunt in San Diego, so child care by a relative is impossible. But this is not necessarily true for the rest of society. As noted, nearly half the (non-mother) daycare used in the United States is provided by family members or relatives.

The death of the extended family has been greatly overstated. A child's grandmother or aunt may no longer live in the same house with the child, but may well live in the same neighborhood or town.

Mothers on AFDC in the inner-city are likely to have particularly strong kinship networks in their neighborhoods. For a low-income mother trying to escape from welfare dependency, a child's grandmother or aunt is often the ideal daycare provider. These kinship networks are a strong, positive social resource to assist families in escaping from poverty and welfare dependence. Public policy ought to seek ways to strengthen these networks rather than demean them as many daycare advocates do.

Objections to the Act for Better Child Care

The ABC bill would provide $3 billion per annum to build a new federal daycare system. Advocates of the bill quietly admit that this is merely the tip of the iceberg. The full costs of creating a "quality" federal daycare system have been estimated at from $75 to $100 billion per annum.[22]

ABC advocates contend that the bill offers parental choice by supporting a wide range of child care options. In reality, ABC would subsidize care only in formal daycare centers. Although state governments would have the option of providing part of the funds to parents as vouchers, it is unlikely that any significant portion of the funds would be allocated in this manner. For example, daycare funds under the existing Title XX Social Service Block Grant Program may, according to current law, also be provided to parents as vouchers. But most Title XX funds are provided as direct grants to daycare centers—few, if any, funds are diverted to vouchers.

In theory, neighborhood "family daycare" providers, caring for six children or less, are also eligible for ABC funding. In practice, they will receive little or no funding. The average family daycare provider is a young mother who, in her own home, cares for her own child as well as one or two other children from the neighborhood. It is ludicrous to believe that many such mothers would be successful in applying for a direct grant or loan from state governments. If states offered a voucher program, family daycare providers could be paid with vouchers from parents. But family daycare providers would be eligible to receive vouchers only if they were licensed and had received government training. Some 90 percent of family daycare providers are not licensed.[23]

ABC proponents argue that the availability of ABC funding will entice family daycare providers to undergo the often difficult licensing process in order to become eligible for ABC vouchers. But family daycare providers may currently receive federal funds through the Child Care Food program if they become licensed, yet few have chosen to do so. Overall, little if any ABC funding will actually reach family daycare providers despite the fact that they provide a substantial portion of the daycare in the United States.

Children cared for by grandparents and other relatives could also, in theory, receive support through an ABC voucher program. But the grandparents would have to be licensed and trained by the state to be eligible to receive vouchers. Clearly few, if any, children who are cared for by grandparents while their mother is employed would receive support through the ABC bill.

Far from maximizing parental choice in child care, the bill does exactly the opposite. For practical purposes, ABC denies support to low-income children who are cared for by mothers, fathers, grandparents, "family daycare" providers, and actively religious daycare centers. Overall, no more than one preschool child in ten currently attends the type of secular daycare center which would be directly subsidized through ABC.

The alleged goal of the advocates of federal daycare subsidies is to help low-income families obtain daycare. But families earning up to $46,000 per year would be eligible for subsidized daycare under the ABC bill, while most low-income families would not receive assistance, since they are unlikely to use licensed institutional daycare. The ABC bill does state that low-income families should be given "priority" in receiving daycare, and that subsidies should be provided on a "sliding scale" with low-income families receiving higher subsidies. But these terms are left deliberately undefined and thus will have little actual effect on who receives subsidized daycare. The bill does not require that any specific portion of its funding be spent on low-income families.

In the hearings on the ABC bill in the House Education and Labor Committee, an amendment was offered to limit eligibility for ABC's subsidized daycare to families earnings less than 200 percent of the poverty threshold (roughly $22,000 for a family of four). While Republicans were unanimous in supporting this amendment, all the Democratic committee members, except one, voted against it.

Liberal proponents of the ABC bill claim that middle-class families have been made eligible for ABC assistance merely to expand political support for the bill. But this argument is paradoxical since the bill's principal opponents are in favor of giving assistance *only* to low-income families. The argument that subsidies must be provided to the middle class in order to muster political support is clearly untrue; it is merely a fig leaf to camouflage the real goal of the ABC legislation, which is to erect the cornerstone for a vast new middle-class entitlement program.

Another extremely objectionable aspect of the ABC bill is its discrimination against religious daycare, which currently makes up nearly one-third of daycare centers. The Federal Government should not adopt any policy which would deliberately diminish the influence of religion on America's young people, especially when there are other non-discriminatory alternatives available. Under ABC, a daycare center which actively sought to provide religious values to young children through Bible stories, prayers, songs and other activities would be barred from receiving funds. These centers would either be forced to purge the religious content from their programs or they would be forced to compete without subsidies against heavily subsidized secular centers, and would thus be driven out of much of the daycare market.[24]

Many of these centers, even if they did not take one dime of federal money, would be forced to comply with federal standards which would, among other things, control their staff selection, forcing them to replace a director with a degree in Christian education with one with a degree in child development, for example. The ABC regulations would also raise the costs of daycare in the religious centers, driving many out of business.

This would be a tragedy, especially in the inner city where many parents prefer to have their children raised in a religious environment. If we look at black male teenagers in the inner city today, comparing those teenagers who have religious values with those who do not, we find that teenagers with religious values are: 47% less inclined to drop out of school; 54% less likely to use drugs; and 50% less inclined to engage in criminal activities.

But the ABC plan would deliberately make it difficult if not impossible for poor parents to put their children in a religious daycare setting if they wish. Under a tax credit policy, on the other hand, any parent who wishes to use the funds to pay for religious daycare would be free to do so.

The Real Problem Facing
America's Families: Over-Taxation

If the Federal Government wishes to help families with young children, it should focus on the number one problem facing families today: over-taxation. The Federal Government used to have a policy of protecting families with children from excessive taxation, recognizing that those families are literally building America's future. That policy is long gone.

In 1948, a family of four at median family income paid two percent of its income to the Federal Government in taxes. Today that same family pays roughly 24 percent. Even low-income families don't escape. In far too many cases, this excessive taxation means that mothers are forced into the workforce to compensate for the loss of family income when they would prefer to remain at home to care for their infant children.

Eugene Steuerle, a tax analyst with the Treasury Department, has noted that between 1960 and 1984 the average tax rate for single persons and married couples with no children did not increase, but for a married couple with two children it climbed 43 percent; for a family with four children, tax rates increased 233 percent. The major cause of this growing anti-family distortion of the tax code was the erosion of the value of the personal exemption, as is illustrated in Charts D and E. In 1948, a personal exemption of $600 equalled 42 percent of the average personal, per capita income, which was then $1,434. Over the next three and one-half decades, the personal exemption lagged far behind, while incomes rose and inflation shrank the value of the dollar. The Reagan tax reform of 1986 did raise the value of the exemption finally to $2,000, but this only partially offset the damage done during the preceding 30 years. To have the same value relative to income in 1948, today's personal exemption would have to be raised to $6,468. As the value of the personal exemption fell, the share of taxes paid by families increased dramatically. To no small degree, the "Great Society" was funded by an ever larger tax burden on families with children.

The George Bush Proposal

President Bush and others have proposed strong policies of tax relief for working class families with children. This tax relief would be focused on families with young children, first, because they generally face the greatest financial pressure, as the family must either forgo the mother's salary while she is busy at the vitally important job of raising infant children, or will face daycare costs.

President Bush has proposed a $1,000 tax cut to parents for each child under age four and cash supports through an expanded Earned Income Tax Credit for very low-income families who pay little or no taxes. The tax cuts would first be directed to families earning less than $20,000 per year, but would be expanded to cover higher-income families as soon as this becomes financially feasible. The key to helping families with young children is to reduce the present tax assault on the family's weekly paycheck. Parents would be free to use the income from the tax cuts to meet family priorities which they, not the government, determine. The funds could be used to pay for more and better daycare, to enable the mother to be employed less and be with her children more, or simply to help meet the grocery bill.

Four specific criticisms have been directed at the tax credit proposal. First, critics claim that tax relief will do little to help low-income families since those families do not pay taxes. This charge is simply untrue; low-income families pay not only income taxes but heavy Social Security taxes. The Bush plan would specifically help low-income families by providing cash assistance through an expansion of the Earned Income Tax Credit.

A second criticism is that a tax credit is inadequate because it would only provide a lump sum refund at the end of the year rather than providing funds during the year when they are needed. But families would not need to wait till the end of the year to receive the credit. The credit would be refundable against the income tax and employee and employer Social Security tax contributions. The withholding of these taxes from the parent's paycheck would be reduced or eliminated according to the value of the new credit owed to the family. This would result in an immediate increase in the family's weekly take-home pay. (The parent, however, would continue to receive full credit toward retirement under the Social Security system, even though the taxes he pays into the system would be reduced.) Cash payments would be made for those families where the value of the new credit or the expanded Earned Income Tax Credit exceeds the total tax liability. These payments would be available on a monthly or weekly basis through the employee's paycheck, using the same payment process as the current Earned Income Tax Credit.

Third, critics have charged that the tax credit proposal fails to provide real parental choice in child care. They argue that a $1,000 per child tax cut would not enable the average mother to quit her job and remain at home with her children. This may be true, but the tax cut will make it attractive for many mothers working at low wages to remain at home, since the net gain from employment for such women after daycare and other work related expenses may be relatively low. The tax cut could enable other mothers to be employed less and to spend more time with their children, if they choose. More importantly, the tax credit approach would give desperately needed tax relief to hundreds of thousands of low-income traditional families who are struggling to keep their heads above water on one salary, while the mother remains at home to care for infant children. The ABC bill ignores the needs of these families entirely and provides support only if a mother leaves her children in the care of strangers and enters the workforce.

Finally, critics contend that a $1,000 tax cut is insufficient to pay for the full cost of daycare in a formal daycare center, which averages about $3,000 per year. This criticism ignores the substantial daycare subsidies which the Federal Government already provides, ostensibly for low-income families. Under the Title XX Social Service Block Grant, $660 million is provided to states to pay for daycare. Another $746 million is provided through the Child Care Food program. Although these programs are supposed to offer assistance to low-income families, in reality, much money is diverted into subsidies for the middle class. In Massachusetts, for example, "low income" families earning up to $28,000 per year are eligible for daycare subsidies under the Title XX program.

These funds should be re-directed to assist "working poor" families. Assistance under the Title XX and Child Care Food program could be limited to working families earning less than 150 percent of the poverty threshold (roughly $17,000 for a family of four). If existing funds were re-directed in this manner, a tax credit plan would provide to families in this income range more than $3,000 in combined tax credits and daycare subsidies for each child under age five currently using paid daycare — while costing no more over the next four years than the ABC bill.

While the ABC bill might provide fully subsidized daycare for a few low-income families, it would ignore the needs of most low-income families in order to subsidize daycare centers for the middle class. ABC exacerbates the tendency of existing daycare programs to divert funds allegedly intended for poor families to the middle class. The Bush tax credit plan, on the other hand, directs its assistance exclusively to families in the greatest financial need.

Different Families, Different Priorities

The Act for Better Child Care represents the industrialization of childhood, the belief that the family as an institution for raising infant children is both obsolete and economically inefficient. The ABC bill would assist only parents who hire others to care for their children. It would practice "Robin Hood in reverse," taxing low-income traditional families in order to pay for daycare subsidies for affluent two-earner families.

Tax cut policies, on the other hand, recognize that different families have different priorities. Tax cut policies seek to give parents the greatest possible choice in determining how their children will be raised. While these policies would provide needed tax relief to help low-income families to pay for daycare, they would not discriminate against families which make an economic sacrifice so that a mother can remain at home to raise her own young children.

The tax cut approach recognizes that the key to helping families with children is to stop taking so much of their hard-earned money. It is rooted in the belief that parents, not bureaucrats and Congressional staffers, should determine what type of child care is best for the children they love.

The government should adopt a policy which truly assists families in their vital task of raising children. A sound pro-family policy on child care should be based on the following principles:

1. The policy would support *all* young children, not just the small number of affluent children who use paid professional daycare. The policy would treat all families with young children equally; it would not financially discriminate against families where the mother makes an economic sacrifice to remain at home to care for her own children.

2. To assist parents in the difficult task of raising children the government should reduce the excessive tax burden it places on families. The foundation of a pro-family child care policy must be to provide substantial tax reductions to families with young children.

3. Tax cuts would place increased financial resources directly in the hands of parents, instead of funding bureaucrats and social service professionals. Parents would be free to use the added income for any purpose they chose: to raise the family's standard of living; to enable the mother to be employed less and to spend more time with her children; or to pay for more or better quality daycare. Parents, not government bureaucrats, know best how to meet family needs.

4. The policy should give the greatest support to low-income employed families with children.

5. The policy should maximize options available to parents who wish to provide daycare for their children. Parents would be free to select the type of daycare which is best suited to their children's needs, including care by relatives or care by unregulated neighborhood daycare providers. Funds provided through

the policy should not be restricted to use in professional day-care centers.

6. The policy should not discriminate against religious day-care centers. Such discrimination is inevitable in any policy which subsidizes daycare facilities directly or through vouchers. Anti-religious discrimination can be avoided only through a tax cut policy which increases income available to families to pay for daycare while leaving parents completely free to select the type of daycare they deem best for their children.

7. Regulation of daycare should be left to state governments; there should be no federal regulation of daycare. There should be a recognition that much current regulation raises costs and restricts supply without improving the quality of care.

Notes

1. The Earned Income Tax Credit currently provides a cash refundable credit equal to 14 percent of earnings for families with children with incomes below $7,000 per year. The value of the credit is incrementally reduced for families with incomes between $10,000 and $20,000.

2. Bureau of the Census, U.S. Department of Commerce, *Who's Minding the Kids?*, Household Studies, Series P-70, No. 9 (May 1987). The number of children under five with employed mothers was divided by the total number of children under age five in the U.S. at the time of the census survey to produce an estimate of the overall percentage of children with employed mothers. See also, Bureau of Census, U.S. Department of Commerce, *Marital Status and Living Arrangements: March 1987*, Current Population Reports, Series P-20, No. 423 (April 1988), p. 43.

3. In a 1987 poll, 88 percent of mothers with children under age 18 agreed with the statement that "If I could afford it, I would rather be at home with my children." By nearly a two-to-one margin, women under age 44 said that they did not regard the increase of children in daycare as positive. Source: "Opinion Roundup," in *Public Opinion* (July-August 1988).

4. In husband and wife families where only the husband is employed, the mean husband's salary is $29,556. In husband and wife families where both spouses are employed, the mean husband's salary is $27,074. Thus, there is an eight percent difference in the husbands' incomes. Source: unpublished Bureau of the Census data for 1987.

5. Susan Rose-Ackerman, "Unintended Consequences: Regulating the Quality of Subsidized Daycare," *Journal of Policy Analysis and Manage-*

ment, 3:1 (1983), p. 15; Sandra L. Hofferth and Deborah A. Phillips, "Child Care in the United States, 1970 to 1995," *Journal of Family and Marriage* (August 1987), p. 565.

6. Sandra L. Hofferth, statement before the Select Committee on Children, Youth, and Families (July 1987), p. 9.

7. U.S. Department of Labor, *Child Care: A Workforce Issue*, Executive Summary, Report of the Secretary's Task Force, p. 10.

8. *Table: Numbers of Latchkey Children*:

Age Level	Children in Self-Care	Children Cared for by Another Child Less Than 14 Years Old
5 to 7	69,595 (0.75%)	217,923 (2.36%)
8	76,637 (2.52%)	111,915 (3.68%)
9	160,949 (5.17%)	75,960 (2.44%)

Source: Virginia S. Cain and Sandra L. Hofferth, "Parental Choice of Self-Care for School-Age Children," paper presented at the Annual Meeting of the Population Association of America, Chicago, (May 1987), p. 25.

9. *Ibid.*, pp. 19-20.

10. U.S. Department of Health and Human Services, *Family Daycare in the United States: Summary of Findings* (September 1981).

11. *The Wall Street Journal* (September 5, 1984).

12. Estimated from Stephen R. Redmond, M.D. and Michael E. Picichero, M.D., "Hemophilus Influenzae Type B Disease: An Epidemologic Study With Special Reference to Daycare Centers," *Journal of the American Medical Association*, 252:18 (November 9, 1984), pp. 2581-2584.

13. *Ibid.*

14. *The Wall Street Journal*, *supra*.

15. "The Impact of the Federal Regulations in the ABC Bill," *Child Care Review* (April-May, 1988), pp. 5-8.

16. Lawrence M. Mead, *Beyond Entitlement: the Social Obligations of Citizenship* (New York: The Free Press, 1986).

17. Suzanne H. Woolsey, "Pied-Piper Politics and the Child-Care Debate," *Daedalus* (Spring 1977).

18. *Ibid.*

19. Daniel Friedlander *et al.*, *Arkansas: Final Report on the Work Program in Two Counties* (New York: Manpower Demonstration Research Corporation, 1985).

20. Interview with Clarence V. Boyd (April 18, 1988).

21. Woolsey, *op. cit.*

22. Edward Zigler, "A Solution to the Nation's Child Care Crisis: the School of the Twenty-First Century," paper delivered at the tenth anniversary of the Bush Center in Child Development and Social Policy (September 18, 1987).

23. Karen Lehrman and Jana Pace, "Daycare Regulation: Serving Children or Bureaucrats?", *Cato Policy Analysis*, 59 (September 25, 1985).

24. Dr. Robert L. Maddox, Executive Director of Americans United for Separation of Church and State, "Americans United Press Release" (July 29, 1988).

Chart A

End of the Ozzie and Harriet Family?

Does it take two incomes to give families the standard of living that one used to?

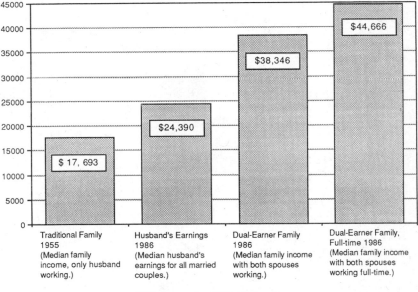

(All figures in 1986 Dollars.)

Chart B

Patterns of Childcare for Children Under Five

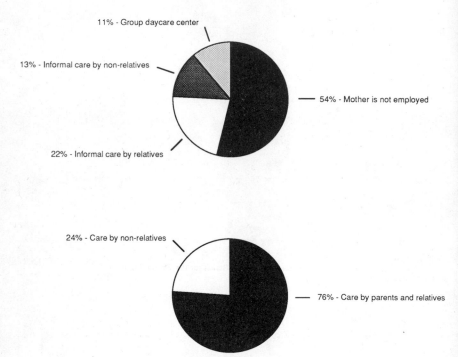

11% - Group daycare center

13% - Informal care by non-relatives

54% - Mother is not employed

22% - Informal care by relatives

24% - Care by non-relatives

76% - Care by parents and relatives

29% - Mother is employed full-time

54% - Mother is not employed

17% - Mother is employed part-time

Chart C

Effect of Lower Child-Staff Ratios on Day Care Availability

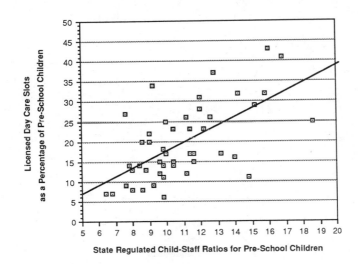

State Regulated Child-Staff Ratios for Pre-School Children

The graph shows the relationship between the strictness of state daycare regulations and the availability of licensed daycare within a state. The X-axis represents the average staff-child ratio for children aged one to five established by existing regulation within each state. The Y-axis represents the number of licensed daycare slots within a state as a percentage of the number of preschool children within that state.

Each dot on the graph represents the daycare situation within a particular state. The line on the graph was calculated by linear regression. It represents the average mathematical relationship between the child-staff ratio mandated by regulations within a state and the number of daycare slots available as a percentage of state's total preschool population. The correlation of the two variables was 0.54.

This interstate comparison clearly shows that, on average, those states which require low child-staff ratios in daycare centers have markedly less daycare available to their populations than do states with less rigorous regulation. By forcing many states to reduce staff-child ratios in daycare centers, the ABC bill would diminish the amount of licensed daycare in those states.

Data used in the graph were derived from "Are State Standards Too High for Child Care?" in *Child Care Review*, April 1987.

Chart D

Value of Personal Income Tax Exemption
Measured in Constant Dollars

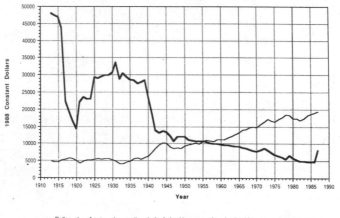

Dollar value of personal exemptions in the federal income tax for a family of four, in constant 1988 dollars.
Per capita gross national product, in constant 1988 dollars.

Chart E

Ratio of Value of Personal Income Tax Exemptions
to Per Capita Gross National Product

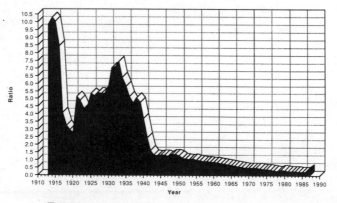

Value of personal exemptions for a family of four divided by per capita gross national product.

Chapter 17

THE GOVERNMENT'S
CHILD CARE DILEMMA

by Douglas J. Besharov

A lawyer and scholar discusses the child care issue from the viewpoint of Capitol Hill in Washington, D.C., including the difficulty of coping with controversies over family statistics, child care costs, targeting upper-income or lower-income couples, church-state questions, and tax equity.

Douglas J. Besharov is a lawyer and a resident scholar at the American Enterprise Institute for Public Policy Research in Washington, D.C., where he directs the Project on Social and Individual Responsibility. He was the first Director of the U.S. National Center on Child Abuse and Neglect, from 1975 to 1979. Before that, he was Executive Director of the New York State Assembly Select Committee on Child Abuse.

Currently on the Adjunct Law Faculties of both Georgetown and American Universities, Mr. Besharov has taught family law, torts and criminal law at New York University, the University of Maryland, the College of William and Mary, and Osgoode Hall Law School in Toronto, Canada.

Mr. Besharov has written or edited eight books, including The Vulnerable Social Worker: Liability for Serving Children and Families *(National Association of Social Workers, Silver Spring, Maryland) and* Juvenile Justice Advocacy *(Practicing Law Institute, New York City). He has written more than 75 articles, and regularly contributes to* The Wall Street Journal *and* Public Opinion *magazine. In the area of social welfare policy, his current research interests include the relationship between family breakdown and family poverty, child support enforcement, child abuse and neglect, and welfare reform. In the area of legal policy, his current research interests include professional and products liability, tort reform, and the legal implications of rationing access to advanced medical techniques. Mr. Besharov shares child-rearing responsibilities with his wife for their two children.*

We have seen over the last year an evolving debate about child care. The issues and our understanding of them have become progressively more sophisticated. I called my talk "The Government's Child Care Dilemma" because Washington can't decide who should care for children. This is a self-imposed dilemma because, when you get right down to it, it's generally not the government's business. Parents should decide who cares for children. That's why I think we should change the terms of the debate from child care to caring for children.

The Census Bureau tells us that 16 percent of all care for preschoolers is provided by fathers. In fact, more than 65 percent of all child care is provided by informal sources, relatives, fathers, etc. About 25 percent is provided in formal centers or nursery schools.

I believe in child care. I believe in child care by mothers, I believe in child care by fathers, and I actually do believe in child care by nurseries and centers, etc., because somebody has to take care of children, almost 24 hours a day, until they are old enough to take care of themselves. My wife is employed part-time. We have a 17-year-old and a ten-year-old and I can tell you that, on Monday and Wednesday mornings, I wake up hoping my daughter is not sick, because those are the two days I'm responsible for changing my schedule if she can't go to school. These are serious problems that really do affect American families.

I will discuss five aspects of child care action here on Capitol Hill and in Washington. The first will be ABC-type bills—specifically, the Act for Better Child Care; second, tax-based solutions to child care; third, employer-provided daycare services; fourth, the Head Start program and other services for low-income families; and lastly, important aspects of the federal role in child care.

A little more than a year ago, the atmosphere in Washington suggested that some version of the ABC bill would be passing very soon. With more and more mothers employed outside the home, with a third of both Houses co-sponsoring the ABC bill, with Republicans clearly on the defensive on this and other gender-gap issues, it looked as if the only question was whether President Ronald Reagan would veto the bill after it passed. As most of you know, the bill was killed as much by the Democratic leadership as by conservative opposition. What happened?

First, and I think foremost, was cost. The ABC bill said that $2.5 billion was authorized for the first year and "such sums as are necessary in the future." In Washington when you hear the words "such sums as are necessary," put your hand on your wallet! The estimates by supporters of federalized daycare were that, when fully implemented, a bill like ABC would cost from $30 to $100 billion a year. That's still a great deal of money. That's as much as Medicare and Medicaid combined. That's ten percent of the federal budget; and that's a third of the Pentagon's budget. So cost was the first problem with the bill.

The second problem was that, no matter how much money was spent, it was going to be very poorly targeted. That is to say, a disproportionate amount of the funds would have gone *not* to low-income families struggling to make it in today's high-powered economy, *not* to single mothers struggling on their own to make ends meet, but to two-employed-parent families making an average of almost $40,000 a year. In fact, in some states, the upper limit of eligibility for aid under the ABC bill would have been as high as $46,000.

At a time of fiscal constraint, it is very hard to think about a bill reaching so many higher-income people when it is supposedly designed to help low-income families. $46,000, by the way, may not seem like a great deal of money here inside the Beltway; but for those who don't think that's a lot of money in this country, I remind you about the debate on the Congressional pay raise. People still think $46,000 is a great deal of money. Median family income in this country, by the way, is about $30,000, and the income cut-off under the ABC bill would have been much, much higher.

What's Wrong With Federal Standards?

Another problem would have been the imposition of federal standards on child care. In the present atmosphere, which I think exaggerates the danger of sexual abuse in daycare facilities, it would have been very difficult — I think it will still be very difficult — for Congress to pass any kind of daycare grant-in-aid program that does not have federal standards attached — federal standards about child-staff ratios, about safety, or whatever. Here we have a real problem because, if the standards are needed, that means that they will change the way daycare is provided. I can assure you that they will not make daycare less expensive. Standards will make daycare more expensive.

The problem is that we are not really sure what a good standard in child care is. We surely don't know how to regulate grandmothers who provide child care. The original ABC bill would have had the effect of regulating and setting standards for the provision of child care by relatives.

We all want the best and safest child care for our children, but no one knows what a good daycare standard is. No one knows whether it should be six children per caregiver or, like the Japanese, 32 children per caregiver. In this day and age when we like everything Japanese, maybe we should have a child-staff ratio of 32 to one. Of course, that is silly! But remember, every time you fiddle with that percentage, even a little bit, you spend half a billion dollars.

What's worse is that you drive up the cost of child care with no real evidence that that's necessary. When my 17-year-old was age two and three, we belonged to a parents co-op, and all of us had to contribute one-half a morning a week. I did it, too. We had our co-op in the basement of a church; the paint was peeling, there was plaster broken here and there. I didn't see any fire extinguisher. Then I looked around at the parents; we were all well-paid professionals; many were Wall Street lawyers! You can imagine what federal standards would have done to our program.

Yet another problem was the separation of church and state. The original bill drew a line saying that no federal funds could go to any facility that looks like a church, quacks like a church, and so forth. You may be able to tell that, with a name like Besharov, I am not a Baptist; but our daughter went to the Bethesda-Chevy Chase Baptist Child Care Center in the basement of the church. It was a nonsectarian daycare center used by the community. In fact, nationwide between 25 and 50 percent of all center-based care takes place in churches.

The original ABC bill would have required, among other things, that all the religious artifacts would have to have been covered, and all the statements about God hidden. Now, I can see some reason for some of that, but the notion of walking into the basement of the church with shrouds over the cross on the lawn, etc., seemed a little extreme, not just to me but to folks here on the Hill; so the ABC bill was revised substantially. Instead of almost totally prohibiting aid to church-based center care, it was made much easier — so much easier, in fact, that the other side of the argument felt betrayed. So there arose very great opposition from, for example, the National Education Association and other folks who thought that we should maintain a very high wall of separation between church and state.

I don't know how that problem can be solved. Congressman Augustus Hawkins (D-CA) has introduced a revised bill. It tries to deal with this problem by saying that the rules about funding Head Start programs, many of which are located in churches, would apply to what you might call the "son" of ABC (or the "daughter," depending on your political approach to these things). I don't think that's going to be enough to deal with the problem because I think that, underlying these technical issues about ABC, there are more fundamental social and political dynamics that were misunderstood a year ago.

One Third, One Third, One Third

There has been a misleading misuse of child care statistics. If I hear one more politician telling me that the times of Ozzie and Harriet are over, I will choke myself! The Bureau of the Census statistics say that, of all American mothers with pre-schoolers, 43 percent are at home taking care of their children full-time while their husbands are employed; 17 percent are working part-time; and 34 percent of two-parent households have the mother employed full-time. Not quite even thirds — but my point is made.

What allows the politicians and the daycare advocates to say we are in a revolution, with all these mothers out working, is the explosive growth of female-headed households. There has been a massive change in labor-force participation by American mothers, but a large part of it is driven by divorce and out-of-wedlock births, and the second part of it is driven by the tax code.

Yesterday I spoke to members of the freshman class of the 101st Congress, at a seminar sponsored by the American Enterprise Institute, the Brookings Institution and the Congressional Research Service, in Williamsburg. We started talking about the political dynamics of the child care debate. They understood the issue well enough to know that one-third of American mothers are employed full-time, one-third stay home full-time, and one-third are employed part-time, some as little as two or three hours a week and some as much as 20 to 30 hours a week.

The assumption was that the part-time mothers identified with the full-time employed mothers, and that's where you get the assumption that 60 to 70 percent of American mothers are employed. In fact, part-time mothers seem to identify with stay-at-home mothers, viewing their role as mothers as being primary. They are more concerned about home issues than job issues — and that changes the political dynamic greatly.

The statistics on employed mothers with young children that we hear most often can distort policy because they mask deep differences among mothers. Government policy should reflect these differences in the work arrangements and needs of American mothers. While addressing the needs of mothers who work outside the home, it should also recognize the contribution of mothers who work at home and care for their children.

Despite all the talk by advocates, by politicians and by journalists about "the crisis in affordable, quality child care," in fact, the majority of American parents don't put child care issues at the top of their list of concerns. That doesn't mean that people aren't concerned about child care. This morning, when I discovered that my daughter was sick, I would have loved to have had a government number to call to say, "Please take care of my child who's sick, has a cold and a cough. I can't send her to school. I'm going to run downtown for two hours, give a speech, and then go back home."

What it means is that, in poll after poll, Americans — including American parents — identify other problems as much more serious. What are they? Drug abuse, especially drug abuse in schools; schooling in general; affordable housing; and affording college. It turns out that child care is not that important a political issue. When they did polls during the presidential election and asked Americans what were the most important issues on their minds—asking an open-ended question that didn't say, "Is child care an important question to you?"—less than one percent of American voters identified child care as an important concern. These are important political realities here on the Hill which, I think, the Members of Congress understood by the time the issue of child care came to a head.

Perhaps almost as big an obstacle to the passage of an ABC-like bill was committee jurisdiction in Congress. As of now, the majority of daycare funds are the responsibility of the Ways and Means Committee in the House and the Finance Committee in the Senate. The ABC bill would have vested jurisdiction over what would become a tremendously costly daycare program in the House Education and Labor Committee and the Senate Labor and Human Resources Committee. When you start moving turf like that, you get important committee chairmen angry at you. The ABC bill was, in effect, killed last year by giving it what's called an unlimited referral from the House Education and Labor Committee to the House Ways and Means Committee, even though it had no provision concerning taxes. They said, "Chairman Rostenkowski, here you are. Do what you want with the bill." And what happened to the bill was . . . nothing.

Tax-Based Solutions

The second topic that I want to discuss is tax-based solutions needed to help Americans with child care. In essence, they come down to doing one of two things: either increasing and making refundable the Child and Dependent Care Credit or expanding the Earned Income Tax Credit (EITC). The EITC lowers the tax burden on low-income employed families and, in some situations, gives them a cash grant above and beyond what they earn. Someone in the family must be employed to get the EITC; if no one is employed, no money is given to them, so it's not a welfare program. It is tax-based assistance for employed parents.

That's both the strength and the weakness of the tax-based solution to child care. Its strength is that it attacks the problem, not the symptom. Many of us feel that the problem underlying the putative child care crisis is that many American families need additional income to make ends meet, and that mothers take jobs to bring more money into the home.

A tax-based solution can bring more money into the home whether or not the mother is employed. This is a more efficient solution from a broad, macro-economic point of view and it avoids the very serious problem that exists with other kinds of proposals, that is, it does not create yet another government incentive for mothers to leave the home. It neutralizes that question. It says, we the government will help you, a family, whether or not the mother is employed; it does *not* say that the government will help you only if the mother is employed. That's a very important difference. It is why I support tax-based solutions. But that is also its weakness because it is not a daycare program.

When candidate George Bush announced his support for an expanded child care credit, which would be a great boon to low-income families, the response of many people was, "That's wonderful but it's not a child care program." I think an appropriate response is that child care is also performed by mothers who stay at home, not just by paid employees of daycare centers.

I think that some kind of tax-based bill is going to pass, and I think so for a number of reasons. Last year, Republicans especially were vocal about the tax-based solution to the child care issue. They kept saying that the way to deal with this problem is to give income relief through the tax code by expanding the child care credit, etc. George Bush endorsed the idea, by the way, to fairly impressive editorial acclaim. Now that the election is over and George Bush is President, I think that the Democrats on the Hill will take the Republicans up on their offer. Congressman Tom Downey (D-NY) in the Ways and Means Committee has already drafted a bill that, in effect, provides a major child care credit for all American families whether or not the mother is employed. That's a terrific victory.

Now the question is whether this will happen. I think it will happen, first, because this will be a Ways and Means Committee bill; remember what I said about jurisdiction. Second, I think that there are two other issues surfacing on the Hill which will give added steam to a tax-based solution. The first is the minimum wage. We can expect a major effort to raise the minimum wage. But the minimum wage is a very cumbersome and inefficient way to raise the income of low-income families. Less than a majority of those at the minimum wage are heads of household; large numbers are teenagers. It is much more efficient to help low-income families through tax relief. So that will be a second reason why people on the Hill and in the Administration will be talking tax relief for low-income families.

There is yet a third reason. If we decide to reduce the deficit, it is clear that it will be through a combination of spending cuts and tax increases. The tax increases are likely to be either sin taxes, that is, taxes on cigarettes, alcohol, etc., and perhaps a gasoline tax. Those kinds of taxes are highly regressive. That is, they affect low-income families proportionately much more than they affect upper-income families. There is a general understanding that, if those kinds of "sin" taxes pass, there will have to be income tax relief for low-income families.

So, I don't think it is a very brave prediction to say that, when you have three separate, big reasons for giving some kind of child care credit and income relief to low-income working families, something is likely to happen. The only open question is the size of that tax relief.

Some say that the tax-based solutions (which I think are the best solutions) are open to the criticism that they are not daycare programs, that if we just let families have that money, they might not buy daycare. To which I say, "That's right. They might buy food; they might pay for education; and yes, they might even buy some gin, or whatever."

Subsidies for Upper-Income Couples

Mandated employer-provided child care benefits are the most complicated area and one in which everything we do probably has unintended consequences. It is an area of great interest to politicians because it is, in effect, a hidden tax. You can mandate fringe benefits without any of the money going through the U.S. Treasury. That's the argument right now about mandating health benefits for employees. You can, in effect, create a whole new federal insurance system without directly taxing employees, and without people realizing who is paying the bill for what is really a new government program.

The Ronald Reagan White House very seriously considered mandating daycare as an element of every cafeteria plan provided by American businesses, so that anyone working at General Motors in Detroit could have had daycare instead of a medical plan, or in addition to such a medical plan, etc. The problem with such mandated employer-provided benefits is that, not only are they very, very expensive, but they tend to be discriminatory.

We at the American Enterprise Institute provided a daycare plan under both Congressional statutory rules and IRS regulations. Employer-provided benefits must be non-discriminatory in their outcome, that is, they must be not only offered *but used* by people with the lowest salaries in the organization as well as those with the highest. Well, it turns out that low- and moderate-income mothers don't want to use those fringe benefits, which are very expensive. They would rather use the money for medical costs, dental costs, etc. So they opted out of our daycare plan. Only those of us who really didn't need governmental help could take the benefit of tax-supported daycare. That is what would happen with federal daycare legislation almost any way we turn, unless we clearly target services for low-income families. Otherwise, it would be the middle-class and upper-middle-class that would benefit most from these programs. Families making more than $35,000 and $40,000 a year would benefit most.

Our tax code and our law in general is filled with all sorts of subsidies for upper-income families. In this time of Gramm-Rudman, however, we should focus our attention and our funds on the most needy among us. That brings us to a discussion of Head Start. George Bush endorsed the program, and said it should be expanded as part of his child care program. Most Republicans are on record as saying they are in favor of expanding Head Start, and most Democrats are, too.

So, on that basis I would predict that there will be a major expansion of Head Start commencing this year. It will be, by the way, easy to do even within Gramm-Rudman targets because, although the expansion that folks are talking about will be in the neighborhood of $1 to $2 billion a year, they will phase it in over a period of four or five years at maybe $200 to $400 million a year. Head Start really can't absorb more money than that in any one year. If the Congress gave more money, it would just have to be banked. You just can't spend it that quickly. So any major expansion of Head Start should come slowly.

I must tell you that I'm a dyed-in-the-wool supporter of Head Start. My son, who is now 17 and has just been admitted to college, started out as a Head Start child. You may know that up to ten percent of all Head Start children can be of any income, so we took advantage of what was a terrific program in New York City 17 years ago. The Head Start program, however, now has many elements that are obsolete. For example, it is a part-time program; in most places it ends by one or two o'clock in the afternoon. In most places it is only nine months a year. So guess what? Employed mothers, even low-income employed mothers, don't find Head Start as helpful as we would like. They must use other kinds of daycare. Localities run around trying to find money to extend the Head Start day. In effect, what's happened is that Head Start has become a ghetto for non-employed mothers. There is a great need to change Head Start by extending it to a full day and making it full-year, so that it can be used by children of mothers who take a job.

As we start implementing workfare, the work and training program under welfare reform, it would be helpful if we could move the Head Start program closer to the workfare-type programs. As we tell young mothers that they should get a job and should get training, we should be providing real support for them. One way to do that is through the Head Start program.

How to pay for expansion? I did a calculation about the existing Child and Dependent Care Credit, one of the most regressive tax breaks we have. The total tax cost for this Child and Dependent Care Credit is about $4.5 to $5 billion, and it is scheduled to rise to $6 or $6.5 billion in coming years. If we were to cap the credit at $50,000 annual income, that is to say that people who are making more than $50,000 would not be allowed to claim this tax subsidy, we would save almost $2 billion a year!

Many Unanswered Questions

There is an important role for the Federal Government in child care. It is, however, not in creating a comprehensive, universal and expensive system. The greatest need is that we not be stampeded into new programs, that we take a look at what the actual need is, what the actual character of the programs is, and that we shape programs to meet those needs. There are a number of very large question marks that we must address. One of them is whether daycare is helpful or harmful to very young children. We really don't know. Professional opinion can be characterized as either mixed or tending toward the notion that very young children are harmed when they are put in day-care, no matter how high the quality. This is an important question that deserves very serious research before we commit the Federal Government's resources to any kind of program that encourages the placing of infants and toddlers in someone else's care. We have no major longitudinal research on this question, and yet it is so important.

Because the political argument about child care is so polarized, and because the issue became focused on the ABC bill, we lost sight of the fact that there are other kinds of needs in child care that aren't called child care. As the parent of a school-aged child, I can tell you that, for many families, the hour and a half before nine in the morning and the time between three and five-thirty or six o'clock in the evening are crucial times. Many school districts are working very hard to accommodate not only employed families but all families. We are changing our style of living. The notion of a 9:00 to 3:00 school day is changing. Even stay-at-home mothers are very supportive of enriched educational experiences for their children. The entire discussion of what all American families want for their schools has been lost in the child care debate.

To summarize, it is very important that we achieve a tax-based solution. American families need help. Families with children are taxed much more heavily now, as a proportion of national income, than they were ten, 20 and 30 years ago. We should stop this. We should encourage families to be families. If mothers want to be employed that should be their decision, and tax codes and government funding should not create an artificial incentive for parents to move into the workforce. Such a program is within reach this year in the Congress, because of the support of the Administration and large elements of both parties, and because it is a potential remedy to other policy issues that will arise this year. We have a real shot at getting substantial tax relief for low-income families—and we should go for it.

Chapter 18

THE POLITICS
OF DAYCARE

by Phyllis Schlafly

A writer and commentator on social, legal, education and political trends describes the several factions that are players in the unfolding drama of daycare as a federal policy issue. She shows how these groups are headed in two fundamentally opposite directions.

Phyllis Schlafly is the author or editor of thirteen books on subjects such as national defense, politics, education, and feminism. Her monthly newsletter, The Phyllis Schlafly Report, *has been published continuously since 1967. Her semi-weekly syndicated newspaper column is carried in 250 newspapers and her syndicated daily radio commentary is carried on 250 radio stations.*

Mrs. Schlafly is a member of the Commission on the Bicentennial of the United States Constitution, by appointment of President Reagan. She is admitted to the practice of law in Illinois, Missouri, the District of Columbia, and the U.S. Supreme Court. She is president of Eagle Forum Education & Legal Defense Fund, founded in 1981, and of Eagle Forum, founded in 1975.

Mrs. Schlafly received her B.A. with Honors from Washington University in St. Louis, her M.A. from Harvard University, and her J.D. from Washington University Law School. She has an honorary LL.D. from Niagara University. She is the mother of six children.

On January 7, 1988, the MacNeil-Lehrer NewsHour proclaimed that "child care" was America's number-one social issue. This was the opening blast of a massive media campaign to convince the American people to support universal federally-financed daycare. This daycare promotion was not designed to help the poor and needy, but to make daycare a middle-class entitlement. One daycare center director interviewed on that program voiced her irritation that the recently-introduced Dodd-Kildee ABC bill would subsidize only families whose income is under 115 percent of the median family income. Such a limit, she complained, would exclude women with higher incomes who want daycare subsidies.

The NBC Today Show soon boarded the publicity train for federal baby-sitting by giving friendly feature interviews to Betty Friedan and Patricia Schroeder. Newspapers climbed aboard by printing a torrent of manufactured "news" about an alleged "crisis" in daycare cost and safety. The cry was for "availability, affordability, and quality," catch words which translate into a demand that the Federal Government build, subsidize, and regulate all daycare.

On February 21, 1988 Dan Rather presented a segment on the CBS-TV Evening News promoting the notion that the Federal Government should finance and regulate daycare. He showed visuals of a Russian daycare center and commented with admiration, "Whatever else the Soviet Union does, it takes care of its children. Daycare is provided for all children from two months of age."

By April of 1988, the Public Broadcasting Service had joined the chorus. PBS-TV proclaimed Federal Daycare Week and spread its message on eight programs, including Sesame Street. A blatantly biased one-hour "documentary" on April 13 not only tried to sell the American people on federal daycare for all children, but featured oh-so-friendly interviews with Senator Christopher Dodd and Democratic Presidential candidate Michael Dukakis without a single opposing spokesman.

In sum, media coverage of the child care issue in 1988 was loaded at least ten to one in favor of initiating federally-funded and federally-regulated daycare.

By the time Congress started to consider the legislative centerpiece of this public relations offensive, the Dodd-Kildee ABC bill, subcommittee chairmen Senator Christopher Dodd (D-CT) and Representative Dale Kildee (D-MI) felt secure enough to stack the hearings without any pretense of fairness to opposing viewpoints. At the House Education and Labor Subcommittee hearing on February 25, 1988, all 22 witnesses supported the bill; not one witness was permitted to testify against it. The Senate Labor and Human Resources Subcommittee hearing on March 15 was similarly staged with 16 pro-federal daycare witnesses and only one against.

As a result of complaints about such bias, a few persons opposed to federal daycare bills, including Secretary of Education William Bennett, were finally permitted to testify before a Kildee subcommittee hearing on April 21. Opponents of the Dodd-Kildee bill labelled it "discriminatory" because the bill would deny all benefits to mothers who take care of their own children, while benefiting only mothers who purchase daycare from federally-approved providers.

Semantics are very important in the politics of child care. The bill's advocates protested the use of the term "baby-sitting," but the bill's opponents use the term in its precise dictionary definition: to take charge of children while the parents are temporarily away. Indeed, the proposed federal daycare bills concern custodial care for infants and preschool children of employed parents; in no sense are they designed as "education" bills or as "welfare" bills. The bill's opponents objected strenuously to the bill's advocates using the terms "working mothers" and "non-working mothers," asserting that there is no such thing as a "non-working mother." The wording should be "employed mothers" and "fulltime mothers."

In the face of the "discrimination" charge, the tide began to turn. The liberal Congressmen and their friendly panelists were very uncomfortable trying to defend the Dodd-Kildee bill's discrimination, which required that the mother be employed and put her children in institutional secular daycare in order to get any benefits, while all other mothers would be taxed but excluded from benefits.

The real shocker came when a Republican Congressman asked a federal daycare advocate at a hearing this question: If an employed mother arranges for her child to be cared for during the day by Grandmother or Aunt Millie (who has already raised three children of her own), don't you think *that* mother should have the same benefit in any federal legislation as the employed mother who puts her child in a daycare center?

The liberal panelist responded: Only if Grandmother or Aunt Millie is licensed, regulated, and has received government training. The implications of that reply rippled through Washington, and one day President Ronald Reagan commented that we certainly can't have any legislation that requires grandmothers to be licensed or registered.

Coalition of Four Interest Groups

The profoundly biased "news" reports to which the American people were subjected in 1988 demonstrated the publicity professionalism of four distinct interest groups which have joined together in a political coalition to promote large-scale federal financing of baby-sitting centers, federal regulation of all daycare, and the establishment of group care for infants and preschool children as the cultural norm and as a middle-class entitlement.

The first leg in this four-legged coalition is the feminists. Their ideology has taught them for years that society's expectation that mothers take care of their own children is unfair, degrading, and oppressive to women. They think this makes women second-class citizens, makes wives a servant class, and impedes women's opportunity to participate full-time in the paid labor force and thereby achieve economic equality with men.

Feminist spokesmen and activists have taught young women to expect men to share equally in changing diapers and other child-tending duties. Since their rising expectations of changing human nature remain unfulfilled, the feminists argue that government must provide daycare for all children outside the home in order for women to have full equality with men in the marketplace.

In November 1977, all the famous feminists gathered in Houston for the National Conference on International Women's Year, chaired by Bella Abzug and funded by the U.S. taxpayers to the tune of $5 million. One of the four "hot-button" resolutions out of the 25 passed at that rowdy conference called for the Federal Government to assume the major role in "universal" child development and daycare programs.

The leading feminist lobby group, the National Organization for Women, passes resolutions year after year demanding public funding of daycare, starting in infancy. The feminist ideology looks toward the elimination of motherhood as a "role" (that's considered a dirty four-letter word) so that child care will become a government responsibility and women can achieve full equality with men.

The notion of universal federal daycare for American children did not originate with the feminists but with the so-called social engineers who used the 1970 White House Conference on Children to recommend that "federally-supported public education be made available for children at age three." That Conference explained in its final report:

> "Daycare is a powerful institution. A daycare program that ministers to a child from six months to six years of age has over 8,000 hours to teach him values, fears, beliefs, and behaviors."

The federal legislative proposal that was designed to implement that White House Conference report was the 1971 Comprehensive Child Development bill, sponsored by Senator Walter Mondale (D-MN) and Representative John Brademas (D-IN). It called for a $2 billion network of federal daycare institutions for "comprehensive child development purposes."

That bill passed Congress, but it was vetoed by President Richard Nixon. His courageous veto message called it a "radical piece of legislation" and "a long leap into the dark" which would "lead toward altering the family relationship." He added, "Good public policy requires that we enhance rather than diminish both parental authority and parental involvement with children — particularly in those decisive years when social attitudes and a conscience are formed, and religious and moral principles are first inculcated."

In 1975 the developmentalists made another try with the Child and Family Services bill, also sponsored by Senator Walter Mondale and Representative John Brademas. That proposal aroused such vehement opposition that it never came to a vote in Congress.

The chief guru of those advocating federal regulation and control of child care is Professor Edward F. Zigler at the Yale University Bush Center in Child Development. At its tenth anniversary dinner on September 18, 1987, Zigler revealed the real plans and purposes of people such as himself whom he calls "developmentalists."

Zigler called for a federal daycare program that will cost "$75 to $100 billion a year." He said he wants the new federal daycare system to "become part of the very structure of our society," under the principle that "every child should have equal access to child care and all ethnic and socio-economic groups should be integrated as fully as possible."

Zigler urged, "The child care solution must cover the child from as early in pregnancy as possible through at least the first 12 years of life." He wants children to be reared by a "partnership between parents and the children's caretakers," headquartered in the public schools.

"Partnership" was the offensive word that helped to defeat the discredited Mondale-Brademas Child and Family Services Bill of 1975. Parents don't want to be mere "partners" with the government in the rearing of their children. The child developmentalists are elitists who sincerely believe they know better than mere parents how to raise children. In the society they seek to develop, most grandmothers would not qualify as child caregivers, and the government would control an integrated "infrastructure" of child care and child rearing.

The third component of this new daycare coalition is the liberal Democrats. The child care issue cannot be rationally discussed without addressing its politics. This issue is political to its core. All media coverage about child care poses the challenge of public policymaking, not private decision-making.

On a January weekend in 1988, 131 Democratic Congressmen went up to the Greenbrier, the fancy resort hotel at White Sulphur Springs, West Virginia, to discuss how to win their 1988 elections. They devised a game plan to use "kids' issues" to help the Democratic Congressmen reclaim constituencies they had lost to the Republicans, who had rather successfully made "family values" their rallying cry during the years of the Reagan Administration.

Stanley B. Greenberg of The Analysis Group, Inc., presented an issue paper called "Kids As Politics: A Proposed Campaign Strategy for Democratic Candidates in 1988." Its theme was that engaging in political rhetoric about "kids" would provide the Democrats with "an enormous opportunity to shape the political discourse, after years of responding to a public debate controlled by the Republicans."

The cold and calculating discussion of children as a technique to get votes was apparent from the rhetoric used by this high-priced campaign consultant: "kids are an umbrella . . . kids are a common currency . . . kids are a common coinage." The paper urged that "Democrats must get voters to focus on their anxieties about the future and make those feelings real and effective. Kids are the best vehicle."

The campaign strategy seemed simple: Just sign on as co-sponsor of the Dodd-Kildee bill — and so scores of Democratic Congressmen did. Others preferred to express a little individuality by introducing their own bills containing a slight variation of the same concept.

The fourth factor in this new daycare coalition is the social service professionals. This is a vast army of tax-salaried people who would like to expand their ranks, their pay, and their turf. The key to doing that is to have more social problems that require more care and more counseling. It's a bureaucracy that feeds on itself.

The social service professionals integrated their network with the other three segments of the new coalition in what they called the Child Care Action Campaign. In order to focus on their legislative objectives, they staged a conference at the Waldorf-Astoria Hotel in New York City on March 17-18, 1988. It was designed to promote a massive expansion of their tax-paid turf by stimulating support for the Dodd-Kildee ABC bill.

The headline speakers were a leading Congressional liberal, Senator Chris Dodd, and a leading feminist, Gloria Steinem, neither of whom has any children. One of the problems with the child care issue is the number of self-appointed spokesmen cavalierly prescribing group care for babies who themselves have never had the care of even one baby, let alone 10 or 20 infants at one time. Most persons advocating group care of babies haven't the foggiest idea of the immense amount of work and love required to care for an infant.

The exciting highlight of the conference was breakfast with Phil Donahue. The board of directors of the Child Care Action Campaign listed on the conference materials included the former head of the National Organization for Women, Eleanor Smeal, and current heads of other radical feminist organizations, the N.O.W. Legal Defense & Education Fund, the National Women's Political Caucus, and *Ms.* Magazine. The Child Care Action Campaign published a newsletter that provided advice on child care from such "experts" as Dr. Ruth.

The stated goal of this formidable coalition is to make daycare part of the "infrastructure" of our society. Each of the four groups in the coalition, for its own purposes, wants to change our culture by persuading the American people to adopt and publicly finance universal group care of preschool children. Relieving women of the "burden" of taking care of their own children is a long-time goal of the feminists. The child developmentalists want to control the minds and the behavior of children. The liberal Congressmen want to win political victories by using "kids" to set the social spending agenda. And the social service bureaucracy wants to create more—and more important—taxpayer-paid jobs.

The Legislative Proposals

The legislative centerpiece promoted by this coalition is the Dodd-Kildee ABC bill, a 62-page $2.5 billion bill first introduced in Congress in 1988, and re-introduced with a few cosmetic changes in 1989. Its objectives are: (1) to make institutional secular government-regulated daycare the norm for all preschool children, even in infancy, by subsidizing only *that* kind of daycare and discriminating against *all* other options; (2) to set up a federal baby-sitting bureaucracy to administer federal daycare regulations which will supersede state regulations and drive unregulated daycare out of existence; and (3) to achieve government control of children by requiring the use of government-trained staff and ultimately a government-prescribed curriculum.

At first, some Republicans were timid about opposing the rolling juggernaut of daycare. They engaged in damage control by dropping bills into the legislative hopper that accepted the liberal daycare premises and purposes, but promised to spend less money. That kind of me-too, stingy liberalism is always a political loser.

The conservative/pro-family movement first set out to analyze the biased assumptions and objectives of the 1988 Dodd-Kildee bill. Let's look at some examples of the rhetoric in this bill's "findings and purpose" and compare it with what *should* be said.

The Dodd-Kildee bill said: "The number of children living in homes where both parents work, or living in homes with a single parent who works, has increased dramatically over the last decade." *What should be said is*: "The number of children living in homes without a fulltime mother, or without any father at all, has increased dramatically over the last decade."

The Dodd-Kildee bill said: "The availability of quality child care is critical to the self-sufficiency and independence of millions of American families, including the growing number of mothers with young children who work out of economic necessity." *What should be said is*: "The availability of mother care is critical to the self-sufficiency and independence of millions of American families, and mothers should not be forced into the labor force out of economic necessity."

The Dodd-Kildee bill said: "High quality child care programs can strengthen our society by providing young children with the foundation on which to learn the basic skills necessary to be productive workers." *What should be said is*: "High quality mother care can strengthen our society by providing young children with the foundation on which to learn the basic skills necessary to be productive workers."

The Dodd-Kildee bill said: "The years from birth to age 6 are critical years in the development of a young child." *What should be said is*: "Mother care is especially needed in the critical years in the development of a young child, from birth to age 6."

The Dodd-Kildee bill said: "The rapid growth of participation in the labor force by mothers of children under the age of 1 has resulted in a critical shortage of quality child care arrangements for infants and toddlers." *What should be said is*: "The rapid growth of participation in the labor force by mothers of children under the age of 1 has resulted in a critical reduction in mother care needed by infants and toddlers."

The Dodd-Kildee bill said: "Making adequate child care services available for parents who are employed, seeking employment, or seeking to develop employment skills promotes and strengthens the well-being of families and the national economy." *What should be said is*: "Easing the economic strain on mothers through tax reduction so they can care for their own children promotes and strengthens the well-being of families and the national economy."

The Dodd-Kildee bill said: "The exceptionally low salaries paid to child care workers contributes to an inordinately high rate of staff turnover in the child care field, makes it difficult to retain qualified staff, and adversely affects the quality of child care." *What should be said is*: "The inordinately high rate of staff turnover in group-care institutions increases stranger anxiety and adversely affects the quality of child care, making it more urgent that mother care be encouraged so that children can enjoy object constancy of the mother as their primary caregiver."

The conservative/pro-family coalition based its approach on the assumptions that (1) as a matter of public policy, we must *not* discriminate against mothers who take care of their own children, or against employed mothers who choose care by relatives, neighborhood daycare mothers, or in religious or unlicensed facilities, and (2) any federal funding must aid children, and not go to bureaucrats, administrators, regulators, or daycare providers.

The Challenge of Child Care Costs

The conservative/pro-family movement recognizes that the challenge of child care costs is real and must be met. Indeed, families do have a problem meeting the costs of caring for children, and that problem is the financial squeeze of higher taxes. So let's tackle the problem, not just the symptoms.

Families are short of cash because their tax burden has dramatically increased. In 1948, an average couple with two children paid two percent of annual income in federal taxes. In 1988, an average couple with two children paid 24 percent of annual income in federal taxes. Families need tax relief—not government handouts. Certainly, families don't need costly tax-financed "solutions" from the same people who have waged this economic assault against families for the last 30 years. Families want to spend their own money, not be directed how to spend subsidies.

When I had my first child in 1950, John brought into our family a $600 income tax exemption, which was at that time 18 percent of the median family income. When I had my first grandchild 30 years later, Tommy brought his parents a $1,000 income tax exemption. Was that more? No, it was less—only four percent of the median family income, which means that a child had been devalued by three-fourths in the income tax code. Yet, I never heard a single Congressman discuss this devaluation during all the years that it was taking place.

The conservative/pro-family proposal to meet the challenge of child care costs is simple, sensible, and cost-efficient: a tax credit for each child. This would give parents 100 percent freedom of choice to spend their money any way they want.

Representative Clyde Holloway (R-LA) introduced the Child Care Tax Reform bill to give a tax credit of up to $400 to each preschool child, and the bill soon had 80 co-sponsors. Senator Malcolm Wallop (R-WY) introduced the companion bill in the Senate. Representative Richard Schulze (R-PA) introduced the Toddler Tax Credit bill to give a tax credit of up to $750 to each preschool child, and Senator Pete Domenici (R-NM) introduced a similar bill in the Senate. Representative Philip Crane (R-IL) introduced the Family Care Package bill to give a $5,000 tax exemption to each preschool child. The tax credit approach gained ground daily.

These conservative bills were fundamentally different from the Dodd-Kildee and other liberal bills. First, the conservative bills were all non-discriminatory; they did not deny benefits to children of fulltime mothers, and so the number of children benefited was vastly greater. Second, they made more money available to each child because no funds needed to be siphoned off for administration, regulation, or a Federal Administrator of Baby-Sitting. Third, they did not discriminate against employed mothers who choose child care by relatives, neighborhood friends, or in unlicensed homes or religious daycare. Fourth, most of these conservative bills were particularly helpful to lower-income families because the tax credit would be refundable (whereas the Dodd-Kildee bill would benefit primarily upper-income, two-earner couples, up to $46,000 in Dodd's state of Connecticut).

The pro-family tax credit approach was incorporated in the Republican Platform adopted in New Orleans in the summer of 1988. It called for "a toddler tax credit for preschool children" and for "a plan that does not discriminate against single-earner families with one parent in the home." For good measure, the Platform also proclaimed that "the best care for most children, especially in the early years, is parental. Government must never hinder it." About the same time, Vice President George Bush endorsed the tax credit approach, calling for a $1,000 tax credit for each preschool child, refundable at the lower income levels through the Earned Income Tax Credit.

When President George Bush delivered his Budget Message to Congress on February 9, 1989, the pro-family tax credit approach came of age. In striking clarity, he said:

> "I support a new child care tax credit . . . — without discriminating against mothers who stay at home. . . . The overwhelming majority of all preschool child care is now provided by relatives and neighbors, churches and community groups. Families who choose these options should remain eligible for help. Parents should have choice."

The conservative/pro-family movement and the Bush Administration are not just reacting to liberal initiatives on the child care issue. Conservatives have been trying for more than six years to get politicians and media to address the issue of tax fairness for families. Now, thanks to the daycare issue, it's all out on the table for public debate.

Child care may, indeed, be the number-one issue of the 1990s. It is central to all other social, economic and political issues. It poses the fundamental question of whether the giant apparatus of government will be pro-family or anti-family. Will we have lower taxes or increased taxes, more government taking over of family functions or less? These issues are crucial to the whole panoply of policies debated by liberals and conservatives.

A National Child Care Policy?

The politicians (both federal and state), the media, and the activist groups all want a piece of the action about child care. The dozens of bills introduced into the 101st Congress can be grouped into two very different types of legislative approaches: (1) The liberal daycare bills, which would create a federal daycare bureaucracy, impose federal regulations, subsidize licensed, secular daycare centers, raise the costs of all daycare, and discriminate against families that care for their own children. (2) The pro-family child tax credit bills, which would give a tax credit to each child and assure 100 percent freedom of choice for parents to select their own child care, including mother care, care by other relatives, neighborhood family care, unlicensed or licensed home care, religious care, or daycare center care.

The conflict between parents who should have the right to select their own type of child care versus overreaching liberals who want to control all child care was illustrated by an eloquent letter to the editor of the *Washington Post* entitled "Someone Reported Me."[1] The writer took her child every day to the home of "Gladys," a good and caring grandmother who cared for children in her home without a license. But someone reported Gladys to the Maryland authorities, since state law defines a daycare provider as anyone who baby-sits more than 20 hours a week. Gladys refused to get licensed because "it's too much paper work" and she doesn't like "people coming into your home." So she told the parents they would all have to find another baby-sitter. The writer of the letter was angry. She wrote, "I have a master's degree in child development, but I didn't need any academic credentials to see that my child is getting good care [from Gladys]. . . . In the name of protecting children, the state law has thrown me back into the pool of anguished parents searching for good daycare, while a superbly competent daycare provider is forbidden to care for children. No wonder there's a crisis in daycare."

The liberal/feminist proposals for dealing with the child care issue refuse to address such problems inherent in their bills as the obvious preference for unlicensed daycare referred to in the "Gladys" letter above, the abundant evidence of daycare disease as an insoluble aspect of group care,[2] and the evidence of sexual abuse of children even in state-run centers.[3] The liberal proposals likewise refuse to recognize the fact that, just because a mother is employed does not mean she wants to turn over the raising of her children to paid caretakers. She is more likely to prefer such options as part-time employment, employment in her own home (which is subject to harassment in so many ways), a shorter work day, flexible hours, job sharing, a "Mommy track" with lower pay and slower advancement,[4] or a "sequential career" which starts after her children are raised.[5]

Here is a check list showing the differences between the two types of pending legislative proposals. The liberal approach to child care policy would:
1. Create a federal baby-sitting bureaucracy.
2. Discriminate against mothers who take care of their own children.
3. Discriminate against relatives who take care of children out of love and without pay.
4. Impose federal regulations and control that will discriminate against religious daycare, interfere with its curriculum, and cause it legal harassment.
5. Impose federal regulations that will raise dramatically the cost of neighborhood daycare, and reduce the availability and affordability of daycare.
6. Help upper-income families proportionately more than low-income families by requiring that mothers be employed, thereby assuring that most of the benefits will go to two-earner couples.
7. Increase taxes every year and lead to a federal daycare system with a potential tax cost of $100 billion annually.
8. Lead to a society modeled on Sweden where most children are cared for in government institutions starting in infancy.

On the other hand, the child tax credit approach would:
1. Assure 100 percent parental freedom of choice in child care, without government incentives that interfere with parental decision-making.
2. Not discriminate against mothers who take care of their own children.

3. Not discriminate against or require the licensing or registration of grandmothers or other relatives.

4. Put 100 percent of the available cash in the hands of parents instead of bureaucrats, regulators, and providers.

5. Not build a federal baby-sitting bureaucracy.

6. Relieve some of the present unfair tax burden on families with children, and move toward tax reduction instead of tax increases.

7. Help low-income families proportionately more than higher-income families through the Earned Income Tax Credit.

8. Not interfere with religious daycare or cause lawsuits or harassment.

9. Not raise the costs of neighborhood daycare.

10. Preserve local control over daycare licensing standards.

Any federal legislation pertaining to children should comply with Executive Order 12606, issued September 3, 1987 by President Reagan: "Does this action by government strengthen or erode the stability of the family and, particularly, the marital commitment? Does this action strengthen or erode the authority and rights of parents in the education, nurture, and supervision of their children? Does this action help the family perform its functions, or does it substitute governmental activity for those functions? Does this action by government increase or decrease family earnings? Do the proposed benefits of this action justify the impact on the family budget? Can this activity be carried out by a lower level of government or by the family itself? What message, intended or otherwise, does this program send to the public concerning the status of the family? What message does it send to young people concerning the relationship between their behavior, their personal responsibility, and the norms of our society?"

In 1986 the White House Working Group on the Family, under Gary L. Bauer as chairman, compiled a splendid assessment of the current status of family integrity and the health of our society. It explained how, for two decades, the federal tax code produced bad news for the American family: "Nearly every special interest group managed to protect itself in tax legislation except for the most important part of our economic and social system: husband, wife, and children."

The report concluded with a simple prescription for our social health: "To help families, the best step government can take is to let them keep more of their hard-earned money."

The complaint is often voiced that the United States is the only Western nation that has no child care policy. We do, indeed, need a child care policy—one that is in harmony with American freedoms, family integrity, and economic growth. That policy should be: Cut the taxes on families with children so they can spend more of their hard-earned money with 100 percent freedom of choice.

Notes

1. July 17, 1988.
2. *E.g.*, "Researchers Say Daycare Centers Are Implicated in Spread of Disease," *The Wall Street Journal* (September 5, 1984); "Study Shows Negative Effects of Full-Time Child Care," *The Washington Post* (April 23, 1988).
3. *E.g.*, An Associated Press Dispatch of February 16, 1989 described a scandal at the Western New York Children's Psychiatric Center in West Seneca, New York where the state administrators permitted 64 instances of sexual activity involving 47 children during 1987 and 1988. A state investigative panel concluded that administrators considered the activity "normal," and so did nothing to stop it.
4. Felice N. Schwartz, "Management Women and the New Facts of Life," *Harvard Business Review* (January-February 1989), pp.65-76. Ms. Schwartz presents the case that, whereas some women are "career primary" and are willing to "remain single or at least childless, or if they do have children, that they be satisfied to have others raise them," the majority of women are "career-and-family women" who are entirely willing to make the trade-off involved in a Mommy track, and that corporations would find it good business to develop new personnel policies to retain talented women who do not want to compete with men in 100 percent commitment to a career.
5. "Medicine + Motherhood," *American Medical News* (February 24, 1989), pp.35-38, describes the lifetime satisfaction of women physicians who first spent 10 to 20 years raising their children and then pursued a medical career after that.

SCHOOL-BASED DAYCARE
FOR ALL CHILDREN
by Edward F. Zigler

A leading child developmentalist explains the goal of daycare for all children, headquartered in the public schools, as part of the very structure of society and at a cost of tens of billions of dollars per year. The following is his testimony to the U.S. House Education and Labor Committee, February 9, 1989.

Edward Zigler has been since 1967 the director of the Bush Center in Child Development and Social Policy at Yale University, and since 1967 has been head of the psychology section of the Yale Child Study Center. Prior to that, he was assistant professor of psychology at the University of Missouri and then held successive posts in psychology as a member of the faculty of Yale University starting in 1959. He was chairman of the Yale psychology department in 1973-74. In 1970-72, he was Chief of the Children's Bureau of the Department of Health, Education and Welfare.

Dr. Zigler received his B.A. from the University of Missouri at Kansas City and his Ph.D. from the University of Texas. He is the recipient of honorary degrees from Yale University and Boston College. He is the author of many books and contributor of many articles to professional journals. He is the recipient of awards from the National Association of Retarded Children and the Social Science Auxiliary, and received the Alumni Achievement award of the University of Missouri. He was an honorary commissioner of the International Year of the Child in 1979.

Dr. Zigler has served on many commissions including Project Head Start, the National Advisory Committee on Early Childhood Education, and the President's Commission on Mental Retardation. He is a member of the American Orthopsychiatric Association, the American Psychological Association, and other professional societies.

Thank you for the opportunity to share with you my concerns about the urgent need for good quality child care and my thoughts how as a nation we can respond to the problem. In the course of these hearings and those held during the 100th Congress, numerous witnesses testified to the need for child care, so you have a sense of the magnitude of the problem and the fact that we have reached a crisis stage.

Today there is an extreme shortage of good quality and affordable child care services. What is of even greater concern, we have no child care system within which we can work to upgrade the quality and availability of services. I see it as a non-system out there. The situation will not improve without intervention. It can only become worse as more mothers work and more children need daycare, and a decade from now we will have 26 million children, or half the population of children, who have either a mother, or both a mother and a father, in the workforce, and these children will be in some type of out-of-home care.

Whether the children will grow up to be healthy, productive members of our society depends very much on the decisions we make now about child care. I say this because a child care facility, whether it is a center or a family daycare home, is an environment in which children spend a significant portion of their day, every day. We know from years of research that the child's environment is a major determinant of the development of children. Environments can be arranged on a continuum of quality, from good to bad. There are certain ingredients which are needed for a good-quality environment. If the environment is lacking in these ingredients, if it is of poor quality, children's development will be compromised.

Today's hearings are an indication that there is an awareness at every level, from parents to policymakers and developmental experts, that the development of tens of thousands of children is indeed already being compromised as we sit here today. There are simply not enough child care slots of good quality to fill the need. Many families have no choice but to place their children in facilities which are inadequate. I have visited some of these facilities and am left with great concern for the children I encountered there.

Mr. Chairman, I support your efforts to address the crisis our nation's families are facing. I understand that you introduced the Child Development Education Act of 1989 as a means of developing a bipartisan consensus on the issue and identifying the Federal Government's role in the solution to the child care problems. For that you are to be commended.

There are many parts of the bill which I endorse. Specifically, the provisions in Title II for school-based child care. Like you, Mr. Chairman, I believe that schools have an important role to play in the solution to the child care problem. The fact is, the problem has reached such crisis proportions that we cannot continue to address it in a piecemeal manner. Rather, we must begin to establish a child care system that is reliable, accessible to all children—I commend the concept of integration, it should be basic—a system that becomes part of the very structure of society. The school, which is a major societal institution with which parents and children are familiar, can provide us with the structure for creating such a child care system, enabling us to offer good quality care to all children.

One aspect of the child care issue that the nation will have to address, and we have not yet done so, is the cost. Nobody really seems to want to look at what the cost of what we're talking about really is. At present we have no firm figure on how much it would cost to put in place a child care system, but we do know that the figure is in the tens of billions of dollars. The question is: How are we going to pay for it? School-based child care figures prominently in the cost issue. We already have a trillion dollar-plus investment in school buildings which can help offset part of the cost of child care. The rest will have to be paid for as follows: (1) through parental fees, (2) through state funds.

I say this because child care, like education, is not mentioned in the Constitution. Therefore, like education, child care must be primarily a state-based system. Finally, besides parental fees and state responsibility for child care, the Federal Government has an important role which is to subsidize the care of needy and handicapped children, as it currently does with Chapter I of the Elementary and Secondary Act in Public Law 94-142. I support a school-based approach to child care because I have seen it work.

Last year I conceptualized a plan for comprehensive school-based child care and family support services. This plan is known as the 21st Century School Program. It has attracted considerable attention across the nation and has been implemented now in two states, Missouri and Connecticut. It is in the process of being implemented in the Columbus, Ohio school district and state-wide in Wisconsin. The 21st Century School Program and Title II of the Child Development and Education Act have much in common. If I may, I would like to share with the committee what I have learned from the implementation of the program about the possibilities inherent in school-based child care.

The 21st Century School Program has five components: (1) all-day child care for three-, four-, and five-year-old children, (2) before and after school and vacation care for both preschool and school-age children. Children who spend a half day in kindergarten would spend the rest of the day in child care if the parents' work schedule made this a necessity. These child care services are provided in the school.

In addition to these services, the 21st Century Program calls for three outreach services. One is a home visitation program beginning in the last trimester of pregnancy up to the child's third year, modeled after the Parents As First Teachers program in Missouri, which offers parents guidance and support to help promote the child's development.

Another outreach service is information and referral to help parents with specific child care needs, such as night care. The third outreach service is support and assistance to family daycare providers in the catchment area of the schools. This latter aspect of the program is of vital importance. Family daycare providers shoulder the awesome task of caring for many of the nation's infants and toddlers. I believe that good quality family daycare is an appropriate setting for very young children. The home-like atmosphere, small group size and individualized attention, which this type of care offers, is conducive to children's development.

However, family daycare providers are often isolated from the child care community. They need opportunity for social support, training and respite that school-based child care services can offer them. In the 21st Century School Program, family daycare homes surrounding the school are combining into a network, with the school's child care system providing the hub of this network. The 21st Century child care program is based on developmental principles and my knowledge accumulated over 30 years' work on the needs of children.

I have specified certain criteria to ensure that the program delivers good quality child care, that it is made available to *all* children in an integrated fashion regardless of family income, that it is operated by individuals who have knowledge and training in child development, and that it emphasize parental involvement. Parts of the 21st Century School Program already exist at some level in communities across the nation. What is unique about the 21st Century Program are: (1) it offers a range of child care support services under one umbrella instead of piecemeal, (2) the services are school-based, providing us with an opportunity to establish a child care system within which we can work to upgrade and expand services as may be needed.

Today we have no real system for child care, but rather a patchwork of different types of services. The test of any plan, no matter how good it is on paper, can be noted in its implementation. What I have to report in this regard about the 21st Century Program is very promising. First, the 21st Century School Program enjoyed a great deal of support and enthusiasm. As with any new idea, it had its share of critics who continue to voice their concerns. However, the interest in this program has been overwhelming, indicating to me a readiness on the part of parents and schools for school-based programs. I have had a request for information and assistance in implementing the program from school districts in Ohio, Wisconsin, Florida, Wyoming, Utah, North Carolina, Colorado, and other states. There appears to be a commitment on the part of school administrators to enhance the development of children and assist families with child care.

Second, as I noted earlier, the program has already been implemented in two states. In my own state of Connecticut, the legislature appropriated $500,000 for startup and operational support of three demonstration programs, one each in an urban, suburban, and rural school district. The Department of Human Resources, which in conjunction with the Department of Education is administrating the program, is providing the subsidies for low-income children so the schools can offer a sliding-scale fee system. In Missouri, the program is initiated by the superintendents of Independence and Platt County school districts. Startup funds were made available by community foundations. Some funds for the school-age programs and for staff training were made available by the Missouri Department of Education. This program, as you can see, is a true public-private partnership in Missouri.

The Missouri program has been in operation since September 6, 1987. A total of 1,400 children are being served in 13 schools. I've visited the Missouri schools recently. The programs are being delivered according to the principles and criteria I have identified. The programs have yet to operate on a sliding scale fee system. This is where the Federal Government can help. The largest problem with the school approach is how do you get the money to pay for poor children who can afford no fee.

I'm especially encouraged by two aspects of the program, namely, parental satisfaction and its cost effectiveness. It appears that the school-based child care program can operate on reasonable fees, once startup costs are provided. For the two school districts in Missouri, startup costs were approximately $180,000. The fees they are now being charged can easily be handled by families who live in the suburbs. They are fees of $45 to $54 a week for all-day child care for preschoolers, and $18 a week for before and after school care. These fees are much lower than the national average. In a middle-class neighborhood, the school-based programs can be self-supportive on parental fees within a relatively short period of time. My colleagues in Missouri tell me they will be in the black within one year, just on fees alone.

There is a need, however, to subsidize the care of low-income families. I would very much hope that this is where the Federal Government would step in. The 21st Century School plan, Mr. Chairman, is a long-term vision in terms of creating a reliable and stable child care system. I see the Child Development and Education Act of 1989 as enabling schools to start initiating these programs across the country and providing the subsidies necessary for low-income children. I believe that our ability to institutionalize a child care system, parental satisfaction, and cost effectiveness are three arguments in favor of school-based child care.

It is for these reasons that I am pleased to see the provisions for school-based programs in Title II of the Child Development and Education Act of 1989. Mr. Chairman, I endorse the Title II provision as written. In particular, the financial support for low-income children, enabling schools to use funds for startup costs, and enabling schools to sub-contract with community-based organizations for services. The one change I would suggest, however, is that services be made to children beginning at age three. At this age, children are ready for group care and, in the school-based programs I have seen, children that age do well. Their families are satisfied and they have the opportunity for continuity of care. Mr. Chairman, I thank you again for the opportunity to testify in support of a school approach to child care. I would like to submit to the Committee, my plan, my complete plan, for the 21st Century School, for the record.

DO WE WANT GOVERNMENT TO BE OUR BABY-SITTER?

by Michael Schwartz

An observer of social policies and trends analyzes proposed daycare legislation, shows the effect it would have on social behavior, and recommends pro-family alternatives. .

Michael Schwartz is resident fellow in social policy for the Free Congress Foundation in Washington, D. C. Well-known as a writer on social issues, he served for nine years as director of public affairs for the Catholic League for Religious and Civil Rights. In 1980 he was the recipient of the Thomas Linacre Award for his study of teenage pregnancy. A native of Philadelphia and graduate of the University of Dallas, he now lives in Germantown, Maryland with his wife and their four children.

The family, and not the individual, is the basic unit of society. Liberalism is inherently anti-family. It regards individuals as integers, equal and isolated, without regard to their status as members of families. It regards the individual as an interchangeable component in a collective social organism, again without regard to the status of each person as a family member.

Individualist liberalism, even if it was the dominant social philosophy in the United States during the Industrial Revolution, has never been implemented in its pure form. This is because America inherited from its European forebears a Christian culture which placed a high value on the family. When the workings of the untrammelled market proved destructive of families, reformers were able to initiate policies that protected families by restricting the labor of women and children, guaranteeing the security of widows, orphans, and old people, and supporting the concept of a family wage through a tax structure that gave preference to families.

After this period of social reform, between World War I and World War II, the family was not a major issue on the political agenda until the 1970s and the rise of feminism. Contemporary feminism has been the most radical and direct attack on the family in American history, and its major achievement, the legalization of abortion, called into being a powerful movement of reaction, especially among Catholics and conservative Protestants. It was this "pro-family" movement which carried Ronald Reagan into the White House in 1980.

The "pro-family" movement was immensely successful in stopping the tide of feminist cultural radicalism. But it must be acknowledged that this movement was essentially one of re-action. It did not advance a clearly-articulated social vision so much as reject the vision of feminism-cum-socialism which was so offensive to the religious and cultural beliefs of the majority of Americans. It was a defensive movement against certain perceived threats to the existing civilization, but it did not success-fully initiate any major reforms of its own.

The one major pro-family reform that was attempted, with-out success, was the acknowledgment of parental rights in edu-cation through tuition tax credits. One victory, but an almost insignificant one, was the doubling of the personal tax exemp-tion to $2,000. This represented just a fraction of the tax advan-tage for families which had been stolen over the previous 35 years through inflation and higher taxation, and it was, to a large extent, offset by the reduced value of most deductions. For most families, the 1986 tax reform was, at best, a wash.

Nonetheless, the political clout of the pro-family movement convinced the feminist/socialist coalition that they had to change their tactics. If nothing else, the family was a rhetorically powerful political symbol, and so the left began to repackage its cultural radicalism and its statism in "pro-family" terms.

That master rhetorician Mario Cuomo kicked off this drive with his famous keynote speech at the 1984 Democratic Con-vention in San Francisco. He used the family as a metaphor for the state in advancing his socialist agenda. Given its inherently anti-family bias, the left can deal successfully with the family only as a metaphor. This is precisely why, at Jimmy Carter's 1980 White House Conference on Families, the definition of the family became a subject of intense conflict. In leftist terminology, the word "family" can never be allowed to mean precisely families, for the existence of families is anathema to feminism and socialism.

Nonetheless, feminists have followed Cuomo's lead and repackaged their anti-family nostrums in "pro-family" garb. The key condition which made this possible was that, by the mid-1980s a majority of American mothers were in the labor market. This is a great burden for most women (a majority of employed mothers say they would rather be able to run their households and raise their children on a full-time basis) and a clear symptom of the failure of the American economy to sustain family life. But for the feminists it was a sociological bonanza. They could, on the one hand, denigrate the normal husband-as-breadwinner family as an aberration, and on the other, label as "pro-family" additional intrusions of the state into traditionally familial functions.

The Ultimate Family Issue

The ultimate family issue in the liberals' new agenda is daycare. Making the state responsible for the care of small children is the *sine qua non* for socializing the family out of meaningful existence. As long as families provide the environment in which children are normally nurtured, families will have a social function. As long as mothers have children at home to care for, it will be difficult to draft them into the labor force. As long as children spend their formative years in the company of unlicensed parents, most of whom lack professional credentials and degrees in psychology, and whose only claim to the care of these young citizens is a biological accident, they are in danger of not being raised properly.

All the "advanced" nations, from Sweden to the People's Republic of China, are sensitive enough to the needs of families to remove children from the inadequate home environment as early as possible, so they can be given the advantage of qualified, professional supervision, while their mother can be released from domestic chores in order to engage in truly productive pursuits such as standing behind a cash register or along an assembly line or filing pieces of paper in alphabetical order.

The avenue to this utopia is called the Act for Better Child Care (popularly, the ABC Bill), sponsored in the House by Representative Dale Kildee (D-MI) and in the Senate by Senator Christopher Dodd (D-CT).

The ABC Bill would establish a federal daycare program under a new Child Care Administration within the Department of Health and Human Services. It would authorize an initial outlay of $2.5 billion in federal funds to be parceled out to the states in grants and matched by $625 million in state funds. Each state would construct its own elaborate bureaucracy to design and supervise a state plan for providing daycare services. Ten percent of the funds would be set aside right off the top for "administration." The next 15 percent would be targeted to the development and enforcement of licensing standards, the training of daycare employees, and salary supplements for these surrogate mothers. Additional sums would provide special services for Indians, for handicapped children, and for the operation of extended-hour programs. For the first time ever, federal minimum licensing standards would be established, and all daycare workers in licensed centers would be required to go through 15 hours a year of in-service training.

The remainder of the money, something over $1.6 billion, would go to qualified providers of daycare who would establish a sliding-fee scale for their services, providing reduced rates for the care of children who live in households with incomes under 115 percent of the median family income in their home state, adjusted for family size. This is the only benefit families would actually receive under the ABC Bill.

Labyrinthine Trickle-Down

It is an astoundingly complicated plan, with layer after layer of bureaucracy and a labyrinthine trickle-down of dollars which, despite its immense cost, actually delivers little or no assistance to its intended beneficiaries. There are currently about 9.5 million children under age 15 whose mothers are full-time participants in the paid labor market and who live in households below 115 percent of the median income. That means the average benefit per eligible child under the ABC bill would be $175 per year. That, of course, is not money the family would actually receive, but simply a discount from the market rate for purchased daycare services.

One reason why this per capita benefit is so low is that the drafters deliberately designed the program as a middle-class entitlement. If middle-class families are the beneficiaries of a social welfare program, they will provide a powerful political constituency for constantly increasing its funding. Nationally, for four-person families, 115 percent of the median income is about $38,000. In Chris Dodd's home state of Connecticut, it is $46,000. People in these income brackets probably do not really need to have their daycare bills subsidized by less affluent taxpayers.

In reality, the average subsidies would probably not be anywhere near as low as $175 per child, because the great majority of eligible children will get no subsidy at all. In the first place, only a small percentage of the children of employed mothers are in organized daycare programs. School-aged children are, of course, in school during most of the hours their mothers are at their jobs.

Most families arrange for child care of preschool children in the following order of preference: (1) at home by the mother (a solid majority of all preschoolers); (2) at home by another relative, usually the father; (3) in the home of a relative or neighbor; (4) in an organized, formal child care program, either preschool or daycare center. Fewer than two million preschool children—about 10 percent of all preschoolers—are in organized programs. In most cases, it is reasonable to assume, that is because none of the preferable options is available to their families.

Even this two million figure does not constitute the number of preschoolers who might receive indirect benefits under ABC. Nearly a third of them are in households above 115 percent of the median income. More importantly, nearly half of them— and for the most part, the poorer half—are in programs operated by churches or on church premises; which raises one of the more interesting points about the ABC Bill.

Anti-Religious Provisions

No funds under the ABC bill may be spent for "sectarian purposes." Funds under ABC are available only for daycare programs that are functionally atheist, just like public schools. If any religious symbols are on the premises, they must be removed or covered up. Children would not be allowed to say milk-and-cookies prayers, or hear Bible stories, or celebrate Christmas or Easter unless they stick strictly to Santa Claus and bunnies.

If capital improvements in the facility are made with ABC funds (and they will have to be made in most church-based centers to comply with the tighter licensing regulations), the space used for daycare services must be restricted *permanently* to non-religious purposes. No preference in admissions or fees may be shown to members of the sponsoring congregation or faith. Any person who teaches in a church-operated school is forbidden from working in the daycare center, while the provision in the 1964 Civil Rights Act which permits churches to give hiring preference to members of their own faith is suspended.

The anti-religious provisions were inserted into the bill at the last minute, on the insistence of the National Education Association (NEA) which, in addition to its long-standing hostility to religion, has an ulterior motive in demanding this anti-religious discrimination. Public school districts are among the eligible grantees for ABC funds, and in many respects the program seems to be tailored precisely to putting public schools in the daycare business. The NEA and other pressure groups interested in strengthening the public school monopoly want to see as large a share as possible of ABC funds directed to public schools in order to create more jobs and more power for the teachers' union.

The anti-religious provisions of the ABC Bill would put most religious daycare centers out of business. Currently, churches run nearly half the daycare centers in the country, and they are especially prevalent in low-income neighborhoods where for-profit centers cannot operate successfully. Many of these church-run centers are conducted as charitable endeavors, offering services at low rates because they do not have luxurious facilities or highly-paid staffs. Very few of these centers will be able to meet the new federal licensing requirements without accepting ABC funds. But if they do accept the funds, they can no longer operate their centers as they wish. Not only that, but they will find themselves in competition with lavishly-funded subsidized public programs. ABC, thus, will force thousands of religious centers to close, thereby further restricting the range of options available to poor parents.

It is on this issue of the eligibility of religious centers for funding that the coalition supporting ABC is cracking apart. Both the NEA and the American Civil Liberties Union (ACLU) insist that they will oppose the bill if any funds are permitted to be used for non-atheist purposes; but there are also about 20 religious groups included in the ABC coalition, and they are equally insistent that some accommodation be made in the bill for religious centers. Rep. Kildee, a former seminarian, appears uncomfortable with the anti-religious fanaticism of some of his bill's bakers, but he needs their support.

Other Defects of ABC

While the religious issue has proved to be a strategic flaw in the ABC Bill, that is but one of its defects.

First, it is expensive. The initial appropriation of $2.5 billion is hefty enough, but it will actually deliver very little to the intended beneficiaries, while raising the expectations of millions of families who use daycare services. If the program were to go into effect, there would immediately be strong demands to increase its funding. Edward Zigler of Yale University's Bush Center for Child Development, one of the masterminds behind the ABC Bill, estimates that it will require $75 to $100 billion a year "to do the job right." Even at the initial $2.5 billion, that would increase the tax burden on the average American family by about $50 a year. At Zigler's ultimate figure, the average increase in taxation would have to be nearly $2,000 per family.

Second, it is inefficient. Nearly a third of the appropriated funds are earmarked for administration, licensing, training and other indirect services. Moreover, the savings to consumers through subsidized fees would be largely offset by the higher cost of providing child care services as a result of the new licensing requirements.

For example, if a center currently maintains a seven-to-one ratio between children and staff and pays its child care workers $10,500 a year, the cost of that worker's salary comes to $1,500 per child. If new regulations mandate a six-to-one ratio and a $12,000 salary, the cost rises to $2,000 per child. This, of course, does not take into account the cost of the facilities, meals, play materials and all of the other expense items in a daycare center's budget, virtually all of which will be affected by more stringent licensing requirements, but it does show how rapidly per-child costs can mount up as a result of even minor regulatory changes. If the average cost of providing daycare services increases by $800 or $1,000 per child, it will take billions of dollars simply to keep the average fees where they are now.

Third, it is monopolistic. Thousands of daycare centers will be driven out of business by the tighter regulations. Religious centers are obviously in jeopardy, but so are many for-profit centers and home-based centers. Not only will their cost of doing business be driven up, but they will also be ineligible for many of the benefits provided under ABC. The only category of centers that will really be better off under ABC are government-run centers, especially those operated by public schools. What that means is that parents using daycare will have fewer and fewer choices, and government agencies will gradually become responsible for the care of more and more children.

Fourth, it is statist. The Federal Government will be regulating, inspecting, and administering daycare centers in both the public and the private sector. Even home-based daycare centers will become subject to federal supervision.

Fifth, it is anti-child. The ABC Bill subsidizes one type of child care — that in licensed centers — to the detriment of every other type of arrangement. It is axiomatic that you get more of what you subsidize. Therefore, one of the inevitable consequences of the ABC Bill would be an increase in the number of children placed in daycare centers. But the strong consensus among psychologists and child development specialists is that non-parental care can be seriously damaging to the physical and emotional well-being of young children.

Daycare Damage to Children

With respect to children under two years of age, the evidence of researchers is unanimous: being separated from parents, and especially mothers, for an extended period of time on a regular basis seriously weakens the child's attachment to his mother, and this weakened attachment results in damage to a child's emotional and intellectual development. Children deprived of parental care in early childhood are likely to be withdrawn, disruptive, insecure, or even intellectually stunted. New research from the Cleveland Clinic even suggests that the depression resulting from separation anxiety in early childhood can cause a permanent impairment of the immune system, making these children prone to physical illnesses throughout their lives.

Leaving aside the psychological factors, daycare centers present threats to the physical health of young children. Daycare centers are notorious breeding grounds for the spread of infectious diseases including diarrhea, jaundice, hepatitis A, and cytomegalovirus which can cause very serious birth defects if a child brings the infection home to a pregnant mother. Public health officials are warning mothers to have their children immunized against certain daycare-linked diseases before enrolling them, while the official recommendation of the American Academy of Pediatrics is that children under two should be cared for only with their own brothers and sisters.

The studies that have yielded these results have not taken place in unlicensed, substandard centers, because most such places will not cooperate with researchers. It is precisely in the top-quality centers that research demonstrates that daycare is risky to the emotional and physical health of children.

The problems do not end there. A recent study from the University of New Hampshire reported that from 1983 to 1985 there were 1,639 confirmed cases of sexual abuse of children at licensed daycare centers. In many instances, children in daycare were used for the production of child pornography. In other cases, boys and girls were physically abused by daycare workers and other adults on the premises, or were forced to perform sexual acts on one another. While the rate of sexual abuse of children at daycare centers was not particularly high, the number of these cases is alarmingly high. In addition, of course, all of these children have homes where they are not sexually abused, so the child abuse at daycare centers represents an additional risk to children.

The conclusion is crystal clear: small children, those under two or three years of age, simply do not belong in institutionalized group care. Even older children, those from three to five years of age, should not be separated from their parents for more than a few hours a day.

The best environment for preschool children, and especially for infants, is obviously at home with their mothers. The next best is at home with another family member. Care in the home of a relative or neighbor with only a small number of other children is far less desirable than keeping the child at home, but not nearly as damaging as placing the child in a large, institutionalized setting.

On this point, scientific research is in complete accord with common sense and consumer preference — and in complete contradiction to the thrust of the ABC Bill, which offers massive subsidies to the worst form of child care at the expense of every preferable arrangement.

Licensing is the panacea put forward by the proponents of ABC. At its first hearing in February 1988, only pro-ABC witnesses, 22 of them in all, were invited to testify. At least half of them recounted the tale of Jessica McClure, the little Texas girl who fell into an abandoned well while under the care of her aunt. The point of this monotonous recitation was that Jessica's accident would not have occurred if there had been tougher regulations. Perhaps they want a federal law requiring every abandoned well in the country to be sealed over. But it is fatuous to expect that federal bureaucrats can foresee every conceivable contingency, and then pass and enforce regulations to prevent any accident from happening. Accidents happen precisely because their potential was not foreseen. Whether the licensing requirements in a given state should be more or less stringent is a separate question which can be debated in the proper forum. But to imagine that a set of detailed federal regulations will turn inherently defective institutions into perfectly safe places is simply folly.

Public policy should be directed at diminishing the need for placing children in organized group care facilities because this is an environment that is not good for children. Daycare is one of the fastest-growing industries in America. The number of children in organized daycare programs is four times higher than it was a decade ago, and those children are at risk of a wide range of developmental and physical problems. Instead of reversing this trend and facilitating child care in more intimate settings, the ABC Bill is aimed at accelerating it and placing even more children at risk.

Sixth, and most importantly, ABC is anti-family. In the majority of families with preschool children, those children are under the care of their mothers. The only thing they get from the ABC Bill is a higher tax burden which will increase the pressure on those mothers to enter the paid labor force. Among families in which the mother participates in the labor market, the most common substitute caregiver for preschool children is the father. In hundreds of thousands of two-earner families, the husband and wife adjust their working hours so that one parent will always be able to stay home and take care of the children. Frequently, this means that the mother is employed only part-time. These families are sacrificing additional income in order to fulfill their parental responsibilities and ensure that their children are not robbed of parental care. They, too, get nothing under ABC but a higher tax burden, which will put more pressure on the mother to increase her working hours.

When it is not possible for at least one parent to remain home with the children, the most common remedy is to have a relative watch the children, sometimes for money and sometimes simply out of love and family solidarity. These arrangements also find no support under ABC. All these situations represent instances of families taking care of their own needs, doing what families are supposed to do, and in the process providing a higher quality of care for children than any paid stranger can. Yet these families are penalized under ABC.

When families are unable to provide care for their own children, they are most likely to turn to their neighbors or their church for assistance. The main reason why they prefer this kind of arrangement over a formal institutionalized daycare center is that it affords more intimacy, a more home-like environment. Neighbors and church are the natural places families go when they need help, and the solidarity of these natural communities is a healthy thing. That solidarity is actively attacked by the ABC Bill.

Only as a last resort do most parents turn to organized daycare programs, but it is only this least desirable of all options that would receive public support under ABC.

The Daycare Scenario

That policy preference for government-supervised daycare centers will set in motion a vicious circle which will tend toward the replacement of parents as the ordinary caregivers of their own children. Here is how the system is likely to work.

Take a hypothetical community which is a microcosm of the nation. Half the mothers of small children work as full-time homemakers. Only about one-third are employed full-time in the market economy. Three-fourths of the children are cared for within their own families, and only about one-tenth in daycare centers. Nearly half the children in daycare are in religious centers. Most of those in for-profit centers come from two-earner households with relatively high incomes.

A grant is extended to the local public school district under ABC for the establishment of a new daycare program offering low-cost services to the poor and middle class. All the other daycare arrangements — in the church-based centers, in private homes, and in the for-profit centers — now have a new competitor for their clientele, one which can offer services at a lower rate to clients. Since the great majority of the employed mothers are in the labor force precisely because they need additional money to make ends meet in their households, the promise of lower fees is very attractive, and a great number of them — more than the new center can handle — apply to enroll their children. The subsidized center now has a demand for services that exceeds expectations, and seeks a larger grant to expand. Congress increases the appropriation under ABC and raises taxes to pay for it.

The other daycare services, especially the unsubsidized church-based and home-based programs, start to lose most of their clients to the subsidized center and find it impossible to remain in business. Their remaining clients apply to the subsidized center, justifying another increase in appropriations. Meanwhile, the sliding-scale fees are still too high for many parents, and they demand lower rates. That demand is satisfied by an additional appropriation. The for-profit center, having to meet stricter licensing regulations, has to raise its rates and begins losing clients to the subsidized center. Within a few years, the only game in town is the subsidized center and a handful of other providers serving a small relatively affluent clientele.

Meanwhile, the families which have been relying on a father or grandmother to watch the children while mother is at her job start asking themselves whether the sacrifice is worth it when free or very cheap daycare is available right at the neighborhood school. Mothers who have not been in the labor force, finding the family budget perpetually squeezed (and now squeezed even more by a few hundred dollars in extra taxes to pay the daycare costs of their neighbors), and finding the marginal value of taking an outside job higher because daycare is so cheap and convenient, are under more pressure than ever to get a job. Before long, a majority of the children in the community are in the public school's daycare program, and the government has replaced the family as the child-rearing institution.

This is not a far-fetched scenario. It is a reasonable expectation of the rational choices people will make under a given set of social circumstances. It is also precisely the scenario that the backers of the ABC Bill envision as the ideal. They want the state to replace the family in the care of children so that more mothers will be able to participate in the labor force and so that social services can be delivered to children in a more organized fashion. As one participant at a daycare conference in March 1988 put it, "We want to free women from their biological destiny."

Some women find no fulfillment in being mothers; they want to pursue some other career. That is fine. Not everyone is called to the same vocation. What is not fine is that many of these women are infected with a feminist ideology that despises motherhood and the very condition of femininity. While we might all join in celebrating the fact that more career choices are open to women than ever before, it seems that the tacit objective of these feminists is to close off the choice of motherhood as a vocation.

Family Outlook for the Future

Among women who hold paid jobs, a substantial majority say they are employed only or primarily because they need the money, and that they would prefer to be employed fewer hours or not at all in order to devote more time to their families. Most employed mothers, like most employed fathers, are not doctors, lawyers, or officers of business enterprises, all of which can be very satisfying careers. Most employed mothers are secretaries, sales clerks, assembly line workers, waitresses, and so forth. A person holding this kind of job can enjoy it; that is mainly a matter of temperament. But few would seriously claim that a job holds a candle to the satisfaction of raising children and managing a household. Little girls do not dream of the day when they grow up and can wait on tables at Schrafft's. They dream of the day when they grow up and can get married and have babies. Far from wanting to be freed from their biological destiny, most women like being women and find their greatest satisfaction in raising their children.

It is a fine thing that women are no longer barred by custom or prejudice from exercising their abilities and ambitions in any vocation they choose. But there is one vocation that contemporary women are increasingly finding closed to them by social circumstances, and paradoxically it is that which most women desire: to be a fulltime homemaker and mother.

It is disgraceful that, in the wealthiest nation on earth, nearly half the fathers of families are unable to bring home enough money to support their families decently, so that their wives are drafted into involuntary servitude and their children are deprived of the presence of both parents. It is idiotic that the self-proclaimed advocates of women's rights can think of no response to this situation except to increase the pressures that are dragging more mothers out of their homes and into the work force.

The participation of mothers in the labor force is accelerating rapidly. In 1965, only 19 percent of women with children under 15 held jobs in the market economy. By 1975, this proportion had doubled to 38 percent. By 1985 it had increased to 57 percent, and the experts predict that by the end of the century three-fourths of all mothers will be in the labor force. One of the proud boasts of the Reagan Administration is that its economic policies have created 18 million new jobs. The other side of that is that two-thirds of those jobs are held by women, and fully half of them by women in the 25 to 44 age range, nearly all of them mothers. This is not a sign of social health, however pleasing it might be to the compilers of economic statistics. Economic growth is not an end in itself, but rather a means to the goal of increasing the strength, stability and security of families. When economic expansion is attained at the cost of family stability, it is not worth it. Worse yet, mothers have been pouring into the labor force during the Reagan years mainly because their husbands have not been able to bring home enough money.

Feminists are wont to sneer that the old "Leave it to Beaver" family — father as breadwinner, mother as homemaker — is extinct. This claim is not so much inaccurate as premature. Still, nearly half the children in America have a mother at home and father as provider. That pattern is becoming less common. The reasons for this are not entirely economic, but they are primarily economic.

The Golden Age

Back in the 1950s families enjoyed a golden age. Economic growth, low inflation rates and a pro-family tax policy combined to make the family wage a norm in our society. It is estimated that four out of five jobs in the economy paid enough to enable workers to bring home a wage sufficient to maintain their families at the prevailing standards of living. Home ownership grew rapidly during these years as the relatively stable currency kept interest rates low. The value of tax exemptions was so great that most working-class families with children did not owe any income tax at all. These were the key material conditions that contributed to creating a pro-family environment during the decade that witnessed the "baby boom," marked by the highest birth rates America has experienced since it ceased to be a primarily agricultural nation. In an industrialized society, the birth rate is probably the best single indicator of the myriad social, economic and cultural factors that contribute to or detract from the overall well-being of families.

Today things are quite different. The past three decades have witnessed technological advances and a general increase in affluence which have produced higher living standards. Wage levels, adjusted for inflation, are somewhat higher than they were in the 1950s, although they have not kept pace with the general economic growth. Taxes are far higher, especially for families with children. Now, only about 40 percent of the jobs in the economy yield a take-home pay that can be considered a family wage. Despite the higher tax burden, government spending at all levels has increased so greatly that it has to be financed by deficits which fuel inflation and high interest rates. Consequently, home ownership has become a crushing financial burden for families. Single persons, retired persons, childless couples and two-earner families are economically better off than they were a generation ago. But single-earner families with children are far worse off, which is one of the major reasons why there are fewer of them. The birth rate now is below the replacement level and only about half as high as it was 30 years ago.

This is the main reason why women are alleged to have "no choice" these days, and why daycare seems to be a pressing need for so many families. Children have become a serious economic liability, and those who take on the task that is absolutely indispensable to the future of society—parenthood—are required to pay heavily for the privilege. If the future of humanity passes by the way of the family, then the restoration of the family wage as a norm is an imperative. In other words, what we need are social policies which will make children an economic asset for their families.

Bad and Good Tax Credits

Federal policy regarding child care lies at the heart of this issue. The present policy is bad in that it encourages mothers to enter the labor force and have their children cared for by strangers, while discriminating against families which care for their own children.

In 1978, at the behest of feminists, Congress passed a tax credit allowing a portion of the money families spent on daycare in order to enable parents to hold a job to be subtracted from their income tax liability. For families earning more than $28,000 a year, the credit is equal to 20 percent of the cost of daycare up to $2,400 for one child or $4,800 for two or more children. For families earning less, the percentage increases to a maximum of 30 percent for families earning less than $10,000. This apparent advantage for the poor, however, is largely illusory. In the first place, a family of modest means is hardly in a position to spend $2,400 per child on daycare; and even if they did spend enough to accrue a large tax credit, their tax liability is likely to be so low that they could not take advantage of the full value of the credit. For a family with a tax liability of $300, a tax credit of $800 is really worth only $300, because it is not refundable.

It is not surprising, therefore, that two-thirds of the money claimed under this Child and Dependent Care Credit goes to families earning more than the median income. In effect, this tax credit is a supplement to the wages of mothers who are the second earners in their families. Less affluent taxpayers pay part of the daycare expenses of more affluent mothers to make it easier and more profitable for them to hold a job.

The effect of this tax credit has definitely been to accelerate the growing work-force participation of mothers and to make it more likely for employed mothers to pay an outsider to care for their children. This federal subsidy to daycare and the employment of mothers is now costing U.S. taxpayers more than $4 billion a year.

Rep. Clyde Holloway (R-LA) authored a reform of this tax credit designed to remove these inequities. His proposal, which won the enthusiastic backing of then Secretary of Education William Bennett, would replace the current credit with an across-the-board credit for every child who has not yet attained school age. Children in families earning less than $18,000 a year would receive a credit of $400 per year, and the size of the credit would decline as family income rises, to a minimum of $150 per child in families earning over $30,000. The credit is not tied to the amount spent by the family for daycare, but is available to all families, including those in which the mother cares for her own children. For low-income families with small tax liability, the credit would be refundable up to the amount the family has paid into the Social Security system. This proposal is virtually revenue-neutral, so it would not add to the budget deficit.

While it is too modest in size to have a significant impact on the employment of mothers, it would remove the tax incentive for mothers to enter the labor force, and it would put in place the principle that having and raising children is socially beneficial and worthy of tax support.

Rep. Richard Schulze of Pennsylvania offered a more expensive proposal along the same lines. His bill would offer an across-the-board credit of $750 for every child under the age of six, while leaving the current tax credit in place for school-age children. The Schulze bill would go a long way toward making children an economic asset for their families and would enable many employed mothers to return home, while helping those who are still working as fulltime homemakers to stay out of the labor market. The down side is that it would reduce federal revenues by an estimated $8 billion.

Constructive Pro-Family Solutions

Both these measures offer a constructive, pro-family solution to the child care issue. They eliminate the discrimination against families which care for their own children and remove the tax incentive for employed mothers to seek commercial child care arrangements. They leave daycare clients free to choose the kind of provider they prefer, including a religious center. They impose no federal licensing standards and create no new bureaucracy. Every dollar achieves 100 percent efficiency, since nothing gets skimmed off for administration or other indirect costs. Either of these measures has the potential to stem or reverse the trends toward more employment of mothers and more utilization of daycare centers, trends that are now aimed at the ultimate extinction of the family.

Reducing the employment of mothers outside the home would be only an indirect effect of the Holloway and Schulze proposals, but that could prove to be one of the key steps in restoring the practice of the family wage.

Survey data strongly suggest that many mothers would drop out of the labor force if they felt they could afford to. If just 10 percent of the mothers now employed were able to return home, that would open up about two million jobs. Some of those jobs would be filled by single men, especially poor young men, who are now unemployed or marginally employed. This would enable some of those young men to marry and establish families, which would marginally contribute to easing welfare and crime problems. (Crime, especially violent crime, is concentrated among unmarried young men who are underemployed, and chronic welfare cases are concentrated among the young women who are not married to those same young men because the men cannot support them.)

Some of the jobs now held by mothers would be eliminated through technological improvements, which, in the long run, contribute to economic growth.

Increase in Wage Rates

Finally, the departure of two million mothers from the labor force would shrink the labor force sufficiently to cause a slight increase in average wage rates, which would bring a few more fathers up to the level at which they earn enough to support their families, thereby enabling still more mothers to leave their jobs. It would be a mistake to expect a reform of this nature to solve all these social problems; but it could reverse the direction of several social trends which are now heading in negative directions. The very factors which are now drawing mothers into the labor force against their will are exacerbated by the increased employment of women, and reversing a vicious circle at any point reverses a whole set of trends.

Increasing average wage rates through the market process will help to restore the standard of a family wage, but as noted above, the erosion of the family wage has not primarily been a consequence of any reduction in the real value of wages. The real culprits are taxes and inflation. In the 1950s, tax policies which gave preference to families with children were one of the chief economic factors in creating a pro-family social environment. Since then, taxes have gone up for everyone, but the increases have been especially crushing for families.

Our tax laws should be rewritten to be pro-family, and this would be the most effective way to restore the family wage as the norm. Some tax reforms that can accomplish this might be: (1) An increase in the standard deduction for married couples, from the current $5,000 to $8,000. (2) A restoration of the value

of the personal exemption for dependent children. That $600
exemption of 1948 would be worth about $6,000 today. (3) A
doubling of the personal exemption for newborn or newly
adopted children for the tax year in which they are added to a
family. (4) A reduction in the payroll tax rate by 1 percent (or
1 ½ percent for self-employed workers) for each dependent child
supported by a worker. This will not only ease the burden of a
severely regressive tax on families, but also help the Social
Security system survive by encouraging more births. (5)
Deductions for educational, medical and insurance expenses for
children. (6) An expansion of the Earned Income Tax Credit
based on family size. Low-income workers now receive a refundable tax credit if they have children, but the credit is the
same whether the worker is supporting one child or six. The
percentage of earnings on which the Earned Income Tax Credit
is based should increase as the number of children increases.

    Taken all together, these family-supportive tax proposals
will enormously increase the disposable income of families with
children, and will certainly make having children an economic
asset. For the great majority of mothers, these reforms will
eliminate the perceived need to enter the labor force. That will
enable more mothers to devote themselves to the nobler and far
more valuable task of raising their children, and will thereby
shrink the market for daycare to a manageable proportion.

CHILD CARE
SEMINAR SPEAKERS

Mr. Gene Armento
85 Copley Avenue
Teaneck, New Jersey 07666

Dr. Reed Bell
97 Shoreline Drive
Gulf Breeze, Florida 32561

Dr. William J. Bennett
Office of National Drug Control Policy
1825 Connecticut Avenue, Room 1015
Washington, D.C. 20009

Mr. Douglas J. Besharov
American Enterprise Institute
1150 17th Street, N.W.
Washington, D.C. 20036

Dr. Eric Brodin
Box 219
Buies Creek, North Carolina 27506

Dr. Allan C. Carlson
The Rockford Institute
934 North Main Street
Rockford, Illinois 61103

Dr. Bryce J. Christensen
The Rockford Institute
934 North Main Street
Rockford, Illinois 61103

Mrs. Midge Decter
Committee for the Free World
211 East 51st Street, Suite 11A
New York, New York 10022

Mrs. Wendy Dreskin
10 East Court
San Anselmo, California 94960

Mr. George Gilder
Tyringham, Massachusetts 01264

Mrs. Barbara M. Hattemer
International Foundation for the
Preservation of the Family
440 Spinnaker Drive
Naples, Florida 33940

Mrs. Brenda Hunter
Home by Choice
9086 Wexford Drive
Vienna, Virginia 22180

Dr. Raymond S. Moore
The Moore Foundation
Box 1
Camas, Washington 98607

Mr. Robert Rector
The Heritage Foundation
214 Massachusetts Avenue, N.E.
Washington, D.C. 20002

Dr. Donald B. Rinsley
Veterans Administration
2200 Gage Boulevard
Topeka, Kansas 66622

Mrs. Phyllis Schlafly
Eagle Forum
Box 618
Alton, Illinois 62002

Mr. Michael Schwartz
Free Congress Foundation
721 Second Street, N.E.
Washington, D.C. 20002

Dr. Harold M. Voth
Veterans Administration
2200 Gage Boulevard
Topeka, Kansas 66622

Mr. Karl Zinsmeister
718 7th Street, S.E.
Washington, D.C. 20003

INDEX

Eagle Forum Education & Legal Defense Fund is a nonprofit educational organization which conducts research, studies, seminars and surveys on the civil, legal, economic, moral and social rights of traditional families. It seeks to promote fair treatment for traditional family values in the economy, the media, the schools and universities. Its major projects are:

Constitution Bicentennial. Both of Eagle Forum's two elaborate programs to alert and educate Americans about the U.S. Constitution in honor of its Bicentennial were "officially recognized by the United States Commission on the Bicentennial":

- "Standing Proud for the Constitution," a 60-second musical public service announcement aired during 1987 on more than 700 radio stations; and

- "We the People," a 35-minute Slide Program on the Constitution was given by 500 local Bicentennial chairmen to community and school groups of all kinds, reaching an American audience of at least a million, and is now available on video.

Phonics Reading Program. Some 5,000 parents have been helped to teach their own children to read by the Forum's Headstart Reading Program to combat illiteracy.

Educational Conferences. Eagle Forum has sponsored and conducted numerous educational conferences and seminars featuring addresses by national experts on such topics as Child Care and Daycare, Comparable Worth, Federally-Mandated Parental Leave, and Parents' Rights in Education.

Parents Advisory Center. This office supports and counsels parents in defending the rights of their schoolchildren. Eagle Forum's monthly publication called *Education Reporter,* the "newspaper of education rights," is a major line of communication for news about public school curricula and how parents are asserting their rights.

Fulltime Homemaker Awards. Each year, Eagle Forum gives a Fulltime Homemaker Award in each of the 50 states in order to recognize the socially useful work done by the mother who sacrifices her career in order to give her children fulltime care.

American Inventors. The Forum developed an original multi-media production showing how, as a result of economic freedom, American inventors changed the way we live.

***Amicus curiae* briefs**. Some of the most important and successful were in the Supreme Court case *Rostker v. Goldberg* (1981), which preserved the exemption of women from the military draft; and the Ninth Circuit case *American Federation of State, County, and Municipal Employees v. State of Washington* (1985), which held against the concept of wage-control called Comparable Worth.

Radio Commentaries. Eagle Forum's nationally syndicated 3-minute-a-day radio program is carried on 250 stations and has been running for more than five years.

Video Productions. Eagle Forum has produced and distributed original videos on important subjects, including the U.S. Constitution, Parental Rights in Education, Child Care, and Strategic Defense.

Publications. Among Eagle Forum's publications are *Equal Pay for UNequal Work*, a volume of the addresses given at one of the Forum's conferences on Comparable Worth; and a *Bibliography on Contemporary Issues*.

Eagle Forum Education & Legal Defense Fund is a publicly supported educational organization described in Section 501(c)(3) of the Internal Revenue Code. Tax-deductible contributions are invited from individuals, corporations, companies, associations, and foundations. It was founded in 1981 as an Illinois not-for-profit corporation and maintains offices in both Alton, Illinois and Washington, D.C.